D0432655

ODD TOM CORYATE

THE
**PAUL HAMLYN
LIBRARY**

DONATED BY
THE PAUL HAMLYN
FOUNDATION
TO THE
BRITISH MUSEUM

opened December 2000

WITHDRAWN

ODD TOM CORYATE

The English Marco Polo

R.E. PRITCHARD

WITHDRAWN

SUTTON PUBLISHING

First published in the United Kingdom in 2004 by
Sutton Publishing Limited · Phoenix Mill
Thrupp · Stroud · Gloucestershire · GL5 2BU

Copyright © R.E. Pritchard, 2004

All rights reserved. No part of this publication may be reproduced,
stored in a retrieval system, or transmitted, in any form, or by any
means, electronic, mechanical, photocopying, recording or otherwise,
without the prior permission of the publisher and copyright holder.

R.E. Pritchard has asserted the moral right to be identified as the
author of this work.

British Library Cataloguing in Publication Data
A catalogue record for this book is available from the British Library.

ISBN 0-7509-3416-6

THE
BRITISH
MUSEUM
WITHDRAWN
THE PAUL HAMLYN LIBRARY

910.92 COR

Typeset in 10.5/14pt Melior.
Typesetting and origination by
Sutton Publishing Limited.
Printed and bound in England by
J.H. Haynes & Co. Ltd, Sparkford.

Contents

List of Illustrations   vi
Acknowledgements   vii

1. Preamble   1

2. Fair Stood the Wind for France   14

3. The Paradise of Travellers   34

4. The Virgin City   51

5. Venetia and the Gray Confederacy   81

6. Through the Mountains   96

7. Down the Two-Horned River   108

8. To the Hollow Land   133

9. Home and Away: Prose, Verse and Worse   153

10. Sailing to Byzantium   184

11. A Passage to India   216

12. To the Field of Bones   237

Bibliography   262
Index   265

List of Illustrations

1. Frontispiece of *Coryats Crudities*
2. Henry, Prince of Wales
3. The route of Coryate's European tour
4. Mountebanks in St Mark's Square, Venice
5. Coryate meeting a Venetian courtesan
6. The clock tower of Strasbourg Cathedral
7. Coryate on the Great Tun of Heidelberg
8. Punishment on the wheel
9. *The Martyrdom of St Ursula and 11,000 Virgins*
10. Coryate's letter to Sir Michael Hicks
11. Alciati's version of the ass bearing the image of Isis
12. A battle with Barbary corsairs
13. Map of the Eastern Mediterranean and the Levant
14. The Sultan's Seraglio, Constantinople
15. A Turkish Janissary
16. A Turkish Dellee
17. A Dervish
18. Turkish punishments in Constantinople
19. Jerusalem
20. Sir Robert Sherley in Persian dress
21. Sir Thomas Roe, Ambassador to the Mughal Empire
22. Sir Thomas Roe's map of the Mughal Empire
23. Title-page of *Thomas Coriate, Traveller*
24. The Emperor Jahangir, his son and woman
25. Frontispiece of Edward Terry's *A Voyage to East-India*
26. The English factory in Surat

Acknowledgements

I am indebted to Michael Strachan's *The Life and Adventures of Thomas Coryate*; also to Nicholas Wood, Roger Winterbottom and William C. Walterhouse, who traced some things for me.

Preamble

On 14 May 1608, in the fifth year of the reign of James I, a young man of (to adopt a style he would have appreciated) more wit than wealth, and yet of more wealth than wisdom, embarked from Dover on a career that was to bring him fame in his lifetime and also, eventually, to an early death, far away, at the end of a dusty road in northern India. This was Thomas Coryate, known as Odd Tom Coryate, partly because he constantly told everyone that he came from the village of Odcombe in Somerset, and partly because he was indeed odd. A minor figure on the fringe of the Court and London literary worlds, he was generally known, from King James to John Donne and the pot poets of Bankside, as an amiable, whimsical eccentric, a comical pedant wandered out of *Love's Labours Lost*, who might well have said with Falstaff, 'I am not only witty in myself, but the cause that wit is in other men'. One popular versifier, John Taylor, later mocked him:

> His head was a large poudring tub of phrases,
> Whence men would pick delites as boys pick daisies . . .
> Admired learning took his heads possession,
> And turnd his wit a wandring in progression.

(A powdering tub contained meat or fish to be salted or pickled.) What these people did not yet know was that Tom Coryate was courageous, determined, enquiring, observant, tireless, ambitious and irrepressible.

Tom Coryate was to become one of the country's best-known travellers, travelling alone, unarmed, with little money and for much of the way on foot (and with only one pair of shoes), to visit and write about, in a way that nobody had done before, early seventeenth-century France, Italy, Switzerland, Germany and the Netherlands. He went on to become the first Englishman to take a serious interest in the plains of ancient Troy, the first to visit India out of sheer curiosity, the first European (since Alexander the Great, who went with an army) to walk all the way from the Eastern Mediterranean through Persia and Afghanistan to India. His book, *Coryats Crudities* (1611), some 800 quarto pages long (including some 150 pages of his father's writings) and the size of a small brick, provides glimpses of European life in the brief period of relative peace after the cessation of hostilities between England, France, Spain and the Netherlands, and before the outbreak of the terrible Thirty Years War. His later notes (most of which were lost), scattered through Samuel Purchas's *Purchas his Pilgrimes* (1625) and various pamphlets, tell of his experiences and the splendours and brutalities of life in the vast Ottoman, Persian and Mughal empires. He was a remarkable man, 'who', as Edward Terry, who knew him in India, wrote, 'while he lived was like a perpetual motion, and therefore now dead should not be quite forgotten'.

Some of Tom's characteristics – verbal facility and a gift for languages, literary ambition, irrepressible impudence – seem to have been inherited from his father, George. George Coryate was born about 1545 in Salisbury, and went to Winchester College; while there, he wrote some Latin verses addressed to Queen Elizabeth, which he nailed to the door of the Bishop's Palace (without equalling the effect of Luther's theses nailed to the door of Wittenberg Cathedral, but nevertheless receiving a very generous gift of £5 from the Queen). In 1560, in the usual progress for Wykehamists, he went up to New College, Oxford, where he was awarded a fellowship, and, according to Anthony à Wood in *Athenae Oxonienses*, became a good Latinist and addressed a poem to the Queen urging her to a prompt marriage (advice she never welcomed). In 1566, when the Queen visited the College, he even delivered a welcoming oration in Latin, which won him some praise and a purse of gold. Having taken Holy Orders, he resigned his fellowship, and became Rector of Odcombe, near Yeovil in Somerset. Here he continued a modest literary career, writing a Latin poem descriptive of England, Scotland and Ireland, and a Latin translation of the Psalms (both unpublished). He wrote some Latin verses for Lord Burghley, who sent him £2 (*noblesse oblige*), and an elegy on the death of Lord Pembroke: the second Earl, also Lord Lieutenant of Somerset, made him family chaplain. More verses followed, to Archbishop Whitgift, and epitaphs for the Archbishop of York and Bishop Jewel. Persistence paid off, and in 1594 he was presented to the prebendal stall of Warthill in York Minster, and awarded a moiety of the Rectory of Axminster in Devon. Despite all this, there was not a lot of money in Odcombe Rectory. It appears that he married twice, first, Henrietta Cooper, and then Gertrude (Williams?), Tom's mother, presumably considerably younger (she outlived him by thirty-five years).

It is not certain when Tom was born: Winchester College records suggest that, like his classmates, he was born in 1579, whereas Wood says he was born in 1577; in the 'Epistle to the Reader' in *Crudities* Coryate suggests that in 1608 he was 32, and the frontispiece of 1611 claims to show him aged 35. In any case, he went up to Gloucester Hall, Oxford (now part of Worcester College), where he studied for three years. There were four terms in the year, lectures beginning at 8 a.m., with failure to attend or to make notes receiving small fines (*autres temps, autres mœurs*). Latin was the essential subject for study (the *sine qua non*, one might say) as a preparation for all careers, and occupied most of the students' time. Latin grammar was taught on Tuesdays and Fridays, logic and rhetoric (Cicero and Quintilian, useful for future orations) on Mondays and Thursdays. Greek and Hebrew were the only other languages taught (in connection with biblical studies). Rather ungenerously, Wood admits that Coryate 'attained by the help of a great memory to some competency in Latin, but more by far in the Greeke tongue, and humane learning'. Coryate (like about one third of students) left before taking a degree – possibly simply because the money ran out, or because it did not seem worth the extra expenditure if he were not going to enter the Church.

After this, he went home, back to Odcombe and the Rectory, apparently uncertain as to what to do with himself, apart from keeping in with the local gentry. We know some of what he did, as he wrote about it later in his second book, *Coryats Crambe*. (Original, seventeenth-century spelling and punctuation, in all their variety and inconsistency, are here retained in quotations – one gets used to them very quickly; with almost equal inconsistency, they are occasionally silently modernized, in the interests of easy readability.) In 1606, the funds of Odcombe Church were nearly exhausted (down to sixteen shillings), and the churchwardens (and, no doubt, his father) asked Tom to come up with a money-raising scheme,

> seeing they knew that I was well acquainted in the countrye. Hereupon I resolved to muster up out of the Parish one hundred choise and able men, as were fit to beare armes in the field [Falstaff's unlikely warriors in *Henry IV, Part II*, Mouldy, Shadow, Wart and Peter Bullcalf o'the Green, come shambling irresistibly to mind], and by a time limited, even the Whitson-day following, about sixe of the clocke in the morning, appointed them to meete me at Odcombe Crosse. Which they did according to my appointment, being furnished with munition for a kinde of warfare. For some of them had muskets, others Calivers [very light muskets], some Partizans [long-handled spears], some Halberts, with diversity of other weapons. Likewise we had good Martiale Musicke and military officers. I my selfe being their Captaine, was mounted upon a goodly milk-white steed.

They then marched towards the neighbouring town of Yeovil, being met by two groups,

> one Masculine, and another Foeminine, which incountered us like a company of Amazones, & after there had been some two or three volleyes of shot discharged on both sides with a prettie kinde of

velitation or light skirmish, we descended a hill called Henford, and entred the towne. In the market place whereof nere to the Crosse, wee had one skirmish more, but umbraticall [a shadowy representation] and imaginarie. Then I ascended an eminent and conspicuous place about the Crosse, where was erected a kind of Canopy, under the which I advanced my selfe above, and after the warlike Musicke was ended, having two or three times brandished my naked Sword, I spake this Oration following to the Evillians, and at the least two thousand people more.

Both father and son Coryate appear to have enjoyed the sounds of their own voices, and making speeches. This, Tom's earliest recorded oration, began by urging people to spend their money here in Yeovil, hoping that they would also spend their money in Odcombe. Then followed a review of religious festivals among the ancient Greeks and Romans and early Christians (which his rustic audience must have found very improving), and a defence of the institution of church-ales (money-raising events of the kind more soberly enjoyed today) if purged of 'drunkennesse, gluttonie, swearing, lascivious-ness, with many more, which indeed I must needs confesse seeme to be the inseparable accidents and individuall adjuncts of Church-ales' (and very much the heart of the matter, for most people there); the anti-carnivalesque sentiments Coryate expressed were not peculiar to him, but in line with the Church's current drive for greater sobriety of behaviour. He concluded by urging everyone to sober enjoyment and spending of money 'without any base whinching or murmuring, for the emolument of your Church'. Some time later, the people of Yeovil paid a return visit to Odcombe, only to be greeted by another oration by Coryate, this time providing his earliest recorded eulogy of his beloved Odcombe. Despite being set on 'a hilly and sterill countrie . . . wanting many comfortable helpes of life', Odcombe had 'a most wholsome and pleasant ayre' and 'sweet and wholsome springs', its wool being 'so famous for the singular finenesse thereof that we dare boldly avouch, that no place whatsoever in England yeeldeth better, saving only Lemster in Herefordshire'.

The church on the hill could be seen for miles around, rather like the Pharos lighthouse in Alexandria (the similarity must have been remarkable), while most important was 'the unity and perfect love amongst our selves . . . firmly knit together in an indissoluble knot of friendship'. It is to be hoped that the visitors were impressed by all this, as Coryate had to admit that the village had nothing much to offer by way of entertainment, except the menfolk parading with their weapons (echoes of Wart exercising his caliver – 'O, give me always a little, lean, old, chopt bald shot'). He does not report how much money was raised.

Such excitements could not satisfy for long, clearly, and Tom had to cast about among friends and acquaintances for gainful occupation. Some contacts came in useful, particularly the Phelipses of nearby Montacute House. Tom was named after Thomas Phelips, Squire of Montacute and his godfather; Edward Phelips, the youngest son, was responsible for the building of Montacute House by 1601 (Tom's standard for judging architectural quality); both Edward and his son Robert were among the many knighted by King James in 1603. In 1604 Edward was made Speaker of the House of Commons, but, more to the point as far as Coryate was concerned, Robert was made Gentleman of the Privy Chamber Extraordinary at the newly established Court of the young Prince of Wales, Prince Henry; and Robert introduced Tom, and got him in, somehow. A Protestant activist, strong-minded, serious-minded, interested in war, foreign affairs and diplomacy, Henry grew up to control an entourage of energetic young men, remarkable, like most young courtiers, more for their wealth, liveliness and self-esteem than for seriousness and sensitivity. Here, young Tom Coryate, provincial, essentially modest and with little money, had to make his way – which he did by amusing them, with wit, wordplay and clowning, as a sort of unofficial court jester. Thomas Fuller wrote of him, 'Prince Henry allowed him a pension [at a rate of £10 a year], and kept him for his servant. Sweetmeats and Coryate made up the last course of all court entertainments. Indeed he was the courtiers' anvil to try their wits upon; and sometimes the anvil returned the hammers as hard knocks as it received, his bluntness repaying their abusiveness. . . . Few would be found to call him fool, might none do it save such who had as much learning as himself' (and there would not be many of those there). Coryate had established himself, not only as a comic but also as someone to be taken notice of, remarkable and independent, with a place among them, whilst not being altogether of them.

Tom's career as a courtier at Prince Henry's court (or courts, for the Prince had three, at Richmond, St James's and Nonsuch palaces, with a household of nearly 500 people) was sadly interrupted by the death of his beloved father, on 4 March 1607, at the age of 62. The death may have been sudden and unexpected, for there was no will (there may not have been a lot to bequeathe). An extraordinary episode now ensued: the funeral and interment were delayed, Wood relates, for nearly six weeks, 'Tom, upon some design, preserving his [father's] body from stench above ground' somewhere unknown, possibly in a cave nearby, 'till the 14th April following, [the body being] then buried in the Chancel of the Church at Odcombe', at a service conducted by the new incumbent. There is no explanation for this bizarre behaviour; it may have been an attempt to delay the funeral until the money to pay for it was available; he may have wanted the service performed by his father's successor; it may have been an attempt to postpone the new man's occupation of the rectory. In any case, Gertrude had to get out of her home, but remained in Odcombe; Tom went off, probably back to Court and London.

A little money was available, not much, but something could be done now – perhaps had to be done. He was not really getting anywhere, so perhaps the answer was to go somewhere: to go on an extraordinary journey, alone, across Europe, well publicized at Prince Henry's court (Henry approved of educational foreign travel) and among the chattering classes of Jacobean London, then to write it up and

gain some moderate fame and fortune. A few years earlier, a
professional clown, Will Kemp, seeking publicity to strengthen
a wobbling career, had danced – over a period of twenty-three
days – from London to Norwich, recording his exploit in a
little book, *Nine Daies Wonder. Performed in a Dance from
London to Norwich* (1600); it would be a pity if an educated,
energetic and inventive young man such as Tom Coryate could
not do as well, and better.

Of course, more and more Englishmen had been going to
mainland Europe in recent years: some young men went to
distinguished foreign universities, such as Padua or Heidelberg
(Hamlet went to Wittenberg); many had gone as soldiers to the
wars in northern France and the Netherlands; wool merchants
set up offices in Flushing; others in the import/export business
went off to the Baltic and Russia (the Muscovy Company was
founded in 1553) and to the Eastern Mediterranean (Elizabeth
granted the Levant Company its charter in 1581, renewed by
James I in 1605). In the intervals of European wars, young
gentlemen, often accompanied by tutor-guides, had started
going on early versions of the European Grand Tour, to see
some culture, meet foreign gentlemen and learn foreign
languages before embarking on glittering careers: Sir Philip
Sidney (for two years, with companion, money and letters of
introduction to important people everywhere), his brother Sir
Robert Sidney, Sir Henry Wotton, Sir Thomas Roe, Sir John
Harrington. In 1606 Sir Thomas Palmer made a point of
dedicating his *Essay on . . . our Travailes into forraine
Countries* to Prince Henry, noting how 'the people of Great
Britain, of all other famous and glorious Nations separated from
the maine Continent of the world, are by so much the more
interessed to become Travailers'.

This was the sort of thing that intellectuals such as Francis
Bacon approved of, as in his essay 'Of Travel' (published too
late for Tom to have read it):

Travel, in the younger sort, is a part of education. . . . That young
men travel under some tutor, or grave servant, I allow well; so that

he be such a one that hath the language and hath been in the
country before . . . Let diaries . . . be brought in use. The things to
be seen and observed are: the courts of princes . . . the courts of
justice . . . the churches and monasteries, with the monuments
which are therein extant; the walls and fortifications of cities and
towns, and so the havens and harbours; antiquities and ruins;
libraries, colleges, disputations, and lectures, where any are;
shipping and navies; houses and gardens of state and pleasure,
near great cities; armories; arsenals; magazines; exchanges; burses;
warehouses; exercises of horsemanship, fencing, training of
soldiers, and the like; comedies, such whereunto the better sort of
persons do resort; treasures of jewels and robes; cabinets and
rarities; and, to conclude, whatever is memorable in the places
where they go. . . . As for triumphs, masques, feasts, weddings,
funerals, capital executions, and such shews, men need not to be
put in mind of them; yet are they not to be neglected.

It is remarkable how much of this daunting programme,
intended for future members of the governing class, Coryate
managed to carry out, despite his restricted time and limited
financial and social resources. The traveller Fynes Moryson
put it on a higher, almost spiritual plane:

They seeme to me most unhappy, and no better than Prisoners,
who from the cradle to old age, still behold the same walls, faces,
orchards, pastures, and objects of the eye, and still heare the
same voices and sounds beate in theire eares . . . Running water
is sweet, but standing pooles stinke . . . Men were created to
move, as birds to flie . . . We are citizens of the Whole World; all
our Life is a Pilgrimage.

On the other hand, not everyone thought travel altogether A
Good Thing. For every one who thought that travel broadens
the mind, there was one who knew that the traveller changes
his sky but not his mind (so why go to the expense? – though
one intransigent traveller, William Lithgow, actually boasted
this on the title page of his own travel book: '*Coelum non
Animum*'). Sir Roger Ascham, once Queen Elizabeth's tutor,
thought it positively harmful, in exposing young men to vice,

recommending that one should read Machiavelli at home, and avoid meeting Machiavellians abroad; others, not without cause, feared imprisonment by the Inquisition, or, worse, conversion to Catholicism.

Travellers were accused of falsity and pretentiousness. As Rosalind put it, in *As You Like It* (1599): 'Farewell, Monsieur Traveller; look you lisp and wear strange suits, disable all the benefits of your own country, be out of love with your nativity, and almost chide God for making you that countenance that you are; or I will scarce think that you have swam in a gondola.' Thomas Nashe in his *Pierce Penniless* (1592) sketches a vivid picture of such a poseur:

> All Italianato is his talk, and his spade peak [beard] is as sharp as if he had been a pioneer before the walls of Rouen [besieged 1591–2]. He will despise the barbarisme of his own country and tell a whole *Legend of Lies* of his travels unto Constantinople. . . . You shall see a dapper jack, that hath been but over at Dieppe, wring his face round about, as a man would stir up a mustard pot, and talk English through the teeth, like Jacques Scabbed-hams or Monsieur Mingo de Mousetrap; when, poor slave, he hath but dipped his bread in wild boar's grease, and come home again.

It was Nashe's entertaining and aptly titled adventure story *The Unfortunate Traveller* (1594) that told Englishmen what to expect of the dubious characters they might expect to encounter on the other side of the Channel. Here, an exiled Englishman gives the young hero fair warning, of what all Englishmen knew:

> Countryman, tell me, what is the occasion of thy straying so far out of England to visit this strange nation [Italy]? If it be languages, thou may'st learn them at home; nought but lasciviousness is to be learned here . . .
>
> The first traveller was Cain, and he was called a vagabond runagate on the face of the earth . . . He that is a traveller must have the back of an ass to bear all, a tongue like the tail of a dog to flatter all, the mouth of a hog to eat what is set before him, the ear of a merchant to hear all and say nothing . . . Let others tell you

strange accidents, treasons, poisonings, close packings in France, Spain and Italy; it is no harm for you to hear them, but come not near them.

What is there in France to be learned more than in England, but falsehood in fellowship, perfect slovenry, to love no man but for my pleasure, to swear Ah par la mort Dieu when a mans hams are scabbed? . . . Yea, and peradventure this also, to esteem of the pox as a pimple, to wear a velvet patch on their face, and walk melancholy with their arms folded. . . .

Italy, the paradise of the earth and the epicures heaven, how doth it form our young master? It makes him to kiss his hand like an ape, cringe his neck like a starveling, and play at heypass, repass come aloft [wave arms like a conjuror] when he salutes a man. From thence he brings the art of atheism, the art of epicurising, the art of whoring, the art of poisoning, the art of sodomitry. The only probable good thing they have to keep us from utterly condemning it is that it maketh a man an excellent courtier, a fine close lecher, a glorious hypocrite. It is now a privy note amongst the better sort of men, when they would set a singular mark or brand on a notorious villain, to say he hath been in Italy.

With the Dane and the Dutchman I will not encounter, for they are simple honest men, that with Danaus daughters [condemned to an eternity of collecting water in sieves], do nothing but fill bottomless tubs and will be drunk and snort in the midst of dinner.

Rosalind thought that foreign travel might be little more than a waste of time and money: 'A traveller! By my faith, you have great reason to be sad. I fear you have sold your own lands to see other men's; then to have seen much and to have nothing is to have rich eyes and poor hands.'

Coryate, however, would have proudly echoed Jaques's reply: 'Yes, I have gain'd my experience.' There was also the hope of a modest profit.

First of all, there were formalities to go through, particularly the obtaining of a passport or licence to travel, for which one had to declare the goal, purpose and proposed length of time of one's journey, how many servants and horses might go, and indicate the amount of money one might take out of the country. In the early seventeenth century this normally varied between £10 and £20; for further expenses people depended on 'bills of exchange' or letters of credit, based on a deposit with a merchant trading abroad (often a goldsmith) that could be exchanged abroad. The average expectation for a gentleman travelling in modest comfort was an annual rate of £50 to £80 a year, and up to £150 a year with a servant and horses. Such amounts were beyond Coryate's reach, but there was one thing he could do like other travellers: 'putting out', a kind of travel or life insurance.

This was a practice that seems to have developed originally in the Netherlands early in the sixteenth century, when a pilgrim intending to go to the dangerous Holy Land would arrange a will-cum-contract, bequeathing a certain sum in the event of his death, on the understanding of receiving double or treble that sum if he returned alive. The traveller Fynes Moryson (1566–1630), a Fellow of Peterhouse College, Cambridge, who spent six years from 1591 travelling widely in Europe, put out £100, to be paid £300 on his eventual return; in 1595 his brother Henry put out £400 at the same rate, for his journey to Constantinople and Jerusalem, but unfortunately lost both his life and his deposit in Syria in the following year. The practice was well known, and increasingly mocked. In *The Tempest* (written in 1611), Gonzago refers to any untruthful traveller as 'each putter-out of five for one', and in Ben Jonson's *Every Man Out Of His Humour* (1599) a comic character, Puntarvolo, says he is 'determined to put forth some five thousand pounds, to be paid me five for one, upon the return of myself, my wife, and my dog from the Turk's court in Constantinople'. Even Will Kemp claimed to have 'put out some money to have three-fold gaine', for tripping to Norwich. Fynes Moryson suggested that the practice was no longer respectable for gentlemen: 'bankerouts, Stage-players and men of base condition have drawne this custome into contempt.' Nevertheless, Tom did deposit £40 with Joseph Starre, a Yeovil linen-draper, for a bond of 200 marks (equivalent to £133 6s. 8d.), in a 'bill of adventure', to be paid on his return. Having said farewell to Gertrude and friends, and hidden his cash in various secret pockets (the linings of one's belt or jerkin were generally recommended), together with some writing materials, but otherwise apparently magnificently unprepared, he was off. The Elizabethan poet Barnabe Googe probably expressed his apprehensions and hopes well enough:

O blest of God thou Pleasaunt Ile,
    where welth her self doth dwell,
Wherein my tender yeares I past,
    I byd thee now farewell.
For Fancy dryves me forth abrode,
    and byds me take delyght
In levyng thee and raunging far,
    to se some straunger syght,
And sayth I was not framèd heare
    to lyve at home with eas,
But passynge foorth for knowledge sake
    to cut the fomyng seas.

Fair Stood the Wind for France

Coryate embarked at Dover at about 10 in the morning, on Saturday, Whitsun-eve, 14 May 1608. The average ferry boat or passenger boat was about 60 tons and 60 feet long, single-decked, capable of taking up to seventy passengers; supposing it avoided any cruising Dutch pirates, or even far-ranging corsair raiders from the Barbary coast, it might carry its passengers across in as few as four or five hours, or, in stormy weather, as many days. The fare was about five shillings, plus extra charges if the ship could not get into harbour, and the passengers had to be carried ashore in small boats, or by wading porters. Tom got in to Calais at about 5 that afternoon, after, as he wrote in the facetious, self-mocking style his Court and London friends expected,

> I had varnished the exterior parts of the ship with the excrementall ebullitions of my tumultuous stomach, as desiring to satiate the gormandizing paunches of the hungry Haddocks (according as I have hieroglyphically expressed it in the front of my booke) with that I had superfluously stuffed my selfe at land, having made my rumbling belly their capacious aumbrie [store-cupboard].

Having arrived in Calais (in French hands for some fifty years, after two centuries of English rule), all passengers had to report to the Deputy Governor (Coryate rather regretted not meeting the Governor, who, he tells us, had a wooden leg). Coryate stayed there that night and the following day, taking the opportunity to attend a Catholic Mass, of which, as a sturdy Protestant, he found much to disapprove, 'for I saw the Priest minister the Sacrament to the lay people under one kind only, namely that of bread, defrauding them of the Wine, contrary to the holy institution of Christ and his Apostles'. He was able to observe an unfamiliar ceremony appropriate to the day:

> About the middle of their Masse there was an extreme crackling noise from a certain hollow place in the vault of the Church. This is the same place, as I take it, where they let up and downe their Bels. After the noyse there was powred downe a great deale of water, immediately after the water ensued a great multitude of Wafer-cakes, both white, redde and yellow: which ceremony was done to put them in minde of the cloven tongues that appeared that day of Pentecost to the Apostles (Acts 2) in Hierusalem.

In the church there was also an unusual 'Doom' wall-painting, showing Christ seated on a rainbow, 'with the soules of the Saints and the godly on the right hand of him, and the devil on the left hand, with a gaping mouth, devouring the soules of the wicked'. While in the church he took the opportunity to copy out a memorial to an English lady; his tour was to be marked by his faithful transcription of well-nigh innumerable inscriptions in churches and public buildings: they will not appear here. (It was also his practice, whenever possible, to precede his accounts of the cities he visited with descriptive Latin verses by the fifteenth-century humanist scholar Julius Caesar Scaliger: these also will be omitted.) Coryate also described the Rice-bank Fort there, named after some shrewd business by an English sea captain in 1540, who, having captured a ship-load of rice from some Dunkirk pirates, was allowed by the Governor to keep half, which he sold and fed to the fort's garrison in place of their usual rations, 'whereupon the said little Fort hath ever since been called the Rice-banke, of the abundance of Rice, battered and boiled in Pottage, which at that time was eaten in it'.

Presumably having written his first notes overnight (as Fynes Moryson recommended that travellers should), Coryate walked out of Calais at about 11 o'clock, reaching Boulogne,

16 miles away, at 7 that evening (averaging 2 miles an hour;
later, having got into his stride in his walking career, he would
double that speed). It is perhaps worth remembering that the
roads he would travel over the next five months were often
little more than tracks, stony, muddy after rain, rutted and,
unless they were originally Roman, often without proper
foundations. Some small paintings by Jan Breughel in the
Pinakothek in Munich give a fair idea of seventeenth-century
roads. The earth track is hardly to be distinguished from the
surrounding terrain; travellers are mostly peasants on foot,
farmers' wives carrying their baskets to market, a few carts, the
occasional horseman. In winter, the holes are full of water, the
horses up to their hocks, the cartwheels sunk in mud;
pedestrians, shepherds and pigs have retreated to the banks
beside the way. On the way, Tom saw two churches and two
monasteries that had been destroyed in the recent wars; in
Boulogne he was pleased to notice the first monks that he had
ever seen. Early the next morning he set off for Montreuil:

A little beyond Boulogne there is a Gallowes, consisting of two
goodly faire pillars of free-stone [fine-grained sandstone or
limestone], where there is no Cross beame as upon our English
gallowes, but that crosse beame is erected when any are hanged,
and taken downe againe immediately after the execution. No
[minor] offendours are hanged there, but only fellons. A little
beyond that there is a place of execution made of timber, at the
toppe whereof there is a wheele, whereon the bodies of murderers
only are tormented and broken in peeces with certain yron
instruments, wherewith they breake their armes first, then their legs
and thighes, and after their breast: If they are favoured their breast
is first broken. That blow on their breast is called the blow of
mercy, because it doth quickly bereave them of their life. . . .
Againe, a little beyond that place there is a little chappell made
conduitwise, wherein is erected the picture of Christ and the Virgin
Mary; there I saw three women and a man praying to that picture.

In England, felons were not publicly broken on the wheel, but
Coryate would have been familiar with public hangings (there

were over 1,000 annually in England and Wales); in Protestant England, such religious images had long been banned.

Just before Montreuil,

> there was a Whitsuntide foole disguised like a foole [a cunning disguise], wearing a long coate, there were many severall peeces of cloth of divers colours, at the corners whereof there hanged the tailes of Squirrels; he bestowed a little peece of plate [metal], wherein was expressed the effigies of the Virgin Mary, upon every one that gave him money; for he begged money of all travellers for the benefite of the Parish Church.

At Montreuil itself, a strongly walled and guarded town, with a long history in Anglo-French fighting, he stayed overnight, leaving at 6 a.m. in a covered cart, 'according to the fashion of the country', and as shown in his title page; passing through the Forest of Veronne, the passengers were warned to take their swords in their hands (not that Coryate had one), as there were gangs of murderous thieves in the area, 'that lurke under trees and shrubbes, and suddenly set upon travellers, and cut their throtes, except the true men are too strong for them. Also there are wild Bores and wild Harts in that Forrest; but we saw none of them.' He left Abbeville at about 1 p.m. and walked to the village of Picquiny, 14 miles distant, having chatted on the way with a young friar. 'We entered into many speeches of divers matters [in Latin; in those days, the educated throughout Europe could converse in Latin – conveniently for Coryate, who, like most Englishmen then and since, was weak on modern languages], especially of Religion, wherein the chiefest matter that we handled was about the adoration of Images.' It was as well that the friar was 'a very good fellow and sociable in his discourses', as Coryate was little inclined to moderation in religious debate. Others were worse: the Scotsman William Lithgow (1582–1645, a great traveller, for whom the term 'dour Scotsman' might have been invented, and known in his native Lanark as 'cut-lugged Willie' after the brothers of a Miss Lockhart cut off his ears – it might have

been worse) was proud to say that he quarrelled with his
continental travelling companions because they were
Catholics, and made a point of tearing garments off religious
images, rather than 'with indifferent forbearance wink at the
wickedness of idolaters'. While France had been relatively
relaxed since the recent improvement of relations with
England, and the succession to the throne of ex-Protestant
Henri IV who had granted liberty of conscience in 1598, it was
as recently as 1572 that thousands of Protestants had been
massacred in Paris, on St Bartholomew's Day, and one did well
to show some restraint. In Italy, one really needed to be
careful: there, the Inquisition not infrequently arrested and
imprisoned Protestants. In 1608 an Englishman, John Mole (or
Molle), an outspoken critic of the Roman Church (and
unfortunate to be employed as tutor-companion to two young
aristocrats, who simply left him and moved on), was arrested
by the Inquisition, eventually dying in prison in Rome, aged
80, after thirty years' imprisonment.

Thursday 19 May Coryate spent in Amiens, staying at 'the
signe of the Ave Maria'. He was impressed by the cathedral,
with its many pictures, an elaborately carved and gilded pulpit,
and a large, complicated brass globe depicting the earth and
stars, planets and astrological signs. The chief relic here
(Protestant Coryate was fascinated by religious relics) was
supposed to be the forepart of John the Baptist's head, enclosed
in gold and precious stones and kept in a crystal cabinet (but, he
was told, only displayed at 6 a.m. in 'a certaine little high
Chappell', with lots of cockle and mussel shells, beads and
'other religious reliques' outside the door). There was also some
needlework by Carmelite nuns (to whose nunnery he had earlier
been refused entry), whom he saw – again, an exotic sight for a
Protestant Englishman – in church, at Vespers, 'in two rowes
opposite to each other. They wore white vailes about their
heades, and blacke over the same which covered their whole
body to their feete: one of these was a very beautifull woman.'
Also at Amiens he encountered his first authentic pilgrim, a bad
Latinist by Coryate's standards ('a country Scholler in England

should be whipped for speaking the like'), walking from Compostella in north-west Spain to Rome (not by an obvious route), with staff in hand, a bead chain (presumably a rosary) about his neck, and a box with a picture of the Virgin and Child. At Mont Faucon there was 'the fayrest Gallowes that ever I saw, built upon a little hillocke . . . which consisteth of fourteene fair pillars of free-stone: this gallowes was made in the time of the Guisian massacre, to hang the Admiral of France, Chatillion, who was a Protestant, Anno Dom. 1572'. Actually Châtillon was murdered in the Louvre; his head was sent to the Pope, and his body, after it had been dragged through the streets of Paris, was hanged here, by the feet.

Coryate liked to insert stories into his travelogue, and here at Amiens, as at Calais, he had a story of the recent wars. The high point of the story was how the Spanish commander besieging the city in 1597 disguised forty or fifty soldiers as peasants, 'with fardels upon their heads and shoulders, and pistols and daggers under their coates'. Early one morning they followed a farm cart going through the city gate, and

> as soon as ever the cart was gotten under the portcullice, one of the peasants untied closely a sacke of walnuttes which he carried, and let them all fall out; and while the corps de garde which kept the gate were scrambling to gather them up, another of these disguised souldiers cuts the hairness of the horse, and so with cart and horse barricadoed and stopped the passage of the gate: and then the rest drew forth their weapons, seised upon the rest that guarded the gate, and made themselves the masters of it.

The rest of the Spanish force, previously in hiding, now entered and seized the town 'whiles the people were at the sermon'. When the Spanish force were themselves eventually forced out, their 2,500 soldiers marched out with all their bags and baggages – 160 laden carts and 'some thousand women of the town'. The remaining population held a celebratory Mass and sang the *Te Deum*.

The next afternoon he set off by coach (still not a very common form of transport in England) through Breteuil,

Clermont (where there was a gibbet with a picture of a wanted man hanging from a gallows, to show what they would like to do if only they could catch him), St Leu, St Brice and St Denis, through rich and fertile country, 'full of corne, especially rie, meadowes, pastures, wooddes, many sweete rivers, a great multitude of goodly and sumptuous houses', arriving in Paris early in the evening of 22 May. Here he stayed in the suburb of St Germain with a French Protestant, 'who in the civill warres fought against the Papists, and was most grievously wounded, who showed me his wounds'. In St Germain Abbey church he 'saw a gray Frier shrift a faire Gentlewoman, which I therefore mention because it was the first shrifting that ever I saw'. He was also introduced to the famous scholar Isaac Casaubon, and talked to him about his books, which pleased the old man, who suggested, as Coryate reported at length, that someone ought to write a biography of Queen Elizabeth.

Early in his account of Paris (the first city he was able to introduce with Scaliger's verses), he recalls the city's Roman name, Lutetia, 'being so called from the Latin word Lutum, which signifieth durt, because many of the streets are the durtiest, and so consequently the most stinking of all that ever I saw in any citie in my life'. Coryate was not to be the last British tourist to be sniffy about French drainage. An anonymous versifier (perhaps Sir John Suckling, whose father had written verses for *Coryats Crudities*) wrote in 1623 of

> Paris on the Seine,
> Its wondrous faire, but nothing cleane,
> 'Tis Europe's greatest Towne:
> How strong it is, I need not tell it,
> For all the world may easily smell it,
> That walke it up and down.

William Lithgow was even less complimentary:

Paris I confess is populous, a masse of poore people, for lacqueys and pages, a nest of rogues, a tumultuous place, a noctuall den of theeves, and a confused multitude: Where contrariwise London is adorned with many grave, prudent and provident Senators, civill, well taught, and courteous people, and absolutely the best governed City on the whole face of the earth, as well by night as by day, and nothing inferiour in quantity to it.

The second sentence is not strictly relevant here, but it is not often that one finds a Scotsman saying anything complimentary about the English, so it seemed worth preserving. However, Coryate was impressed that Paris (unlike London, which was largely built of brick and timber, or wattle and daub) was mostly constructed from 'faire white freestone' – the newer building, anyway – and admired a nearly completed bridge, the Pont Neuf, begun in 1599 (a few years later, the world-travelling businessman Peter Mundy (1596–1667) saw it completed, with an elaborate fountain house with a clock and carvings, 'also the Statue of a maide cast in brasse with a buckett in her hand, wherewith she seemeth to poure out the water, which . . . by Pipes is conveyed to the Louvre or Kings house').

Coryate described the Louvre at some length, praising the many statues, great staircases, elaborately carved and gilt roofs, particularly the main gallery, that

excelleth in my opinion, not only al those that are now in the world, but also al whatsoever that ever were since the creation thereof . . . The roofe of most glittering and admirable beauty, wherein is much antique work, with the picture of God and the Angels, the Sunne, the Moone, the Starres, the Planets, and other Celestiall signes. Yea, so unspeakably faire it is, that a man can hardly comprehend it in his minde, that hath not first seene it with his bodily eyes.

He also admired the gilding and inlaid marble at the Tuileries, where he found the garden 'the fairest garden for length of delectable walkes that ever I saw, but for variety of delicate fonts [fountains] and springes, much inferior to the Kings garden at Fountaine Beleau'. Gardeners were busy working on a knot and herb garden, and at the end of the garden a man sang to activate 'an exceeding fine Eccho'.

On the feast of Corpus Christi he attended Mass at Notre Dame Cathedral, itself 'nothing so faire as our Lady Church of Amiens: for I could see no notable matter in it'. He remarked, not altogether approvingly, on the richness of the priests' vestments (the Bishop 'with his crimson velvet gloves and costly rings upon his fingers, decked with most glittering gemmes'), and was shocked by the way that the little boy choristers had their heads clean shaven,

> for they had not a quarter so much haire left upon their heads as they brought with them into the world out of their mothers wombs, being so clean shaved away round about their whole heads that a man could perceive no more then the very rootes. A spectacle very pitifull (me thinks) to behold, though the Papists esteeme it holy.

The processions around the city streets provided more spectacle; the streets were generally 'sumptuously adorned that day . . . from the pentices [overhanging, sloping roofs] of their houses to the lower end of the wall hanged with rich cloth of arras, and the costliest tapistry that they could provide', whilst 'they garnished many of their streets with as rich cupboards of plate as ever I saw in my life. For they exposed upon their publique tables exceeding costly goblets, and what not tending to pompe that is called by the name of plate. Upon the middest of their tables stood their golden Crucifixes, with divers other gorgeous Images.' The processions, led by the Bishop and priests, were treated with great reverence:

> For whereas the Bishop carried the Sacrament, even his consecrated wafer cake, betwixt the Images of two golden Angels, whensoever he passed by any company, all the spectators prostrated themselves most humbly upon their knees, and elevated their handes with all possible reverence and religious behaviour, attributing as much divine adoration to the little wafer cake, which they call the Sacrament of the Altar, as they could doe to Jesus Christ himselfe, if he were bodily present with them.

In the Abbey Church of St Denis he was able to view images of the kings of France, and the royal regalia – crowns, sceptres and crucifixes of gold, carbuncles and rubies – and tombs of marble and alabaster; also 'one of the nayles wherewith Christ was crucified, as they affirme: that nayle I saw set in a faire peece of silver plate double gilt, at the top whereof there was a silver Theca or Sheath which contayned the nayle'. Equally remarkable were 'an Unicornes horne valued at one hundred thousand crownes, being about three yardes high, even so high that I could hardly reach to the top of it', and the shroud of St Denis, the patron saint of France. 'I saw St Denis his head inclosed in a wonderful rich helmet, beset with exceeding abundance of pretious stones: but the skull it selfe I saw not plainly, only the forepart of it I beheld through a pretty crystal glasse by the light of a waxen candle'. Suckling (or anon.) was there a few years later, not overly impressed or credulous:

> And to St Denis first we came
> To see the sights at Notre Dame.
>   The man that shews them snuffles:
> Where who is apt for to believe,
> May see our Lady's right-hand sleeve,
>   And her old pantofles. . . .   [slippers]

> There is one of the Cross's nailes,
> Which whoso sees, his bonnet vailes, [doffs respectfully]
>   And if he list may kneele:
> Some say its false, 'twas never so,
> Yet feeling it, thus much I know,
>   It is as true as steel. . . .

> There's one saint there has lost his toes,
> Another his head but not his nose,
>   A finger and a thumb:
> Now when we had seen these holy rags,
> We went to th'inne and tooke our nags,
>   And so away did come.

Early on the morning of Saturday 28 May, Coryate rode out to the Palace of Fontainebleau, where the King and his family were in residence. 'On the way my [hired] horse began to be so tiry, that he would not stirre one foote out of the way, though I did even excarnificate [make bloody] his sides with my often spurring of him, except he were grievously whipped.' Seeing this, another man, Mr I.H., helpfully 'tooke great paines with him to lash him', before he 'drew out his Rapier and ranne him into his buttocke neare to his fundament, about a foote deep very neare'. This did not greatly improve matters, and later Mr I.H. attempted to stop the copious bleeding by washing the horse, but 'lost his labour, as much as he did that washed the Aethiopian: for the bloud ranne out afresh'. When the guide and owner discovered this, he was 'extreame cholericke', and in the end Mr I.H. had to buy him off with 'sixe French crownes' – no small amount. Coryate thought the incident worth recounting, but made no comment whatever.

At Fontainebleau, Coryate was particularly taken with the gardens (designed by Claude Mollet), remarking on the fountains, fishponds with great carp, elaborate knot gardens, large beech trees, and sculptures, particularly of Romulus and Remus with the wolf, 'Savage men' and Sphinxes: 'the face of a maide, the body of a dogge, the winges of a bird, the nailes of a Lyon, and the taile of a Dragon, which was called Sphinx, according to which form these sphinges were made.' Among the living animals in the gardens were storks (of which he was to see many more, later, in Flushing), birds reputed to cherish and feed their aged parents, even carrying them on their backs, 'a notable example for children to follow', and also ostriches,

such birds that (as Historians doe write of them) will eate yron, as a key, or a horse shoe [a wide-spread myth: Shakespeare repeated it in *II Henry VI*, 'I'll make thee eat cast iron like an ostrich, and swallow my sword like a great pin']; one male and two female . . . a very foolish bird: for whereas hee doth sometimes hide his necke behind a bush, he thinks that no body sees him, though indeede he be seene of every one. Also he is said to be so forgetfull, that as soone as he hath laid his [*sic*] egges, he hath cleane forgotten them till his young ones are hatched.

With the Royal Family being in residence, Coryate was not able to see as much of the Palace as he had hoped, but got involved with the Royal Guards, a large body (of no doubt large bodies) comprising 1,600 footsoldiers, 400 on duty at a time, with fifty archers at the gate, and including detachments of French, Swiss and Scots guards. The Scotsmen did get him in to see some of the Palace, especially the great Presence Chamber, where he was very impressed by 'the fairest chimney that ever I saw, being made of perfect alabaster' richly carved, which cost 'fourescore thousand French crownes, which amount to foure and twenty thousand pound starling'. He also caught sight of some of the family, particularly the young 'Dolphin . . . about seven yeares old . . . His face full and fat-cheeked, his haire black, his looke vigorous and couragious, which argues a bold and lively spirit' (in two years' time, following the assassination of his father, Henri IV, he would become Louis XIII, governed first by his unintelligent Italian mother, Marie de Medici, and then by the very intelligent Cardinal Richelieu). Coryate was amused by the guards' fancy uniforms:

The Switzers weare no Coates, but doublets and hose of pane[l]s intermingled with red and Yellow and Blewe Sarcenet [fine, soft silk] rising up between the Panes, besides Codpieces of the like colours, which Codpiece, because it is by that merie French writer Rablais [in *Gargantua and Pantagruel*, book III, chapter 8] stiled the first and principall piece of Armour, the Switzers do weare it as a significant Symbole of the assured service they are to doe to the French King in his Warres, and of the maine burden of the most laborious imployments which lye upon them in time of Peace, as old suresbyes [reliables] to serve for all Turnes . . . I noted many of them to be very clusterfisted lubbers. As for their attire, it is made so phantastically, that a novice newly come to the Court, who never saw any of them before, would half imagine, if he should see one of them alone without his weapon, hee were the Kings foole.

On 29 May he rode post-horse to La Chapelle la Reine, before continuing on foot; he remarked on the fertility of the land on the way — walnut trees, rye fields, hemp fields, vineyards; 'a little on this side Montargis I saw a very dolefull and lamentable Spectacle: the bones and ragged fragments of clothes of a certaine murderer remayning on a wheele, whereon most murderers are executed: the bones were miserably broken asunder, and dispersed abroad upon the wheele in divers places'. He saw the Loire, broad, with little islands, bordered by great open meadows; at Briare he noted the French custom of putting wooden shutters on the inside of the lower parts of windows, where there was no glass. He also remarked on the 'road rage' of French postillions: 'If they happen to be angry with a stranger upon the way upon any occasion, they will say to him, le diable t'emporte, that is, The divell take thee. This I know by mine own experience.' It would be nice to know what lay behind that last sentence. On 31 May he lunched at La Charité, and that evening arrived at Nevers.

Here, after recording various pictures, tombs and inscriptions in the cathedral, he was made somewhat apprehensive by a large gathering of gypsies.

> For both their haire and their faces looked so blacke, as if they were raked out of hel, and sent into the world by great Beelzebub to terrifie and astonish mortall men: their men are very Ruffians and Swashbucklers, having exceeding long blacke haire curled, and swords or other weapons by their side. Their women also suffer their haire to hang loosely about their shoulders, whereof some I saw dancing in the streets, and singing lascivious vaine songs; whereby they draw many flocks of the foolish citizens about them.

He also saw lots of wooden clogs for sale, at twopence farthing a pair, which he thought worth recording. 'Thus much of Nevers.'

The next day he rode post-horse again, to St Gérand; at Moulins, on the way, he could hardly get to his inn for lunch because of the great herds of oxen and cows brought into town for the cattle market; that afternoon he saw more evidence of the disorder caused by the recent wars, 'one very ruefull and tragicall object: ten men hanging in their clothes upon a goodly gallows made of freestone about a mile beyond Moulins, whose bodies were consumed to nothing, onely their bones and the ragged f[l]itters of their clothes remained'. Presumably by 'goodly' he meant well constructed, rather than admirable.

From St Gérand he could see the jagged peaks of the Alps rearing up, about 40 miles away; the road became more mountainous and stony, bordered by fields with black sheep, and increasing numbers of pine trees. At an 'obscure towne called Tarare' he was not able to get a fresh post-horse, and had to walk 6 miles 'in my boots' before he could get one; then it rained very heavily, so that he was 'drooping wet to my very skinne when I came to my Inne' (a rare instance of Coryate complaining of the weather) at Lyons, on 3 June. Here he had to pass through three gates, and declare his business and where he came from, to the porter at the third gate, who gave him 'a little ticket' as a warrant permitting him to stay in the city.

The great city got the full treatment in his book: verses by Julius Caesar Scaliger, an outline of its history from Roman times, a summary description, with speculation as to the origin of the names of the rivers, a list of thirty-nine churches, nunneries and friaries, and comments on ruins. Coryate stayed at 'The Three Kings', the best and smartest inn in Lyons, and therefore without doubt the most expensive, not as a rare self-indulgence but as an attempted investment, 'for the Earle of Essex [a young nobleman of great family, whom Coryate claimed as fourth cousin] lay there with all his traine before I came thither: he came thither the Saturday and went away the Thursday following, being the day immediately before I came in' – Coryate just missed him. Coryate's frustration can be imagined – the encounter with His Lordship could have proved quite profitable, in either the short or long term. Not that the smart set of High Renaissance Europe were necessarily reliable patrons; by the hall of one courtyard was written 'this pretty french poesie: On ne loge ceans à credit: car il est mort, les mauvais paieurs l'ont tué. The English is this: Here is no lodging upon credit: for he is dead, ill payers have killed him'.

One guest at the inn ('with his traine') when Coryate was there was the French Ambassador, formerly at Constantinople, now proceeding to his new post at Rome.

> Amongst the rest of his company there were two Turkes that he brought with him out of Turkey, whereof one was a blacke Moore, who was his jester; a mad conceited [witty, imaginative] fellow, and very merry. He wore no hat at all eyther in his journey (for he overtooke us upon the way riding without a hat) or when he rested in any towne, because his naturall haire, which was exceeding thicke and curled, was so prettily elevated in length that it served him alwaies instead of a hat: the other Turke was a notable companion and a great scholler in his kinde: for he spake six or seven languages besides the Latin, which he spake very well.

The Turk told Coryate about Constantinople, where he was born (and which may well have whetted Coryate's appetite for future travel), before, unfortunately, the conversation turned to religion.

> I had a long discourse with him in Latin of many things, and amongst other questions I asked him whether he were ever baptized, he told me, no, and said he never would be. After that wee fell into speeches of Christ, whom he acknowledged for a great Prophet, but not for the Sonne of God, affirming that neither he nor any of his countrey men would worship him, but the onely true God, creator of heaven and earth: and called us Christians idolaters, because we worshipped images; a most memorable speech if it be properly applied to those kind of Christians which deserve that Imputation of Idolatry. At last I fell into some vehement argumentations with him in defence of Christ, whereupon being unwilling to answer me, he suddenly flung out of my company.

Exasperation was the least of the reactions Coryate might provoke in religious disputes, notable as they were on his part for assertive dogmatism (characteristic of most religious debate at the time) and obtuseness; like many contemporaries, he would probably have been proud of such behaviour.

Coryate's other encounters in Lyons included the French king's mules, with willow nosebags and trappings with the royal arms, a man being whipped through the streets, and another pilgrim proceeding (possibly homeward) from Compostella to Rome, this time via Avignon (he still seems to have been out of his way): 'I had a long discourse with him in Latin, who told me he was a Roman born. I found him but a simple fellow, yet he had a little beggarly and course Latin, so much as a Priscianist may have.' (Priscian was used for a standard Latin grammar text – see *Love's Labours Lost*, Act V). More important during Coryate's two-day stay was the making of arrangements for travelling over the Mont Cenis pass into Italy. First, there was the obtaining of bills of health,

> without the which we could not be received into any of those cities that lay in our way toward Italy. For the Italians are so curious and scrupulous in many of their cities, especially those that I passed through in Lombardy, that they will admit no stranger within the wals of the citie, except he bringeth a bill of health from the last citie he came from . . . the Venetians are extraordinarily precise herein, insomuch that a man cannot be received into Venice without a bill of health, if he would give a thousand duckets.

Coryate then joined a group of travellers proceeding with the assistance of a guide to take them up through the mountains along the narrow, difficult passes on the way from Lyons to Turin; it would be many years before an adequate carriageway would be built. In the evening of Tuesday 7 June he arrived at Pont de Beauvoisin: 'at this Pont de Beauvoisin France and Savoy doe meet, the bridge parting them both. When I was on this side the bridge I was in France, when beyond, in Savoy.'

An independent duchy since the fourteenth century, with its capital in Chambéry, Savoy was to become a province of the kingdom of Sardinia in 1720, before being ceded to France in

1860. All through the mountains here, Coryate noticed immense fertility and profusion of animal life: 'red snailes of extraordinary length and greatnesse', an 'admirable abundance of Butter-flies . . . by the hundreth part more then ever I saw in any countrey before', barley ready for mowing two months earlier than in England, corn and rye-fields, many chestnut trees, above all

> infinite abundance of vineyardes planted at the foot of the Alpes . . . I doe not remember I saw halfe the plenty in any part of all France in so short a space . . . for the space of ten whole miles together, a man could not perceive any vacant or wast place under the Alpes, but all beset with vines: in so much that I thinke the number of these vineyardes on both sides of the Alpes was not so little as foure thousand. I admired one thing very much in those vineyards, that they should be planted in such wonderfull steepe places underneath the hils, where a man would thinke it were almost impossible for a labourer to worke, such is the praecipitium of the hill towards the descent.

The main impression of his journey through the Savoy territory, however, is of the sheer nervous and physical strain produced by the steep, narrow, winding tracks edged with unnerving, vertiginous precipices. He began by climbing Mount Aiguebelette, starting at 10 a.m. and finishing on the other side, towards Chambéry, about 1 p.m., a mile and a half up, he reckoned, and half a mile down.

> I went up a-foote, and delivered my horse to another to ride for me, because I thought it was more dangerous to ride then to goe a foote, though indeede all my other companions did ride: but then this accident happened to me. Certaine poore fellowes which get their living especially by carrying men in chairs from the top of the hill to the foot thereof toward Chambery, made a bargaine with some of my company, to carry them down in chaires, when they came to the toppe of the Mountaine, so [on condition] that I kept them company towards the toppe. But they being desirous to get some money of me, led me such an extreme pace towards the toppe, that how much soever I laboured to keepe them company, I

could not possibly performe it: The reason why they led such a pace was because they hoped that I would give them some consideration to be carryed in a chaire to the toppe, rather then I would leese their company, and so consequently my way also, which is almost impossible for a stranger to finde alone by himselfe, by reason of the innumerable turnings and windings thereof, being on every side beset with infinite abundance of trees. So that at last finding that faintnesse in my selfe that I was not able to follow them any longer, I compounded with them for a cardakew [cardecu, an old French silver coin], which is eighteene pence English, to be carryed to the toppe of the Mountaine, which was at least half a mile from the place where I mounted on the chaire . . . but such was the miserable paines that the poore slaves willingly undertooke for the gaine of that cardakew, that I would not have done the like for five hundred. The ways were exceeding difficult in regard of the steepnesse and hardnesse thereof, for they were al rocky, petricosae & salebrosae [stony and rugged], and so uneven that a man could hardly find any sure footing on them. When I had tandem aliquando [at last] gotten up to the toppe, I said to my selfe with Aeneas in Virgil:

– Forsan & haec olim meminisse juvabit.
[Perhaps one day this too will be pleasant to remember]

then might I justly and truly say, that which I could never before, that I was above some of the clowdes.

It is notable that it is the unusual achievement – of being above cloud level – that appears to excite him; the romantic pleasure in the sublime, in dramatic vistas or wild nature, are after his time, and unknown to him. Later he records the violent currents running through a lake at Lezere, with torrents tearing off huge rocks, but acknowledges no excitement, only 'the horrible and hideous noyse thereof [like] the river Cocytus in hell'.

He rode out of Chambéry at 6 a.m. on 9 June, reaching Aiguebelle, 10 miles further on, by noon:

The worst ways that ever I travelled in all my life in the Sommer were those betwixt Chamberie and Aiguebelle, which were as bad as the worst I ever rode in England in the midst of Winter. . . . On every Alpe I saw wonderfull abundance of pine trees, especially about the toppe, and many of them of a very great heigth; and betwixt the toppe and the foote there are in many of those mountains wilde Olive trees, Chesnut-trees, Walnut-trees, Beeches, Hasel trees, &c. . . .

It seemeth very dangerous in divers places to travel under rocky mountains, because many of them are cloven and do seeme at the very instant that a man is under them minare ruinam [to threaten to fall]; and by so much the more fearefull a man may be, by how much the more he may see great multitudes of those stones fallen downe in divers places by the river, and the side of the way from the mountains themselves, & many of them foure or five times greater then the great stone of Hamdon hill [in Somerset, very near Odcombe – of course].

The feete of the Alpes that are opposite to each other are distant one from another . . . in some places halfe a mile, or something more, but scarce a whole mile: and in some places they are so neare together, that they are but little more then a Butte-length [arrow-shot] asunder.

'A man' was definitely getting unnerved; further on, he remarked, 'the waies on the sides of the mountaines whereon I rode were so exceeding high, that if my horse had happened to stumble, he had fallen downe with me foure or five times as deepe in some places as Paules tower in London is high'; so prudent Thomas got off and walked his horse for a mile and a half.

At Aiguebelle itself he saw many people with great throat goitres, 'such as we call in Latin strumas, as bigge as the fistes of a man, through the drinking of snow water, yea some of their bunches are almost as great as an ordinary foote-ball with us in England'. Up in the Grande Chartreuse range of mountains, 'exceeding is the abundance of woodden crosses in Savoy, and a marvailous multitude of little Chappels, with the picture of Christ and the Virgin Mary, and many other religious persons, wherein I did oftentimes see some at their devotion'. In Lasnebourg, the last Savoyard town he stayed in, he noticed the women's fashions, of an extremely high girdle and large, elaborate headdresses; also, 'the heigth of their beds: for they were so high that a man could hardly gette into his bedde without some kind of climing, so that a man needed a ladder to get up as we say here in England'. In Savoy, it seemed to be all climbing: up and down the mountains (Mont Roche-Melon was 11,640 feet high – not 14 miles, as he thought, but high enough), in and out of bed, on and off the road. But, as the rocky tracks twisted and turned, down Coryate and his fellow travellers went

headlong. The waies were exceeding uneasie. For they were wonderfull hard, all stony and full of windings and intricate turnings, whereof I thinke there were at the least two hundred before I came to the foot. Still I met many people ascending, and mules laden with carriage, and a great company of dunne kine driven up the hill with collars about their neckes.

The air seemed warmer; there were different scents; in the distance, coming closer, were the softer hills and the gentle green plains of northern Italy.

The Paradise of Travellers

The descent from Mont Cenis Pass proved particularly tedious and leg-aching, as Coryate had to walk down the foothills for 7 miles; but at 1 o'clock, on Saturday 11 June, he arrived in Novalesa in Piedmont. After lunch he rode on to San Giorgio, avoiding the walled and fortified town of Sura, where travellers were relieved of any money in excess of what was legally permitted. The appearance of the country people he found charming:

> In many places of Piemont I observed most delicate strawen hats, which both men and women use in most places of that Province, but especially the women. For those that the women weare are very prety, some of them having at the least an hundred seames made with silke, and some pretily woven in the seames with silver, and many flowers, borders, and branches very curiously wrought in them, in so much that some of them were valued at two duckatons, that is, eleven shillings.

The oxen that drew carts were covered with white linen cloths around their bodies, as protection from the flies 'which would otherwise much infest them'. He saw rye being reaped on Sunday, about six weeks earlier than it might be in England, 'infinite abundance' of walnut trees, 'wonderfull plenty of corne' and 'store of vines that grow not so low as in France, but upon high poles or railes, a great deale higher from the ground'.

In Turin, reached late in the afternoon of 12 June, the travellers said farewell to their *vetturino*, or guide, but Tom saw little of the city, as he was unwell with an inflammation in his face and hands, caused, he thought, by drinking 'the sweet wines of Piemont', which led him to warn all future English travellers in Italy to water their wine. His account of the 'faire city', with its well-fortified citadel and cathedral, is brief and almost entirely potted history. His condition encouraged him to continue his progress by coach, and on Monday evening he arrived in Cigliano. Once again he delighted in the fertile land – 'goodly spacious grounds . . . wonderfully replenished with corne, Vineyards, Orchards, and a singular exuberancy of all manner of fruits'. The vines, he noticed, were trained on trees, usually maple, but also walnut, willow and elm, with stakes set in the earth so that the grapes hung from them very accessibly. He also observed that

> many of their women and children goe only in their smockes and shirts in divers places of the countrey without any other apparell at all by reason of the extreme heat of the clymate [which in general he does not remark on, or appear to be inconvenienced by]; and many of their children which doe weare breeches, have them so made, that all the hinder parts of their bodies are naked, for the more coolnesse of the ayre.

Fynes Moryson had a different explanation: 'the Italians clothe very little children with doublets and breeches, but their breeches are open behind, with the shirt hanging out, that they may ease themselves without helpe.'

Early next day, restored, Coryate rode on, reaching Vercelli in mid-morning, where he saw the festival of John the Baptist. At the west gate of the city there was erected 'a faire bower covered with green boughs newly cut, under the which there stood a cupboord furnished with the pictures of Christ and our Lady, and with great abundance of exceedingly costly plate'. There was also a procession through the streets, with singing boys, and priests and men and women carrying candles. 'They went all in couples very orderly. But I never saw in all my life such an ugly company of truls and sluts as their women were. Withall there was an exceeding shooting of squibs in every street where the Procession passed.'

He had previously suffered from an excess of the local wine; now he complained of the habit of sprinkling food with cheese, 'which I love not so well as the Welchmen doe', which put him off his food. One of their dining habits, however, greatly interested him: the use of forks. Throughout Europe, on the dining tables there might be wooden or pewter plates or, often, just slices of stale bread, trenchers, to soak up any liquid. In company, the food was laid out in a large dish on a table, for people to reach in and get for themselves whatever they might want, usually with a knife, which often caused nasty accidents (in Middleton's *The Changeling* of 1621, Deflores, displaying a murdered man's severed finger, remarks, 'A greedy hand thrust in a dish at court I In a mistake, hath had as much as this'). While one could eat with spoon and knife, often people used their fingers (Montaigne admits to sometimes biting his fingers in his hasty eating).

I observed a custome in all those Italian Cities and Townes through the which I passed, that is not used in any other country that I saw in my travels, neither doe I thinke that any other nation in Christendome doth use it, but only Italy. The Italian and also most strangers that are commorant [resident] in Italy, doe alwaies at their meales use a little forke when they cut their meat. For while with their knife which they hold in one hand they cut the meate out of the dish, they fasten their forke which they hold in their other hand upon the same dish, so that whatsoever he be that sitting in the company of any other at meale, should unadvisedly touch the dish of meate with his fingers from which all at the table doe cut, he will give occasion of offence unto the company, as having transgressed the laws of good manners, in so much that for his error he shall be at the least browbeaten, if not reprehended in wordes. This forme of feeding I understand is generally used in all places of Italy, their forkes being for the most part made of yron or steele, and some of silver, but those are used only by Gentlemen. The reason of this their curiosity is, because the Italian cannot by any means indure to have his dish touched with fingers, seeing all mens fingers are not alike cleane.

Coryate was very taken with this novelty, forks, as he said, being hardly known in England (though Ben Jonson refers to them in his Venice-set comedy *Volpone*, in 1605: 'Then must you learn the use I And handling of your silver fork at meals'), and promptly adopted the practice, not only while in Italy but on his way home through Germany, and back in England, 'being once quipped for that frequent using of my forke, by a certain learned Gentleman, a familiar friend of mine, one M. Laurence Whitaker, who in his merry humour doubted not to call me at table furcifer, only for using a forke at feeding, but for no other cause' (the word, deriving from the forked yoke worn by Roman criminals, normally being used abusively). Forks were slowly introduced into Europe in the sixteenth century, though not everyone approved: a German preacher condemned them as sinful – God would not have given us fingers if he had wished us to use forks. The earliest painting of a fork is in a Last Supper by Jacopo Bassano, in 1599. Coryate was certainly one of the earliest English users of the word 'fork' and of the thing itself, which he probably introduced to his friends meeting at the Mermaid Club in London. The earliest mention of a fork in England is in a will inventory of 1660; it was about a century before the use of forks became anything like general.

If Coryate had been charmed by Piedmont, he was enraptured by Lombardy:

Surely such is the fertility of this country, that I thinke no Region or Province under the Sunne may compare with it. For it is passing plentifully furnished with all things tending both to pleasure and profit, being the very Paradise and Canaan of Christendome. For as Italy is the garden of the world, so is Lombardy the garden of Italy, and Venice the garden of Lombardy. It is wholly plaine, and beautified with such abundance of goodly rivers, pleasant meadowes, fruifull vineyardes, fat pastures, delectable gardens, orchards, woodes, and what not, that the first view thereof did even refocillate [revive: *OED* cites this as the first use of the word] my spirits, and tickle my senses with inward joy. To conclude this introduction to Lombardy, it is so fertile a territory, that (as my

learned and eloquent friend M. Richard Martin of the middle
Temple once wrote me a most elegant letter) the butter thereof is
oyle, the dew hony, and the milk nectar.

At 11 a.m. on Wednesday 15 June he rode into the great city
of Milan, where, despite being there no more than twenty-
seven hours, he managed an extraordinary amount of
sightseeing: the Church of St Ambrose, the Cathedral, the
Palace, the Library, the Monastery and the Citadel (the city
being part of a Spanish Dukedom and governed from the
Citadel by Spaniards: 'There is such an extreme hatred between
the Milanois and the Spaniards, that neither the Milanois doe
at any time come into the Citadel, nor the Spaniards into the
City, but only in the evening'). One should acknowledge that
not infrequently Coryate fleshed out his own observations with
material from other guidebooks. Certainly parts of his Italian
writings are indebted to Fra Girolamo da Capugnano's edition
of François Schott's *Itinerarium Italiae* (Vicenza, 1601).

The Church of St Ambrose (where the saint stood to prohibit
'the Emperor Theodosius to enter the Church after hee had
committed that great slaughter of seven thousand men at
Thessalonica') provoked some righteous indignation in the
travelling Protestant, when he was shown a monument

which is the auncientest of al Christendome, if that were true
which they report of it. For then it would be three thousand five
hundred yeares old: namely the brasen serpent which Moses
erected in the wildernesse as a type and figure of Christ . . . It is
erected upon a goodly marble pillar of some twelve or sixteene
foote high in the body of the Church on the left hand as you come
in from the great gate. Verily I wonder that the Papists can be so
impudent to delude the people with these most palpable mockeries.
For it is a meere improbability, yea and an impossibility that this
should be the true Serpent, because we read in the holy Scriptures
(2 King 18.4) that the godly King Ezekias caused it to be broken in
pieces, because the children of Israel did burne incense to it . . . Yet
maugre the authority of Gods word, these people doe not sticke to
say that they have the selfe same serpent.

The Cathedral was also supposed to contain 'one of the nayles wherewith Christ was crucified, as they affirme', like the one he was shown in Paris, but Coryate was not able to see it, and made no comment. However, he climbed almost to the top of the Cathedral tower (which can still be done),

> wherehence I surveyed the whole citie round about, which yeelded a most beautifull and delectable shew . . . there also I beheld a great part of Italy, together with the lofty Apennines [which, being mountainous and not urban or fertile, rated no commendation] . . . The territory of Lombardy, which I contemplated round about from this Tower, was so pleasant an object to mine eyes, being replenished with such unspeakable variety of all things, both for profit and pleasure, that it seemeth to me to be the very Elysian fields, so much decantated and celebrated by the verses of Poets, or the Tempe or Paradise of the world. For it is the fairest plaine, extended about some two hundred miles in length that ever I saw, or ever shall if I should travell over the whole habitable world; insomuch that I said to myselfe that this country was fitter to be an habitation for the immortal Gods then for mortall men.

His brief account of the Palace of the Viscounts of Milan is almost entirely potted history; he went to the Library of the Cardinal Borromaeus, which contained no books, as it was not yet completed (until 1609); then on to the Ambrosian monks' monastery, the Augustinian monks' church, a rich merchant's house ('even fairer then the Viscounts Palace') and 'the Hospitall', where 'foure thousand poore people are relieved . . . The yearelie revenues of it are said to be at the least fifty thousand crownes.'

The Spaniards' moated citadel in the Castello Sforzesco interested him, so large that it seemed more like a separate, enclosed town, with marketplaces and 'many spacious and goodly greene courts, wherein the Spaniards dwell with their families'. The river running through the citadel drove two mills, one for grinding corn, the other for gunpowder, and could be blocked off to deprive and control the townspeople below. 'Neare to one of these Rivers', he noted, 'I saw a pretty amorous sight; a woman naked from the middle upward sitting at her worke'. Such notes serve as aides-mémoire. The Citadel was well supplied in case of siege, with corn and oil to supply soldiers for three years (the garrison comprising 500 men). Francis Bacon had recommended travellers to examine arms and fortifications, and Coryate for once rose to the occasion, going round inspecting, and counting, even on only one walk, 'twenty great peeces, besides those of the lesser sort, as Sakers [light cannon]' as well as a demi-culverin, a whole culverin [a long cannon firing shot of 17–20 lb] 'which was said to carry a bullet at the least eight miles, which I could hardly beleeve to be true', together with 'an exceeding huge Basiliske [a large brass cannon capable of firing 100lb shot], which was so great that it would easily contayne the body of a very corpulent man'. It is hardly surprising that this examination provoked 'a certain Spaniard' to express 'many tokens of anger' against Coryate, causing him to make a rapid departure.

About 2 p.m. the next day he took a slow coach journey to Lodi, about 20 miles away, arriving at 9 p.m.; unfortunately, the town gates were already locked for the night. Unable to get to his inn, he retreated to one out in the suburbs, only to find that every bed was taken, and he had to pass the night as best he could in the coach that he had arrived in.

This seems as good a place as any to touch on differences in telling the time.

The Italians beginne the day after the Sunne is set [Fynes Moryson explains], 'having whole Clockes striking twenty-foure howers, as our halfe clockes onely strike twelve, so as, not to be weary with telling the clocke, a man had neede of a stoole and a Cushion to sett at ease. The first hower after the Sunne is sett, strikes one, the Noone or midday varyeth daily as the Sunne doth his setting, for when the Sunne setteth at eight in the evening, the next Noone is when the Clocke strikes sixteene, and when the Sunne setts at seven, the next noone is when the Clocke strikes seventeene, and so it differs for the rest of the howers and minutes.

That seems clear enough; Coryate's coach-driver may have been dilatory, or he may have had a different idea of the time of sunset from that of the gatekeepers of Lodi.

Not surprisingly, Coryate rode off in good time the next day, at 4 a.m., arriving at the town of Pizzighettone early in the afternoon. An Italian gentleman showed him round, particularly the castle, where King Francis I of France had been imprisoned for two years nearly eighty years before, and had written on the wall, in Spanish and French, 'Francis King of France'. The gentleman also told the story of how the king, playing tennis ('real' or royal tennis, presumably) with one of his Spanish captors, accidentally struck his opponent with the ball. 'The Spaniard told the king that he played foule play; the king affirmed the contrary, and said to the Spaniard, darest thou contradict a king? and therewithal immediately drew his dagger, and stabbed the Spaniard.' Game, set and match.

The next stage Coryate did on foot, arriving at Cremona that evening, but on the way he saw some things that he admitted some readers might find too frivolous to mention:

The first Italian fannes that I saw in Italy did I observe in this space betwixt Pizighiton and Cremona. These fannes both men and women of the country doe carry to coole themselves withall in the time of heate . . . Most of them are very elegant and pretty things. For whereas the fanne consisteth of a painted peece of paper and a little wooden handle; the paper which is fastned into the top is on both sides most curiously adorned with excellent pictures, either of amorous things tending to dalliance, having some witty Italian verses or fine emblemes written under them; or of some notable Italian city with a brief description thereof added thereunto. These fannes are of a meane price . . . as countervaileth our English groate.

Also many of them doe carry other fine things of a far greater price, that will cost at least a duckat, which they commonly call in the Italian tongue umbrellaes, that is, things that minister shadow unto them for shelter against the scorching heate of the Sunne. These are made of leather something answerable to the forme of a little canopy, & hooped in the inside with divers little wooden hoopes that extend the umbrella in a pretty large compasse. They are used especially by horsemen, who carry them in their hands when they ride, fastning the end of the handle upon one of their thighes, and they impart so long a shadow unto them, that it keepeth the heate of the Sunne from the upper parts of their bodies.

As with the fork, this, with Randle Cotgrave's *Dictionarie* of the same year, appears to be one of the earliest uses of the word 'umbrella' in English, the thing itself not coming into use in England for a century or more (and then to provide shelter from the rain rather than from the sun).

Coryate was in Cremona (also part of the Spanish Duchy of Milan) for only a few hours (from 7 p.m. on the 17th to 5 a.m. on the 18th), and his brief account is mostly history, though he described the city as beautiful, with a church tower reputed to be the highest in Italy ('howsoever the Italians extoll it for the heigth, it is not comparable to the steeple of our Lady Church in Sarisbury, which I take to be at least twenty foote higher then this'). He was too late to see the Augustinian monks' library, but did dine on 'fried Frogges . . . a dish much used in many cities of Italy: they were so curiously dressed, that they did exceedingly delight my palat, the head and the forepart being cut off'.

About 12 miles before he got to Mantua he rode through Mirandula, the birthplace of the Renaissance neo-Platonist philosopher Pico della Mirandola, now

very desolate and unpeopled: the reason is, because the Bandits, which are the murdering robbers upon the Alpes and many places of Italy, make their abode in it as it were their safe Sanctuary and refuge, where they live in the castle of the towne: who because they doe oftentimes violently breake out upon the townsmen and other passengers, depriving them both of life and goods, they minister such occasion of feare to the inhabitants, that there dwell but few people in the towne.

Mantua, despite being the birthplace of the poet Virgil, also received only a flying visit, between 7.30 p.m. and 8 a.m.

Nevertheless he was able to see from the outside the Duke of
Mantua's palace, guarded by Switzers, and the Church of St
Barbara, 'meane without, being built all with bricke, but
within it is exceeding beautifull . . . imbossed with goodly
bosses of gold'; he also 'observed a very stately bricke bridge at
Mantua over the river Mincius, the longest that ever I saw till
then (saving our famous bridge of London)'. Early on the
Sunday morning 'a great multitude of country clowns' came
into town, 'with strawen hats with feathers in them, and every
one had his sithe and hooke in his hand; belike they came to
put themselves out to hire for harvest worke'. Despite the
extreme brevity of his visit to the city, Mantua and the
surrounding area, it seems, almost stole his heart away:

> I saw many stately Pallaces of a goodly heigh: it is most sweetly
> seated in respect of the marvailous sweete ayre thereof, the
> abundance of goodly meadows, pastures, vineyards, orchards, and
> gardens about it. For they have such store of gardens about the
> Citie, that I thinke London which both for frequencie of people
> and multitude of howses doth thrise exceed it, is not better
> furnished with gardens. Besides they have one more commoditie
> which maketh the Citie exceeding pleasant, even the fair river
> Mincius . . . Withall they have abundance of delectable fruites
> growing about the Citie, whereof I saw great variety in the market
> place the Sunday morning when I departed therehence, and no
> small diversity of odoriferous flowers. Truely the view of this most
> sweet Paradise, this domicilium Venerum & Charitum did even so
> ravish my senses with such inward delight, that I said unto my
> selfe, this is the Citie which of all other places in the world, I
> would wish to make my habitation in, and spend the remainder of
> my dayes in some divine Meditations amongst the sacred Muses,
> were it not for their grosse idolatry and superstitious ceremonies
> which I detest, and the love of Odcombe in Somersetshire, which
> is so deare unto me that I preferre the very smoke thereof before
> the fire of all other places under the Sunne.

At Sanguinetto, his next stop, on 19 June, there was the
usual two-hour lunch-break at a travellers' inn, assailed by
swarms of flies that had to be driven off with wooden flaps,

for no sooner could a dish of meate be laid upon the table, but there
would incontinently be a thousand flies in it, were it not for these
flaps. I told my fellow travellers at dinner, that if the Emperor
Domitian had beene now alive, and in that roome with us, he would
have done us some pleasure in driving away those flies. For indeede
Suetonius doth write in his life that about the beginning of his
Empire he would sometimes spend a whole houre alone by himself
every day in some private roome of his Palace in catching of flies.

It seems always the way: whenever you need an emperor as
fly-catcher, there's not one to be found.

That evening, after about five hours' walking, Coryate at last
entered the State of Venice, in the walled town of Legnano,
where he first saw the winged lion 'gallantly displayed in the
wals', and obtained a warrant from the Town Prefect to
proceed further. On 20 June he rode on from Este through rich
farming country ('a very fertile and spacious plaine that
affordeth all manner of commodities, both for corne, vines,
and fruits'), with poplars, poppies in the fields and blue hills
in the distance, and reached Padua at about 7 p.m.

Padua, where Shakespeare's Petruchio came to wive
wealthily and tame his shrew, was the first major city of the
Venetian Republic that Coryate had visited. The Republic,
despite being past its peak of wealth and power, was still
enormously rich (Fynes Moryson estimated an annual income
of two million gold crowns), and retained substantial
territories in northern Italy and the Adriatic, its mainland
borders running along the Alps, down the River Adda to its
junction with the Po and down to the sea, and from near
Monfalcone to the Carnic Alps. As in many cities in the State,
travellers had to pay a toll to enter Padua – six soldi here,
eight for Verona. Coryate stayed at the principal inn, the Stella
d'Oro, in the Piazza della Paglia, or Straw Market, a superior
establishment notable for its 'stove' heating-system in the
Swiss and German style. The English traveller Peter Mundy
recorded staying here for five lire a day (about 2s. 4d.): not
cheap. Coryate was in the ancient, double-walled city,
supposedly founded by the Trojan exile Antenor (a large statue

of the Wooden Horse stood in one of the palazzi), for three days. Moryson described it as having 'very healthfull' air, with a walkway on the inner wall, 'with pleasant shade of trees, where Gentlemen use to play Balloone [a kind of hand-ball]'.

Here Tom was assisted in his sight-seeing by three Englishmen and a scholarly Italian student, whom he met in a bookbinder's shop and who helped in deciphering an obscure inscription. The young man later sent him some friendly Greek verses, enclosed in a letter from a mutual friend, George Rooke (on the staff of the English Ambassador in Venice, and who helped Coryate there), that was addressed '"To the English Gentleman that converteth Jewes, etc. in Venice". The history of which my conversion of the Jewes (being indeede rather a disputation with them then a conversion of them, which I much both desired and endeavoured) I will relate in my observations of Venice.' The other friendly helpers were a Dr Moore and a Mr Willoughby, 'a learned student in the University', which Tom never got round to visiting, being 'so drawen away with the pleasure of other rarities and antiquities'. Willoughby was presumably Richard Willoughby, a former Cambridge don, who left England in 1579, converted to Catholicism, and was at Padua from 1592 until his death in 1617; Sir Henry Wotton, the English Ambassador, described him in a letter as 'an infectious Papist, of a still and dangerous temper' – not that there was much chance of him infecting Coryate.

Coryate really missed out in not visiting the university, which had become one of the most famous and important universities in the Western world, attracting scholars and students from all over Europe, especially to the medical school. William Harvey, the discoverer of the circulation of the blood, studied there in 1598 under the noted biology scholar Fabricius; Queen Elizabeth's future spymaster Sir Francis Walsingham was there in 1555–6, and John Donne's son was there in 1634 (the university was happy to accept Protestant students). Most notably, Galileo (who gave Willoughby a copy of one of his books on astronomy) made some of his most spectacular discoveries there: in 1609 he made a telescope,

and in 1610 saw 'marvels' – the satellites of Jupiter, the rings
of Saturn, and extra stars in the Pleiades. As for 'town-and-
gown' relationships, Moryson expressed concern about the
'liberty and priviledges' of the students, 'as men-slaiers are
only punished with banishment, which is a great mischiefe,
and makes strangers live there in great jealousie of treason to
be practiced against their lives'. William Lithgow,
characteristically, was even more condemnatory about the
morals of the students, who were notorious for their 'beastly
Sodomy . . . as rife here as in Rome, Naples, Florence,
Bullogna, Venice, Ferrara, Genoa, Parma not being exempted
[why, indeed?], nor yet the smallest Village of Italy: A
monstrous filthiness, but to them a pleasant pastime, making
songs and singing Sonets of the beauty and pleasure of their
Bardassi, or buggerd boys'.

The university also established the first botanical garden in
Europe, in 1545; this Coryate did visit, and saw the plane tree,
with which England was not familiar, remarking
characteristically, 'The Poets do faine that Jupiter dallied with
Europa under this kinde of tree [to paraphrase a famous
comment on Milton, one suspects that Coryate saw sex
through the spectacles of books] . . . Also I saw a very prety
fruit which is esteemed farre more excellent than Apricocks,
or any other dainty fruit whatsoever growing in Italy. They call
it Pistachi, a fruit much used in their daily banquets'.

In any case, with the help of his friends, Coryate saw much
more than he might have done, and (perhaps with Schott's
assistance, also) was able to describe at very great length and
mind-numbing detail including measurements, churches,
public buildings, statues (especially of the Roman writer,
Livy, about whose many statues and supposed former home
we are told more than anyone would wish to know),
monuments and tombs. He also saw some 'exquisite pictures
very artificially [skilfully] drawne by the curious hand of that
Apelles of Padua, Titianus' (of whose work he would see
plenty more in Venice), but missed the frescoes by Mantegna
and Giotto. He inspected the Basilica Sant'Antonio, with its

domed turrets, containing the tomb of the saint, which, it was reported,

> hath the vertue to expell Divels, which I doe hardly beleeve. For I saw an experiment of it when I was in the Church which came to no effect. For a certain Demoniacall person praied at the Sepulchre upon his knees, who had another appointed to attend him, that he should not irreligiously behave himselfe at so religious a place. And a Priest walked about the Tombe while the Demoniack was praying, to the ende to helpe expell the divell with his exorcismes, but the effect thereof turned to nothing. For I left the fellow in as badde a case as I found him.

Among the many tombs and epitaphs that he lacked time to describe fully, he found (on his second visit, on his return journey) the resting place of Edward Courtenay, Earl of Devon, who had left England after being imprisoned for his involvement in the Wyatt Rebellion, and died suddenly in Padua in 1556, possibly from poison. 'Truely it strooke great compassion and remorse in me to see an Englishman so ignobly buried. For his body lieth in a poore woodden Coffin, placed upon another faire monument, having neither Epitaphe nor any other thing to preserve it from oblivion.' The forgotten, anonymous grave in a distant foreign land was like a bad dream for him.

However, at the west end of the Senate House there was – and is –

> a very mery spectacle to be seene . . . a round stone of some three foote high inserted into the floore, on the which if any bankerout doth sit with his naked buttocks three times in some public assembly, all his debts are ipso facto remited. Round about the stone are written these wordes in capitall letters, Lapis vituperii & cessationis bonorum [the seat of shame and loss of property] . . . But belike there is a limitation of the summe that is owed . . . otherwise it were great injustice of the Venetians to tollerate such a custome that honest creditors should be cousened and defrauded of the summe of thirty or forty thousand duckats by the impudent

behaviour of some abject-minded varlet, who to acquit himself of
his debt will most willingly expose his bare buttockes in that
opprobious and ignominious manner to the laughter of every
spectator. Surely it is the strangest custome that ever I heard or
read off (though that which I have related of it be the very naked
truth, whereof if some of our English bankrouts should have
intelligence, I thinke they would hartily wish the like might be in
force in England. For if such a custome were used with us, there
is no doubt but that there would be more naked buttocks shewed
in the term time before the greatest Nobility and Judges of our
land in Westminster hall, then are of young punies in any
Grammar Schoole of England to their Plagosi Orbilii, that is, their
whipping and severely-censuring Schoole-masters.).

He went on to admire the 'sumptuous and rich Monastery of
the Benedictine Monkes. I call it sumptuous, because there is
nothing but pompe and magnificence to bee seene there; rich,
because their yearly revenew amounteth to one hundred
thousand Crowns, which make the summe of thirty thousand
pounds sterling.' Here he was shown the coffin and epitaph
verses ('I have often repented since that I had not copied
them') of St Luke the Evangelist:

his bones were brought from Constantinople in an yron coffin
which is inclosed in a great grate of yron, that was likewise
brought from Constantinople together with the coffin. That coffin I
touched with my fingers, but with some difficulty . . . Within a
short space after this coffin was brought to Padua, his bones were
taken out of the olde yron coffin that came from Constantinople,
and laide in a very sumptuous monument hard by, made of brasse
. . . right opposite unto it . . . there standeth the monument of
Matthias, one of the Twelve Apostles.

In the apothecary's room nearby, where medicines were
prepared for the poor, there was

the skin of a great crocodile hanged up at the roofe, and another
skinne of a crocodile in the inner roome. This crocodile is a beast of
a most terrible shape, fashioned something like a Dragon, with

wonderfull hard scales upon his backe. I observed that he hath no
tongue at all; his eyes are very little, and his teeth long and sharp . . .
he liveth for the most part in Nilus that famous river of Egypt, the
Egyptians in former times being so superstitious that they
worshipped him for a god . . . and if it happened that their children
were at any time violently taken away by him, their parents would
rejoyce, thinking that they pleased the God in breeding that which
served for his food.

There were two features of the city that he mentioned. The
first was that almost every street had covered walkways or
arcades, 12ft high and 5ft broad, providing shelter from the
hot sun of summer and cold winds in winter; Lithgow
thought they made Padua 'the most melancholy city of
Europe, the cause onely arising of the narrow passage of the
open streets, and of the long galleries and dark-ranges of
pillars, that goe alwhere on every hand of you'. The other
feature that Coryate noticed was how few people appeared to
be living there, 'so that were the students removed . . . this
citie would seeme more then halfe desolate'. Another feature
of life there that apparently escaped his notice, but not that
of Fynes Moryson, was the habit of some courtesans of
wearing men's clothes. Moryson saw some walking with
some men 'to the Tennis Court in mens Apparell and
Racketts in their handes, most commonly wearing doblets
and Hose of Carnation [flesh-coloured] Satten, with gold
buttons from the Chinne round to the wast behinde, and silke
stockings, and great Garters with gold lace'. Moryson also
tells us later that such sexually provocative cross-dressing
was used by prostitutes in Venice (who 'commonly weare
dobletts and Breches under their wemens gownes',
presumably appealing to all tastes), especially during that
'most licentious time', Carnival, when both men and women
might be *en travesti*; in Jonson's *Volpone*, Lady Politic
Would-be suspected her husband had been with 'a female
devil in a male outside'.

Coryate was quite charmed by Padua, set among the
Euganean hills, which were 'heretofore by Martial and

Catullus esteemed the very receptacle and habitation of the Muses', and cited Constantine Palaeologus, the last Christian Emperor of Constantinople, who used to say that, were it not for the scholars who firmly located Paradise in the East, 'he would otherwise thinke it could not be in any other place of the world but only in Padua. For indeede it is as sweetly seated as any place of the whole world is or can be.'

Now, however, it was time to move on; at 7 in the morning of 24 June, Coryate took a horse-drawn boat down the River Brenta, to Lucie Fesina (modern Fusina), where he took another boat to Venice, shining in the morning light, 5 miles away over the lagoon. Moryson drily records a local saying about the ferry boat to Venice, that 'the boat shall bee drowned when it carries neither Monke, nor Student, nor Cortesan (for they love them too well to call them whores), the passengers being for the most part of these kindes'; there are not many monks on the ferries nowadays. For all that, Venice itself, declared Coryate more lyrically, 'yeeldeth the most glorious and heavenly shew upon the water that ever any mortal eye beheld, such a shew as did ravish me both with delight and admiration'.

More prosaically, he now calculated the distance he had travelled, from Odcombe to London to Dover to Calais to Paris to Lyons to Turin to Milan to Padua to Venice, as 952 miles.

FOUR

The Virgin City

It is remarkable that Coryate begins his account of a city notorious throughout Europe for its thousands of prostitutes by calling it the Virgin City ('for by that title doth the world most deservedly stile her'), a title deriving from the claim that, as yet, Venice had never been taken by enemy forces. Declaring himself 'the unworthiest of ten thousand' to describe the city, Coryate nevertheless determined to try, 'partly because she gave me most loving and kind entertainment for the space of six weekes, which was the sweetest time (I must needes confesse) for so much that ever I spent in my life; and partly for that she ministered unto me more variety of remarkable and delicious objects then mine eyes ever survayed in any citie before, or ever shall'. The sexuality of Coryate's language and imaginative engagement here are very apparent, whatever one may make of that.

He begins, as usual, with the setting and some history:

Such is the rarenesse of the situation of Venice, that it doth even amaze and drive into admiration all strangers that upon their first arrivall behold the same. For it is built altogether upon the water in the innermost gulfe of the Adriatique Sea which is commonly called Gulfo di Venetia, and is distant from the maine Sea about the space of 3 miles. From the which it is divided by a certaine great banke called litto maggior [the Lido], which is at least fifty miles in length. This banke is so necessary a defence for the Citie, that it serveth in steed of a strong wall to repulse and reverberate the violence of the furious waves of the Sea. . . . The forme of this foresaid banke is very strange to behold. For nature herself the most cunning mistres and architect of all things hath framed it crooked in the forme of a bow, and by the Art of man there are five Ostia, that is mouths, or gappes made therein, whereof each maketh a haven, and yeeldeth passage to the ships to saile forth and backe to Venice. . . . Now that whole space which is betwixt this banke and the Continent . . . is the same which we call Gulfo di Venetia . . . in which space are to be seene many fennes, marishes, and other dry places, whereof some are covered altogether with reedes and flagges, others doe shew like faire little greene Islandes, which are the very places that yeelded harbour to divers companies of people, that in the time of the Hunnes, Goths, and Vandals devastation and depopulation of Italy repaired thither with their whole families as to a safe refuge . . . The first place of Venice that was inhabited, is that which now they call the Rialto, which word is derived from rivus altus, that is, a deepe river, because the water is deeper there then about the other Islands. And the first that dwelt in the same Rialto was a poore man called Joannes Bonus, who got his living there by fishing. After this many repaired unto this mans house for the safety of their lives in the time of Radagisus King of the Goths, who with a huge armie of two hundred thousand men invaded Italy, wasting it extremely with fire and sword . . .

He goes on to describe the Grand Canal – 'in the forme of a Roman S. It is in length a thousand and three hundred paces [how did he pace that out?], and in breadth at the least forty, in some places more' – before praising the bordering palazzi:

a very glorious and beautifull shew . . . most being built with bricke, and some few with faire free stone, and partly of Istrian marble. Their roofes doe much differ from those of our English buildings. For they are all flat and built in that manner as men may walke upon them, as I have often observed . . . [Fynes Moryson reports how 'the flooers of the upper roomes are not boorded, but plastred with lime tempred with tiles beaten to dust. The windowes are for the most part very large, the greater roomes lying almost altogether open to receive aire, but the lodging chambers have glasse windowes, whereof the Venetians brag, glasse being rare in Italy, where the windowes are for the most part covered with linnen or paper']. Withall I perceived another thing in their buildings, which is the rarest thing that ever I saw in my life . . . The foundations of their houses are made after a very strange manner. For whereas many of them are situate in the water, whensoever they lay the foundation of any house they remove the water by certaine devices from the place where they lay the first fundamentall matter. Most commonly they drive long stakes into the ground, without [around] the which they doe aggerere molem, that is, raise certaine heapes of sand, mudde, or clay, or some other such matter to repell the water. Then they ramme in great piles of woodde, which they lay very deepe, upon the which they place their bricke or stone, and so frame the other parts of the building. These foundations are made so exceeding deep, and contrived with so great labour, that I have heard they cost them very neare the third part of the charge of the whole edifice. . . . It is said there are in the City of Venice at the least a hundred and twenty goodly Palaces, the greatest part whereof is built upon the sides of this great Channel. So that if you will take a view of the fairest Palaces that the whole City yeeldeth, you must behold these Palaces of the Canal il Grande, either from the Rialto bridge, or passing in a little Boate which they call a Gondola . . .

There is only one bridge to go over the great channell . . . commonly called Ponte de Rialto, and is the fairest bridge by many degrees for one arch that ever I saw, read, or heard of. For it is reported that it cost about fourescore thousand crownes, which doe make foure and twenty thousand pound sterling [so it must be good]. Truely, the exact view hereof ministred unto me no small matter of admiration to see a bridge of that length (for it is two hundred feet long, the channel being at the least forty paces broade as I have before written) so curiously compacted together with only one arch . . . It was first built but with timber (as I have heard divers Venetian gentlemen report) [and as can be seen in a painting by Carpaccio in the Accademia] but . . . they defaced that, and built this most sumptuous bridge with squared white stone, having two faire rowes of pretty little houses for artificers, which are only shops, not dwelling houses. Of these shops there are two rowes in each side of the bridge till you come to the toppe.

Coryate then starts counting: steps, and pillars, and carvings. The bridge was built in 1588–91 by the appropriately named

Antonio da Ponte, after a competition (which he did not enter) that included among its entrants Michelangelo, Sansovino and Palladio. What might have been . . .

After this, Coryate turns to the traghetti ferries, the boatmen at the Rialto arousing his particular wrath: 'the most vicious and licentious varlets about all the City. For if a stranger entereth into one of their Gondolas, and doth not presently tell them whither he will goe, they will incontinently [a well-chosen word] carry him of their own accord to a religious house [i.e. a brothel] forsooth, where his plumes shall be well pulled before he commeth forth againe. Then he may afterward with Demosthenes buy too dear repentance for seeing Lais.' A whole clatter of classical allusions follows, as our latter-day Ulysses heatedly fights off 'Circean cups and the Syrens melody'. Moryson had the same experience, but was cooler and more amused: 'If you call for a boate, and you will goe *a spasso* that is for recreation, howsoever you meane to take the ayre upon the water, he will presently carry you to some Curtezans house . . . as if there were no other recreation but only with wemen . . . it was vulgarly sayde, that when they purposed to builde Tennice Courtes at Venice, the Curtizans paying much tribute [tax] made their suite to the Contrary, lest it should hinder their trading, which at Venice is insteede of all exercises.'

Back on the water, Coryate discussed the lesser canals, 'very singular ornaments to the citie, through the which they runne even as the veynes doe through the body of a man, and doe disgorge into the Canal il Grande, which is the common receptacle of them all'. One of their benefits was to carry away 'all the garbage and filthinesse that falleth into them from the citie, which by meanes of the ebbing and flowing of the water is the sooner conveighed out of the channels, though indeede not altogether so well, but that the people doe eftsoones adde their owne industry to clense and purge them'. In addition to this traditional hit-or-miss sewerage, the many fires and openness to the winds, thought Moryson, helped to make Venice more healthy: 'and though I dare not say the Venetians live long, yet except they sooner grow old, and rather *seeme* then truly *be* aged, I never in any place observed more old men, or so many Senators venerable for their grey haires and aged gravity.' The other benefit of the canals was the easy access to all parts by means of the gondolas. At this time the gondola still had the 'felze' or central covered cabin

with faire blacke cloth . . . to the end that if the passenger meaneth to be private, he may draw downe the same, and after row so secretly that no man can see him: in the inside the benches are finely covered with blacke leather, and the bottomes of many of them together with the sides under the benches are very neatly garnished with fine linnen cloth, the edge whereof is laced with bonelace [lace of linen thread, knitted with bone bobbins]: the ends are beautified with two pretty and ingenuous devices. For each end hath a crooked thing made in the forme of a Dolphins tayle, with the fins very artificially represented, and it seemeth to be tinned over. The Water-men that row these never sit as ours do in London, but alwaies stand, and that at the farther end of the Gondola, sometimes one, but most commonly two; and in my opinion they are altogether as swift as our rowers about London. Of these Gondolas they say there are ten thousand about the citie, whereof six thousand are private, serving for the Gentlemen and others, and foure thousand for mercenary men, which get their living by the trade of rowing.

Coryate was overwhelmed by the 'admirable and incomparable beauty' of the Piazza San Marco:

Truely such is the stupendious (to use a strange Epitheton for so strange and rare a place as this) glory of it, that at my first entrance thereof it did amaze or rather ravish my senses. For here is the greatest magnificence of architecture to be seene, that any place under the sunne doth yeelde. Here you may both see all manner of fashions of attire, and heare all the languages of Christendome, besides those that are spoken by the Barbarous Ethnickes; the frequencie of people being so great twice a day, betwixt six of the clocke in the morning and eleven, and again betwixt five in the afternoon and eight, that (as an elegant author says of it) a man may properly call it rather Orbis then Urbis forum, that is, a market place of the world, not of the citie. [Here] the Venetian long gowned Gentlemen doe meete together in great troupes. For you shall not see as much as one Venetian there of the Patrician ranke without his blacke gowne and tippet [hat]. There you may see many Polonians, Slavonians, Persians, Grecians, Turks, Jewes, Christians of all the famousest regions of Christendome, and each nation distinguished from another by their proper and peculiar habits. A singular shew . . .

He then settled down to pacing out, measuring and counting. The two great pillars at the end of the Piazetta San Marco were too large for him to get his arms around. 'They were brought by Sea from Constantinople for more than foure hundred yeares since. Upon the top of one of them are advanced the arms of Venice, the winged Lyon made all of brasse [probably a bronze Persian chimera with added wings]; on the other the statue of St Theodorus gilt, and standing upon a brazen Crocodile, with a speare in one hand, and a shield in another.' He goes on to tell the story of the third pillar, which fell into the water when being disembarked, and how the others were erected by Nicolas Beratterius, who asked only that men could legally play at dice between the pillars (gambling being otherwise forbidden); the space between the pillars was used for executions (of which, more, later).

The campanile he estimated at 280ft high, and measured at 40ft square:

The staires are made after such a strange manner that not only a man, or woman, or childe may with great ease ascend to the top of it, but also an horse, as it is commonley reported in the citie. [At the top] you have the fairest and goodliest prospect that is (I thinke) in all the world. For therehence you [and your horse] may see the whole model and forme of the citie sub uno intuito, a sight that doth in my opinion farre surpasse all the shewes under the cope of heaven. There you may have a Synopsis, that is, a general view of little Christendome (for so doe many intitle this citie of Venice) . . . [All the main buildings of the city, the Churches, monasteries, market places, the] many faire gardens replenished with diversity of delicate fruites, as Oranges, Citrons,

Lemmons, Apricocks, muske melons, anguriaes [gourds like water-melons], and what not; together with their little Islands bordering about the citie wonderfully frequented and inhabited with people, being in number fifty or thereabout . . . therefore whatsoever thou art that meanest to see Venice, in any case forget not to goe up to the top of Saint Markes tower before thou commest out of the citie . . . on the toppe of the tower is erected a brasen Angell fairely gilt, which is made in the sort that he semeth to blesse the people in his hand.

After St Mark's, the finest street in Venice was the Merceria, running from the Piazza San Marco towards the Rialto:

there is a very faire gate at one end of this street . . . which is decked with a great deale of faire marble, in which gate are two pretty conceits to be observed, the one at the very top, which is a clocke with the images of two wilde men by it made in brasse, a witty device and very exactly done. At which clocke there fell out a very tragicall and rufull accident . . . A certaine fellow that had the charge to looke to the clocke, was verie busie about the bell, according to his usuall custome every day . . . But in the meane time one of those wilde men that at the quarters of the howers doe use to strike the bell, strooke the man in the head with his brasen hammer, giving him such a violent blow, that therewith he fel down dead presently in the place, and never spake more.

Coryate earnestly assures us that, though he did not see this himself, some other Englishmen did, who advised him to mention it in his journal. Like many of his contemporaries, and many tourists to this day, Tom was fascinated by clockwork marionettes, such as the figure of the Virgin Mary behind some doors above a clock on the gate, with two angels lurking behind two more doors: 'These dores upon any principall holiday doe open of themselves, and immediately there come forth two Kings to present themselves to our Lady, unto whom, after they have done their obeysance by uncovering of their heads, they returne againe into their places', leaving behind a broken sentence.

Near St Mark's, his attention was caught by

a certaine Porphyrie stone of some yard and halfe or almost two yards high, and of a pretty large compasse, even as much as a man can claspe at twice with both his armes [the kind of thing Coryate did very frequently, it seems; such column-cuddling must have provoked comment, on occasion]. On this stone are laid for the space of three dayes and three nights, the heads of all such as being enemies or traitors to the State, or some notorious offenders, have been apprehended out of the citie, and beheaded by those that have beene bountifully hired by the Senate for the same purpose. In that place do their heads remain so long, though the smell of them doth breede a very offensive and contagious annoyance . . . I have heard that there have beene twenty thousand duckats given to a man for bringing a traytors head to that place.

He does not mention that this Pietra del Bando was also used for making official proclamations – but that does not produce the same frisson. Likewise he admired a nearby 'marvailous faire paire of gallowes made of alabaster' intended 'to hang the Duke whensoever he shall happen to commit any treason against the State. And for that cause it is erected before the very gate of his Palace to the end to put him in minde to be faithfull and true.'

Coryate also has an unusual account of the carving on the corner of the Basilica, of the so-called Four Moors, that was part of the Venetian spoils of the war against Acre in 1256, and is thought to depict four Roman Emperors as Tetrarchs. For him, this depicts four noble Albanian brothers, who came by ship laden with treasure; two went on shore and two stayed on board. Each couple resolved to poison the other in order to retain the treasure for themselves; after dinner, all four lay dead. 'Whereupon the Signiory of Venice seised upon all their goods as their owne, which was the first treasure that ever Venice possessed . . . and in a memoriall of that uncharitable and unbrotherly conspiracy, hath erected the portraitures of them in porphyrie as I said before in two severall couples consulting together . . . many Gentlemen of very good account in Venice both Englishmen and others reported it unto me for an absolute truth.' He does not sound absolutely confident.

He praised the Treasury, with its 'statues of two monstrous great Gyants opposite to each other with clubs in their hands, which worke was most singularly done in free stone by that rare fellow, Titianus of Padua, who was not only an excellent painter as I have before mentioned but also a very cunning statuary'. Coryate was unusual among travellers of his time in noting the names of artists. Here he counted thirty-one great iron treasure chests, and remembered seeing forty-two others in two rooms in the Rialto, 'so that it is thought all the quantity of money contained in these threescore and thirteene chests doth not amount to so little as forty millions of duckats'. The Doge's Palace he considered 'absolutely the fairest building that ever I saw, exceeding all the King of Frances Palaces that I could see', and provided an exhaustive account, estimating heights, pacing out widths and lengths, counting pillars and arches, detailing carvings of fruit and lions and 'exquisite statues in alabaster of Adam and Eve naked, covering their shame with figge leaves. That statue of Eve is done with that singularity of cunning, that it is reported the Duke of Mantua hath offered to give the weight of it in gold for the Image, yet he cannot have it.' Once again, cost is the measure of quality.

Coryate was not able to see round the Armoury, much to his regret, 'the store being so great that it is thought it can well arme ten thousand men, and the beautie [of the armour] so incomparable that no armoury of Christendome doth match it'. Nevertheless, it provided the occasion for a story of a failed armed coup, when 'a gentleman of the Patrician rank' secretly brought together a large force of armed men:

as he was entering into St Markes place through the sumptuous gate where the clocke standeth . . . there hapned a very disastrous accident that confounded and frustrated his whole designement. For a certaine maide that looked out of the window hard by the gate to see the company, had by chance a pestell of a mortar in her hand, with which she was powning in the said mortar at the very instant they passed by; and whereas she looked out of the window with the other, to see what was doing, her pestell which she then held in her hand, not intending any hurt with it, fell casually much against her will upon the head of the Ring-leader of this company, which strooke out his braines, and so by that dismall chance hee died in the place,

since when the Senate had increased the strength of their armoury. This is a somewhat mangled version of the attempted coup by one Bajamonte Tiepolo on the night of the feast of St Vitus, in 1302. Pausing at the head of his forces by the clockhouse near the Piazza San Marco, he found the populace roused in opposition to him; here an old woman threw a heavy stone mortar out of an upper window at him, which missed him but killed his standard-bearer outright. Tiepolo fled back across the Rialto bridge, destroying it behind him, and eventually succeeded in negotiating a four-year exile in Dalmatia. As a reward, the old woman was promised that her rent would never be increased.

Had Tiepolo been captured, he might have ended in the adjoining prison: 'I thinke there is not a fairer prison in all Christendome,' wrote Coryate, who had a connoisseur's eye for gallows and such things:

It is built with very faire white ashler stone having a little walke without the roomes of the prison, which is forty paces long and seven broad. For I meated [measured] it . . . In the higher part of the front towards the water there are eight pretty pillars of free-stone . . . In the lower part of the prison where the prisoners do usually remaine, there are six windows, three on each side of the dore, whereof each hath two rowes of great iron barres, one without and the other within; each row containing ten barres that ascend in heigth to the toppe of the window, and eighteene more that crosse those tenne. So that it is altogether impossible for the prisoners to get forth . . . it is reported that this prison is so contrived, that there are a dozen roomes under the water, and that the water doth oftentimes distill into them from above, to the great annoyance of the prisoners that lodge there.

The exotic opulence and mysterious atmosphere of the Basilica were beyond him, though he reported as accurately as he could. He was intrigued by the gilt mosaic work – he had never seen any before – and awed by the great gold and enamel Pala d'Oro altarpiece: – 'I think it is worth at the least ten thousand pounds.' Here also Tom was pleased to see a memorial of 'the Popes most barbarous and unchristian tyranny', when in 1177 Pope Alexander was supposed to have placed his foot on the head of the Emperor Frederick Barbarossa, and

> most blasphemously and prophanely abused a notable place of Scripture, which he took out of one of the Psalmes of David, even this: Super Aspidem and Basiliscum ambulabis, & caput Draconis conculcabis [On the asp and basilisk shalt thou tread, and the head of the dragon shalt thou crush]. The Pope pronounced it in that manner as if it were applied properly and peculiarly to his own person, when he did so tyrannically insult upon the good Emperour, though the holy Prophet meant only Christ, and his vanquishing of the Devill and the power of hell.

However, John Julius Norwich, in his *History of Venice*, insists that 'this story is told by no contemporary writer and is inconsistent with all the first-hand evidence that has come down to us' – not that Coryate would have cared about that; as a notorious American newspaper editor said, 'When the fact becomes legend, print the legend.' Coryate was not impressed by a picture of the Virgin Mary attributed to St Luke (who would appear to have been a remarkably prolific artist, especially in the Middle Ages), particularly when it was carried in procession around the Piazza by the Doge, Senators and clergy, in the belief that it would break the current drought: 'For it brought no drops at all with it: onely about two dayes after it rained (I must needes confesse) amaine. But I hope they are not so superstitious to ascribe that to the vertue of their picture. For it is very likely it would have rained at that time, though they had not at all carried their picture abroad.'

Moving eastward, he visited the famous naval arsenal (where he was unsuccessful in an attempt to get an Englishman released from slavery in the galleys):

The richest and best furnished storehouse for all manner of
munition both by Sea and land not only of all Christendome, but
also of all the world . . . in compasse two miles, and fortified with
a strong wall . . . There are continually one thousand five hundred
men working in it, unto whom there is paid every weeke two
thousand crownes which doe amount to sixe hundred pound
sterling, in the whole yeare twenty eight thousand and sixe
hundred pound. Also those workemen that have wrought so long
in the Arsenall that they are become decrepit and unable to worke
any longer, are maintained in the same at the charge of the citie
during their lives. Here are alwaies kept two hundred and fiftie
gallies, each having a severall roome fairely roofed over to cover
and defend it from the injury of the weather, and fifty more are
alwaies at sea.

Fynes Moryson provides details of the standard Venetian
galley and its crew: the forecastle in the prow he paced out at
12 paces long, and the main body and poop at 50 paces, with 4
cannon in the forecastle, 30 more on the sides and 12 in the
poop; 25 oars to each side, with 7 men to each oar. 'When they
are in Port, two sleepe uppon the benche where they use to
sett, two in the place which is under their thighes, and two
where they sette their feete when they rowe, and the seaventh
slept upon the Oare, and uppon a little boarde betweene each
oare three soldiers used to sleepe. So as their being in the
Gallye is nothing commodious.'

Coryate was thrilled by the gilding and cost of the great
1,220-seater state Bucentoro Galley:

It cost one hundred thousand crownes which is thirty thousand
pound sterling. A worke so exceeding glorious that I never heard
or read of the like in any place of the world, these onely excepted,
viz: that of Cleopatra, which she so exceeding sumptuously
adorned with cables of silke and other passing beautifull
ornaments; and those that the Emperor Caligula built with timber
of Cedar and poopes and sternes of ivory. And lastly [it's Please
Your Patron time] that most incomparable and peereless ship of
our Gracious Prince, called the Prince Royall, which was launched
at Wollige [Woolwich] about Michaelmas last, which indeed by

many degrees surpasses this Bucentoro of Venice, and any ship
else (I believe) in Christendome.

He then listed the Doge's 'sumptuous' gilt throne, the five gilt
images of slaves by the throne, the twenty gilt statues along
both sides of the galley, the two gilt winged lions at each end,
and the ten gilt carvings set over the dignitaries' benches when
they attended the ceremony of the Doge marrying the sea by
throwing into it a gold ring.

The Church of St John and St Paul ('Zanipolo' to Venetians)
provided many monuments and epitaphs to transcribe,
especially one that he could not read 'with dry eyes, neither
do I thinke any Christian could be so hard hearted . . . that
can reade the same without either effusion of teares, or at the
least some kinde of relenting, if he doth understand the Latin
tongue'. He transcribed it but, according to his usual practice,
did not translate it, thus sparing the un-Latined. The story (as
Mark Antony said, 'If you have tears, prepare to shed them
now') is of Marcantonio Bragadin, the Venetian commander
of Cyprus when it was besieged by the Turks in 1570; he and
his outnumbered soldiers held out bravely, until the Turks
offered an honourable surrender. While he was returning the
signed accord to the Turkish general, the Turks slaughtered
all the other Venetians (350 heads were heaped outside).
After cutting off his nose and ears, they tortured him for two
weeks, before he was tied naked to a column and flayed alive,
only dying after half an hour as the executioner reached his
waist. His skin, stuffed with straw, was sent back to the
Sultan in Constantinople, where it was hung up on display,
until after twenty years it was stolen and brought to Venice.
The memorial, put up in 1596, is topped by an urn still
containing Bragadin's skin, neatly folded (they checked, a few
years ago).

Nearby is Verrocchio's splendid equestrian statue of the
fifteenth-century mercenary leader Bartolomeo Colleoni, 'who
had his name from having three stones, for the Italian word
Coglione doth signify a testicle' – which would make him

three times better endowed than Hitler was popularly supposed to be; certainly his insignia display three balls. In the churchyard here Tom saw a little bay nag feeding, the only horse he saw during his stay in Venice, where the narrow canal-side walkways and (after the fourteenth century) steeply hump-backed bridges made horses altogether impractical.

So that I now finde by mine owne experience, [he declared indignantly] that the speeches of a certaine English Gentleman (with whom I discoursed before my travels), a man that much vaunted of his observations in Italy, are utterly false. For when I asked him what principall things he observed in Venice, he answered me that he noted but little of the city. Because he rode through it in post. A fiction as grosse and palpable as ever was coyned.

Tom enjoyed himself at the festival in July, when a bridge made of linked boats is made across the great Giudecca canal to the Redentore church, to celebrate the cessation of a plague in 1576.

That day I saw a marvailous solemne Procession. For every Order and Fraternity of religious men in the whole city met together, and carried their Crosses and candlesticks of silver in procession to the Redeemers Church, and so backe againe to their severall Convents. Besides there was much good fellowship in many places of Venice upon that day. For there were many places, whereof each yeelded allowance of variety of wine and cakes and some other pretty junkats to a hundred good fellowes to be merry that day, but to no more: this I know by experience. For a certaine Stationer of the city with whom I had some acquaintance [presumably from buying quantities of writing paper], one Joannes Guerilius, met me by chance at the Redeemers Church, and after he had shewed me the particular places of the Capucins Monastery, brought me to a place where we had very good wine, cakes, and other delicates gratis, where a Priest served us all.

He also attended various religious festivals in the city, most notably one at San Rocco, or 'Saint Roches church, a very sumptuous and magnificent building', where he was enchanted by 'the best musicke that ever I [heard] in all my life . . . which was both vocall and instrumentall, so good, so delectable, so rare, so admirable, so superexcellent, that it did even ravish and stupifie all those strangers that never heard the like'. He was particularly enthralled by a counter-tenor, 'who had such a peerelesse and (as I may in a maner say) such a supernaturall voice . . . that I think there was never a better singer in all the world . . . exceeding happy may that Citie, or towne or person bee that possesseth this miracle of nature'; but Tom would not have been quite so impressed, he said, if the singer had been a castrato.

The Venetians seemed to him very devout, or, rather, 'superstitious . . . at noone and the setting of the sunne, all men, women and children must kneele, and say their ave Maria bare-headed wheresoever they are, eyther in their houses or in the streets, when the Ave Marie bell ringeth'. Coryate's religious interest brought him further encounters. He attended Mass in the Greek Orthodox church, where he admired mosaics, icons and some very large candles (one of his minor interests, it seems), and managed a conversation in Greek ('which by reason of my long desuetude was become almost rusty') with the Greek bishop, who 'spake the purest and elegantest naturall greeke that ever I heard, insomuch that his phrase came something neere that of Isocrates', and praised the English Ambassador, Sir Henry Wotton.

Coryate also went to the Ghetto (the first enforced Jewish residential area to be so named – from an ironworks previously on the site), to which the Jews were transferred in 1516. He estimated a population of 5,000–6,000, European Jews being required to wear red hats, Levantine Jews, yellow turbans. He admired their strict observance of their Sabbath, but was somewhat bemused by their practice at the synagogue, the rabbi reading aloud

not by a sober, distinct, and orderly reading, but by an exceeding loud yaling, indecent roaring, and as it were a beastly bellowing of it forth. And that after such a confused and hudling maner,

that I thinke the hearers can very hardly understand him . . .
One custome I observed amongst them very irreverent and
prophane, that none of them, eyther when they enter the
Synagogue, or when they sit downe in their places, or when they
goe forth againe, doe any reverence or obeysance, answerable to
such a place of the worship of God, eyther by uncovering their
heads, kneeling, or any other externall gesture, but boldly dash
into the roome with their Hebrew bookes in their handes, and
presently sit in their places, without any more adoe.

Whilst lamenting the Italian Jews' failure to convert to
Christianity, which he understood as being partly due to the
confiscation of all their goods upon their conversion (unlike
the practice in other parts of Europe), the people themselves
he was more impressed by (as there were – in theory – no Jews
in England, Edward I having expelled them in 1290, they had
the interest for him of the exotic).

I observed some fewe of those Jewes especially some of the
Levantines to bee such goodly and proper men, that then I said to
my selfe our English proverbe, To looke like a Jewe (whereby is
meant sometimes a weather beaten warp-faced fellow, sometimes a
phrentike and lunaticke person, sometimes one discontented) is
not true. For indeed I noted some of them to be most elegant and
sweet featured persons, which gave me occasion more to lament
their religion.

In the women's gallery he saw

many Jewish women, whereof some were as beautiful as ever I
saw, and so gorgeous in their apparel, jewels, chaines of gold, and
rings adorned with precious stones, that some of our English
Countesses do scarce exceede them, having marvailous long
traines like Princesses that are borne up by waiting women serving
for the same purpose. An argument to prove that many of the
Jewes are very rich.

While walking in the ghetto he fell in with a rabbi who
spoke Latin, and was soon in religious debate, and then

dispute, with him (much as with the Turk in Lyons); Coryate summarised the ding-dong: 'in the end he seemed to be somewhat exasperated against me.'

After there had passed many vehement speeches to and fro betwixt us, it happened that some forty or fifty Jewes more flocked about me, and some of them beganne very insolently to swagger with me, because I durst reprehend their religion: Whereupon fearing least they would have offered me some violence, I withdrew my selfe by little and little towards the bridge at the entrance into the Ghetto, with an intent to flie from them, but by good fortune our noble Ambassador Sir Henry Wotton [whose residence in the Canareggio sestier was near the ghetto] passing under the bridge in his Gondola at that very time, espyed me somewhat earnestly bickering with them, and so incontinently sent unto me out of his boate one of his principall Gentlemen, Master Belford his secretary, who conveighed me safely from these unchristian miscreants, which perhaps would have given mee just occasion to forsweare any more comming to the Ghetto.

This story occasioned a passage in praise of Sir Henry Wotton, from whom Coryate 'received many great favours' (generally, it seems, in advising him what to see, and, probably, in directing him to a house where other young Englishmen lodged). Sir Henry (1568–1639) was another Winchester and Oxford man, with acquaintance in common with Coryate, including John Donne and Richard Martin. Coryate proudly quotes Martin's letter of introduction, either unaware of, or indifferent to, its ambiguities of tone:

To give your Lordship an inventory of his [Coryate's] particular qualities were rather to paint my friend then to praise him . . . I will only say this, that looke what pleasure or contentment may be drawn from good society, liberall studies or variable discourse, are all to be found in M. Thomas Coryate. In the first, *in via pro vehiculo est*, more pleasant then a Dutch waggon [as pleasant as a coach on a journey]; in the second a Universall pretender; in the third amongst his friends infinite, and the last that will be wearied. The end of his voyage (which must be first made knowen to an

Ambassador) is to better himselfe by the increase of knowledge for the good of his Country, wherein he is resolved to begge wisdome among the rich, rather then wealth of riches among the learned; and what the affection of the Gentleman is to learning, I can (if need be) be deposed; but of his ability and judgement therein, I had rather your Lordships sharpe judgement should find him guilty, then mine accuse him. For I hate to betray my friends [but sometimes I just can't help myself]. Two things I have intreated him to carry with him, discretion and money, which commodities are not easily taken up by exchange on the Rialto; he hath promised me to goe well furnished with both, of other things he hopes to be furnished by your Lordships means.

Coryate was never to escape the condescending smirk of his socially superior 'friends'. On the other hand, Laurence Whitaker (as quoted by Edward Terry) wrote, 'My Lord, Good wine needs no bush, neither a worthy man letters commendatory, because whithersoever he comes he is his own epistle.'

Wotton himself had been travelling for many years on the Continent, learning languages and engaging in diplomatic activities, most notably going to Scotland disguised as an Italian, to warn King James VI of a plot to poison him before he could inherit the throne of England; in 1604 James appointed him Ambassador to Venice, where his wit, charm and intelligence made him very effective. Nowadays he is, unfortunately, probably best known for an aphorism written in a friend's album in Augsburg, which was translated as 'an ambassador is an honest man sent to lie abroad for his country', which got him into some trouble at the time. In literary circles he is known for his poetry, particularly the poem addressed to Prince Henry's sister, the Queen of Bohemia, beginning:

> You meaner beauties of the night,
>   That poorly satisfie our eyes
> More by your number than your light
>   You common people of the skies
>   What are you when the sun shall rise?

His influence can still be seen in England, in the architecture of the large country house. He had a particular interest in architecture, sending back to England pictures, books, models and drawings by Palladio (he was to publish *Elements of Architecture* in 1624, promoting neo-classical art and architecture, especially that of Palladio). Not only did he advise Coryate on what to see in Venice; it was under his influence that Coryate wrote about the Palladian buildings in Vicenza and the Veneto. This in turn would have encouraged Inigo Jones's visit there in 1613–14, so affecting Jones's architectural style and that of English mansions in the late seventeenth and early eighteenth centuries.

Coryate recorded some of the amusements of Venice; in the Piazza San Stefano ('two hundred eighty seven paces long, for I paced it; but of a meane breadth, onely sixty one') on Sunday evenings he watched young men playing at Balloon,

> which is thus: Sixe or seven young men or thereabout weare certaine round things upon their armes, made of timber, which are full of sharpe pointed knobs cut out of the same matter. In these exercises they put off their dublets, and having put this round instrument upon one of their armes, they tosse up and downe a great ball, as great as our football in England; sometimes they will tosse the ball with this instrument as high as a common Church, and about one hundred paces at the least from them. About them sit the Clarissimoes of Venice, with many strangers that repair thither to see their game. I have seene at the least a thousand or fifteene hundred people there: If you will have a stoole it will cost you a gazet, which is almost a penny.

He also went to the theatre, not being impressed by the building, acting, costumes or music, but intrigued by the women acting, a practice that he had not seen in England. He spent some time describing the courtesans in the audience, who came

> so disguised, that a man [who?] cannot perceive them. For they wore double maskes upon their faces, to the end they might not be

seene: one reaching from the toppe of their forehead to their chinne and under their necke; another with twiskes of downy or woolly stuffe covering their noses. And as for their neckes round about, they were so covered and wrapped with cobweb lawne and other things, that no part of their skin could be discerned. Upon their heads they wore little blacke felt caps very like to those of the Clarissimoes that I will hereafter speake of. Also each of them wore a black short Taffata cloake. They were so graced that they sate on high alone by themselves in the best roome of all the Playhouse. If any man should be so resolute to unmaske one of them but in merriment, onely to see their faces, it is said that were he never so noble or worthy a personage, he should be cut in pieces before he should come forth of the roome, especially if he were a stranger [does one hear an echo of Coryate being warned off a proposed show-off prank?]. . . . There is but one or two little galleries in the house, wherein the Cortezans onely sit. But all the men doe sit beneath in the yard or court, every man upon his severall stoole, for the which he payeth a gazet.

There is noticeably no mention of any respectable women present in the theatre. In fact, Coryate disapproved of the women's fashions in Venice as immodest or foolish, even though the women wore veils, black, white or yellow, when they went out. Black was worn by wives and widows, white and yellow by young, unmarried women, 'but they weare more white than yellowish' (Coryate was apparently unaware that courtesans were supposed to wear yellow veils); the veils were very thin, so that the women could see through, but frustrating for men: 'you can very seldome see her face at full when she walketh abroad, though perhaps you earnestly desire it, but onely a little glimpse thereof.' Moryson reports Venetian men using bolder methods than Tom could have managed: 'Young Virgins of the Nobility passing the streete, and having their Faces covered with a Vayle like a Nett, so as they might see and be seene tho not fully, gentlemen for a Curtesy would stop their way, standing still before them as amazed at their beauty, and they took pryde to declyne asyde with a smyle and light blushing.' Tom did not always approve of what he could see:

Almost all the wives, widowes and mayds do walke abroad with
their breasts all naked, and many of them have their backes also
naked even almost to the middle, which some do cover with a
slight linnen, as cobweb lawne or such other thinne stuffe: a
fashion me think very incivill and unseemly, especially if the
beholder might plainly see them. For I beleeve unto many that
have prurientem libidinem, they would minister a great incentive
& fomentation of luxurious desires. Howbeit it is much used both
in Venice and Padua.

It is surprising that Coryate was shocked, when such a topless
fashion had been very common in London and Queen Elizabeth's
court only a few years earlier – but perhaps not in Odcombe.

Another feminine fashion that he condemned was the
wearing of *zocoli*, that is, extremely high platform shoes
(called chapineys or chopines in England, where they were not
unknown – see *Hamlet*, II. 2), designed to keep feet and
dresses out of puddles:

so uncomely a thing (in my opinion) that it is pitty this foolish
custom is not cleane banished and exterminated out of the citie.
There are many of these chapineys of a great heigth, even half a
yard high, which maketh many of their women that are very short,
seeme much taller then the tallest women we have in England.
Also I have heard that this is observed amongst them, that by how
much the nobler a woman is, by so much higher are her
Chapineys. All their Gentlewomen, and most of their wives and
widowes that are of any wealth, are assisted and supported eyther
by men or women when they walke abroad, to the end they may
not fall. . . . I saw a woman fall a very dangerous fall, as she was
going down the staires of one of the little stony bridges with her
high Chapineys alone by her selfe: but I did nothing pitty her,
because shee wore such frivolous and (as I may truely terme them)
ridiculous instruments, which were the occasion of her fall.

He also described how every Saturday afternoon the women
of Venice bleached their hair, both with some kind of bleach
and by spreading it out in the sunlight, on the broad brims of
straw hats. Apropos of women's fashions, or fashions in women,

Moryson tells us that 'the Italyans love fatt and tall wemen, and for those causes the Venetian wemen are sayd to be Belle di Bellito, bianche di calcine, grasse di stracchie, alto di legno o zoccole, that is, fayre with painting, white with chalk, fatt with rags (or stuffed linnen) and high with wood or Pantofles (which many weare a foote or more deepe)'.

Description of women's fashions led Coryate on to a lengthy discussion of Venice's most famous – or notorious – residents, the Venetian courtesans, 'because the name of a Cortezan of Venice is famoused all over Christendome [indeed, in London, at the end of the sixteenth century, there was a brothel simply named "Venice"]', though

> all the writers that I could ever see, which have described the city, have altogether excluded them out of their writings [a puzzling assertion, as practically everyone who visited Venice mentioned them. One Elizabethan, John Day, went so far as to call Venice 'the best flesh-shambles [meat-market] in Italy', and another, Sir Roger Ascham, the young Queen Elizabeth's tutor, who briefly visited in 1552, 'saw in that litle tyme, in one citie, more libertie to sinne, then ever I heard tell of in our noble Citie of London in ix [9] yeare']. . . . Onely I feare least I shall expose my selfe to the severe censure and scandalous imputations of many carping Cricticks, who I thinke will taxe me for luxury and wantonnesse to insert so lascivious a matter into this Treatise of Venice.

In the event, everyone made merry at Tom's expense.

He reported the estimated number of whores (expensive and cheap) in Venice and the surrounding islands as at least 20,000, 'whereof many are esteemed so loose, that they are said to open their quivers to every arrow'. Coryate expressed surprise that they should be so tolerated, and the city not fear God's destruction by fire and brimstone, as in Sodom and Gomorrha, but recorded two justifications made to him. The first was that Venetian husbands feared 'that the chastity of their wives would be the sooner assaulted, and so they should be capricornified, (which of all the indignities in the world the Venetian cannot patiently endure) were it not for these places of evacuation'. This argument did not impress him, as he had observed that the Venetian women were always kept cooped up and inaccessible in their houses. Moryson provides some confirmation of this:

> Husbands take straunge liberty in the use of Courtezans (so their Harlotts are called) who live a mery life . . . neither doe the wives marry with any hope to enjoy their husbands alone, but are content if they may have the tythe of their love. . . . the poore wife sitts alone at home, locked upp and kept by old wemen, not having liberty to looke out of the windowe, especially if it be towards the streete . . . Yet by corruption of the old wemen, and by any occasion of having Conversation, though it be with meane men, this strict keeping makes them think it simplicitye not to take the revenge their husbands most feare, even with hazzard of their honors and lives.

As to the consequences of such hazardous revenges, Moryson reports that 'adulteries (as all furyes of Jelousy, or signes of making love, to wives, daughters and sisters) are commonly prosecuted by private revenge, and by murther, and the Princes and Judges, measuring their just revenge by their owne passions proper to that nation, make no great inquiry after such murthers, besides [providing] that the revenging party is wise inough to doe them secretly, or at least in disguised habitts'. The other justification made to Coryate was that the courtesans' taxes paid for a dozen galleys; Moryson also wrote that these taxes exceeded 300,000 crowns a year.

In any case, there they were in great numbers, a bad business doing very good business. Coryate's account of his visit to a courtesan is very lengthy, and unusually vivid – even eloquent.

> For when you come into one of their Palaces (as indeed some few of the principallest of them live in very magnificent and portly buildings fit for the entertainment of a great Prince) you seeme to enter into the Paradise of Venus. For their fairest roomes are most glorious and glittering to behold. The walles round about being adorned with most sumptuous tapistry and gilt leather . . . As for

her selfe shee comes to thee decked like the Queene and Goddesse of love, in so much that thou wilt thinke she made a late transmigration from Paphos, Cnidos, or Cythera, the ancient habitations of Dame Venus [Venus and Venice seem to be blurring into each other, the seductive courtesan the embodiment of the ravishing city]. For her face is adorned with the quintessence of beauty. In her cheekes thou shalt see the Lilly and the Rose strive for supremacy, and the silver trammels [nets, combs] of her haire displayed in that curious manner besides her two frisled peakes standing up like prety Pyramides, that they give thee the true cos amoris. But if thou hast an exact judgement, thou maist easily discerne the effects of those famous apothecary drugs heretofore used amongst the Noble Ladies of Rome, even stibium, cerussa, and purpurissum [it is unlikely that these Venetians used the cosmetics employed in ancient Rome, that Coryate's memory of having read of provided him with a shield and the basis of 'exact judgement' and defence]. . . . Also the ornaments of her body are so rich, that except thou dost even geld thy affections (a thing hardly to be done) or carry with thee Ulysses hearbe called Moly [as a defence against the seductive witch, Circe] which is mentioned by Homer, that is, some antidote against those Venereous titillations, shee wil very neare benumme and captivate thy senses, and make reason vail bonnet to affection [submit to desire]. For thou shalt see her decked with many chains of gold and orient pearle like a second Cleopatra (but they are very little), divers gold rings beautified with diamonds and other costly stones, jewels in both her eares of great worth. A gowne of damaske (I speake this of the nobler Cortizans) eyther decked with a deep gold fringe (according as I have expressed it in the picture of the Cortizan that I have placed about the beginning of this discourse [where Tom is shown greeting her in the correct Italian manner – 'The Italians in saluting one another, crosse the right hand over the breast, laying it upon the heart,' writes Moryson]) or laced with five or sixe gold laces each two inches broade. Her petticoat of red chamlet [a light, expensive fabric of silk and wool] edged with rich gold fringe, stockings of carnasion [flesh-coloured] silke, her breath and her whole body, the more to enamour thee, most fragrantly perfumed . . .

It seems that Tom was having a hard time, but, having brought himself and his reader to the brink with this breathless display and vision of her charms, he reins back: 'Though these things will at the first sight seeme unto thee the most delectable allurements, yet if thou shalt rightly weigh them in the scales of a mature judgement, thou wilt say with the wise man, and that very truely, that they are like a golden ring in a swines snout.' Circe is overcome, herself transformed into an animal. After this, singing to the lute, 'elegant discourse', a tour of her 'chamber of recreation' with its 'curious milke-white canopy of needle worke, a silke quilt embrodered with gold and generally all her bedding sweetly perfumed' may all be brought into play, but all in vain against the mature judgement of the wise man.

Coryate then warns his male reader, heated by this description, that 'if thou shouldest wantonly converse with her', and not pay, the courtesan will 'either cause thy throate to be cut by her Ruffiano . . . or procure thee to be clapped up in the prison'. The frontispiece to the book shows Coryate merely being pelted with eggs, presumably for time-wasting (if the incident happened at all – he makes no mention of it). He concludes with an extended defence of his visit, undertaken in a purely anthropological spirit, 'to see the manner of their life', and also, like Gladstone many years later (as we are told), to 'endevour by perswasive terms to convert her . . . so did I visite the Palace of a noble Cortezan, view her own amorous person, heare her talke, observe her fashion of life, and yet was nothing contaminated therewith, nor corrupted in maner'. As Melville's Ishmael wrote, after surviving his encounter with the deadly white whale: 'And I only am escaped alone to tell thee.'

After feminine flamboyance, masculine self-repression (or a different kind of masking): Coryate approved of the sober, black-gowned gentlemen who met in the Piazza San Marco twice a day, the 'Clarissimos' dressed in black cloth, with gowns faced in black taffeta, whilst the senior men called 'Savi' wore red gowns, all of whom wore 'marveilous little black caps of felt, without any brimmes at all'. All this he preferred to English fashion, new fangled curiosities and ridiculous superfluities of pane[l]s, plaites, and other light toyes . . . For whereas they have but one colour, we use many more than are in the Rain-bow, all the most light, garish and unseemly colours that are in the world. Also for fashion we are much inferiour to them. For we weare more phantasticall fashions then any Nation under the Sunne doth, the French onely excepted; which hath given occasion both to the Venetians and other Italians to brand the English-man with a notable marke of levity, by painting him starke naked with a paire of shears in his hand, making his fashion of attire according to the vaine invention of his braine-sicke head, not to comelinesse and decorum.

Such sober-sides criticism of English fashion was a common theme among conservative and puritan commentators – 'except it were a dog in a doublet, you shall not see any so disguised as are my countrymen of England', wrote William Harrison in his 1587 *Description of England*. Against this might be set Tom's delight in the extravagant falsities and performances of other occupants of the Piazza, the mountebanks or street salesmen, who 'oftentimes ministred infinite pleasure' to him with their bravura rhetoric and sales pitches, performed on benches or small stages (Ben Jonson's Venetian comedy *Volpone* includes a superb parody of a mountebank sales performance).

These Mountebanks at one end of their stage place their trunke, which is replenished with a world of new-fangled trumperies. After the whole rabble of them is gotten up to the stage, whereof some weare vizards being disguised like fooles in a play [or courtesans: the characteristic Venetian combination of display and deception], some that are women . . . are attyred with habits according to that person that they sustaine; after (I say) they are all upon the stage, the musicke begins. Sometimes vocall, sometimes instrumentall, and sometimes both together. . . . While the musicke plays, the principall Mountebanke which is the Captaine and ring-leader of all the rest, opens his truncke, and sets abroach his wares; after the musicke hath ceased, he maketh an oration to the audience of halfe an houre long, or almost an houre. Wherein he doth most hyperbolically extoll the vertue of his drugs and confections . . .

though many of them are very counterfeit and false. Truely I often wondered at many of these naturall Orators. For they would tell their tales with such admirable volubility and plausible grace, even extempore, and seasoned with that singular variety of elegant jests and witty conceits, that they did often strike great admiration into strangers that never heard them before: and by how much the more eloquent these Naturalists are, by so much the greater audience they draw unto them, and the more ware they sell . . . The principall things that they sell are oyles, soveraigne [healing] waters, amorous songs printed, Apothecary drugs, and a Commonweale of other trifles. The head Mountebanke at every time he delivereth out any thing, maketh an extemporall speech, which he doth eftsoones intermingle with such savory jests (but spiced now and then with singular scurrility) that they minister passing mirth and laughter to the whole company, which perhaps may consist of a thousand people that flocke together . . . Also I have observed this in them, that after they have extolled their wares to the skies, having set the price of tenne crownes upon some one of their commodities, they have at last descended so low, that they have taken for it foure gazets, which is something less than a groat.

The wise man got his pleasure from watching the courtesan and mountebank from a distance, but engaged with neither.

Contrasting with these entertaining, essentially harmless rogues were the gangs called Braves, who wandered

abroad very late in the night to and fro for their prey, like hungry Lyons, being armed with a privy coate of maile, a gauntlet upon their right hand, and a little sharp dagger called a stiletto. They lurke commonly by the water side, and if at their time of night, which is betwixt eleven of the clocke and two, they happen to meete any man that is worth the rifling, they will presently stabbe him, take away all about him that is of any worth, and when they have thoroughly pulled his plumes, they will throw him into one of the channels: but they buy this booty very deare if they are after apprehended. For they are presently executed.

Between the two pillars in the Piazetta San Marco was the usual and popular place for extreme punishments and executions. There Coryate saw a very Tragicall and dolefull spectacle . . . two men tormented with the strapado, which is done in this manner. The offender having his hands bound behind him, is conveighed into a rope that hangeth in a pully, and after hoysed up in the rope to a great heigth with two severall swinges, where he sustaineth so great torments that his joynts are for the time loosed and pulled asunder; besides such abundance of blood is gathered into his hands and face, that for the time he is in the torture, his face and hands doe looke as red as fire. . . . [Coryate also reported] one very memorable thing (besides all the rest that I have before named) . . . even the head of a certaine Fryer which is set upon the top of one of their steeples: He was beheaded for his monstrous and inordinate luxury, as some affirme. For I heard many say in Venice that he begat with childe no lesse than ninety nine Nunnes, and that if his courage had served him to have begotten one more with child, that he might have made up the full number of an hundred, his life should have been saved. I asked many Venetians whether this were true, who denied it unto me, but with such a kinde of smiling and laughter, that that denying seemed a kinde of confessing of the matter. Againe some others extenuating the haynousnesse of the crime, told me that that was a meere fable, and said the truth was, that he committed sacriledge by robbing one of the Churches of the Citie, stealing away their Chalices and other things of greatest worth.

Sadly, this does seem more likely (as Coryate probably suspected). Curiously, William Lithgow has a similar story to tell, incidentally revealing the popularity of public executions near St Mark's. Arriving by boat from Ancona, he and his fellow travellers saw a column of smoke in the air:

We began to demand a Venetian what the matter was: who replied, there was a grey Frier burning quicke [alive] at S. Markes pillar . . . for begetting fifteen young Noble Nunnes with child, all within one yeare, he being also their Father confessor. Whereat, I sprung forward through the throng, and my friend followed me, and came just to the pillar as the halfe of his body and right arme fell flatlings in the fire; the Frier was forty sixe yeares old, and had bene Confessor of that Nunnery of Sancta Lucia five yeares.

Most of these young Nunnes were Senators daughters, and two of them were onely come in to learne vertue, and yet fell in the midst of vice.

Fynes Moryson in turn tells of how, when he was living in Venice,

some roaring boyes went out uppon a Wager who should do the greatest villany, and when they had done most wicked things, at last they came all to the window of the Popes Nuntio, where they sang horrible blasphemyes against our Lord, his blessed mother, and the Apostle St Peter [a reflection of the strained relations between Rome and Venice at the time]. The next morning all these Rascalls (so I call them, whereof most notwithstanding were gentlemen) had escaped out of the Citty, only two were taken, whome I did see executed in this manner, their hands were cutt of in fower places where they did the greatest villanyes, their tongues were cutt out under the window of the Popes Nuntio, and so they were beheaded with an axe falling by a Pully [a kind of guillotine], which done, the Scaffold and their bodyes were burnt, and the Ashes throwne into the Sea.

After nearly six weeks, Coryate's money was running out, and it was time to leave this 'most flourishing garland of Christendome'. The latter part of his account of Venice includes an outline of the state and its system of government, and a lengthy account of the complex coinage and monetary system, with warnings about money-exchange problems, which apparently cost him dear. Nevertheless, on his last day there, patriotism was pleased: in the Piazza San Marco he saw a large portrait of King James (England was currently supportive of Venice in its quarrel with Rome), and, at the Rialto bridge, a picture of James, Queen Anne and Prince Henry, with, on the other side, a picture of Henri IV, all of which 'ministered singular contentment unto me'.

He concludes with more lyrical eulogies of 'this Paradise, this Tempe, this rich Diademe', which had provided him, he wrote, 'such infinite and unspeakable contentment' that he

would not have missed it for a gift of four estates in England –
even in Somerset. Reluctantly leaving this 'fairest Lady, yea
the richest Paragon and Queene', virgin-whore and queen-
mother, a visually satiated but financially poorer Coryate at
last pulled away, to set off on what would have to be a more
economical journey home.

FIVE

Venetia and the Gray Confederacy

After, as he noted, six weeks and two days in Venice, Coryate dragged himself away on 8 August, returning by boat to Padua, where he was invited to dinner by young Lord Wentworth (later to make a considerable name for himself, as the Earl of Strafford, abandoned to his fate by Charles I in 1641 – 'hurried hence | 'Twixt treason and Convenience', in what were probably John Cleveland's words) and revisited the church with him and his friend George Rooke, who saw him on his way the next afternoon.

After passing through 'the Guasto, that is, the waste plot', an area deforested by the Venetians as a defensive measure, and a night in what he called 'a solitary house', he arrived in Vicenza early in the morning of 10 August. Here he was shown round the city by two friendly Vicentines, who had nothing better to do, but earned praise for Italians' kindness to strangers: 'Therefore I will ever magnifie and extoll the Italian for as courteous a man to a stranger as any man whatsoever in Christendome.' His account of the city makes good use of Schott's book, but for himself he visited a garden where he was tempted to steal some fruit that made his mouth water, and the monastery of the Dominican friars, where they claimed to possess Christ's crown of thorns – which was also claimed by Paris: with irrefutable logic, Tom pointed out that 'eyther they must prove that Christ had two severall crownes of thornes put upon his head (which is contrary to the history of the Evangelists) or else it must needed follow that one of the crownes is false'. He asked to see it, but was told it was shown only on the feast of Corpus Christi.

Of particular interest to him (and here he was a little in advance of English taste at home, thanks to Sir Henry Wotton) was the neo-classical architecture of Andrea Palladio. Palladio's Basilica, which Coryate called the Praetorium, he described as 'a very sumptuous and magnificent building' (as usual, he paced out its length and breadth); the Villa Capra, which received greater attention,

> built upon a pretty eminent hillocke, and is round (in which respect it is called in the Italian, Rotonda) having foure very beautifull fronts, which doe answere the foure parts of the world . . . Every front hath sixe most stately great pillars, and two paires of staires to ascend to the same . . . The roofe of the house is round [domed] and very pretily adorned partly with curious pictures, and partly with statues . . . Also the roofe is open for the raine to descend into a very convenient place made of purpose in the hall for the receiving thereof. In one of the higher chambers there is the fairest chimney for clowy and jeames [jambs, supporting side-pillars] that ever I saw, saving that of the King of France at his Palace of Fountaine Beleau before mentioned. For it was made of an extraordinary fine marble, beautified with faire veines of divers colours . . . also there is a stately cellar under the Palace, the roofe whereof is vaulted,

with an inscription over the door, reading,

> Antrum non Cumaeum
> Neque Homericum videbis,
> Sed Bacchi;
> Hospes ingredere,
> Laetior abibis.

[Neither the Cumaean nor the Homeric cave shalt thou see, but that of Bacchus; enter, guest, thou shalt depart more happily.]

'But I found not the words of the inscription true; for I went not out more merily then I came in, because the cellarer had not the honestie to bestowe as much as one draught of his wine upon me.'

The Villa Capra was to prove remarkably important and influential, being widely copied in the Continent and later in England, as at Mereworth Castle in Kent and, most notably, at Lord Burlington's villa in Chiswick, which caused Alexander Pope to mock architecture-fashion snobs who inappropriately

> call the winds through long arcades to roar,
> Proud to catch cold at a Venetian door;
> Conscious they act a true Palladian part,
> And if they starve [of cold], they starve by rules of art.

Thirsty Tom concluded his account of Vicenza with 'two memorable Italian sayings', no doubt told him by his Vicentine companions:

> 'Quanti hà Venetia ponti e Gondolieri,
> Tanti hà Vicenza Conti e Cavallieri.

That is, looke how many bridges and Gondoleers Venice doth yeeld, so many Counts and Knights doth Vicenza. The other, of the wine of Vicenza, which is in a manner proverbially spoken of as other commodities are of Italian cities, viz.

> Vin Vicentin,
> Pan Paduan.
> Tripe Trevizan.
> Putana Venetian.

That is,

> The Wine of Vicenza,
> The Bread of Padua.
> The Tripes of Treviza.
> The Cortezans of Venice.'

Moryson praised the Paduan bread, unprompted, and the wine of the area, 'of a red colour and sweet, and howsoever it seems thicke, more fit to be eaten then drunke, yet it is of a most pleasant taste'; Tom had to take most of that on trust.

The next day he set off on foot for Verona; on the way he noticed, rather worryingly, that most of the horsemen he encountered had muskets ready loaded, with touch-boxes and bags of bullets, apparently a common practice in Italy at the time, 'because the people of the country are so given to villainies, that they will rob, rifle and murder passengers, if they are not sufficiently provided to defend themselves' (Coryate had neither gun nor sword, nor − fortunately − obvious signs of wealth). More to the point for him was 'a marvailous violent showre' that afternoon, that persisted during three miles' walking, 'even till I came to my lodging, and made me wet to the very skinne, that I did even rigere frigore [shiver with cold]'. Nevertheless he admired the abundant vineyards, fertile fields and meadows on the way but, true Englishman of his time, noticed the absence of 'one speciall commodity . . . wherwith (God be thanked) England is so abundantly furnished . . . being indeed a thing exceeding necessary for the sustenation of mans life . . . viz. sheepe'.

Verona received the full treatment in his book, with introductory verses by Scaliger (three of whose relatives had monuments there) as well as much potted history ('first founded by the ancient Hetruscans') and extensive borrowings from Schott, with a great many inscriptions carefully transcribed. In those days they did not show off Juliet's window and balcony; but of the various histories that Coryate copied out, one would have been very much to the taste of Jacobean tragedians:

Here also Alboinus the first king of the Langobards died an unnaturall death. For whereas the said King, after he had taken the famous city of Pavie [Pavia] by a long siege out of the hands of Longinus the first Exarch of Ravenna, and solaced himselfe with feastes and banquets: he compelled his wife Rosamunda to drinke one day at table of the skull of her father Cunimundus, whom a little before he had slaine: for the which his Queene intending to be revenged upon him for that most inhumane and barbarous injury, conspired with one Hemichildus a noble Longobard, to kill the King her husband, with promise both to

Frontispiece of *Coryats Crudities* (1611), by William Hole. The incidents illustrated are
annotated in verses by **Ben Jonson** and **Laurence Whitaker** (see p. 161). In the lower centre,
France holds bunches of grapes, Italy is bare-breasted like the Venetian women Coryate saw,
and drunken Germany, who has a miniature wine-tun on her head, vomits over him.
(Bodleian Library, Oxford: J.-J. Drayton e. 83)

HENRICVS PRINCEPS

Muscular Protestantism. Henry, Prince of Wales, exercising with the pike, by William Hole, in Michael Drayton's *Polyolbion* (1612). *(Bodleian Library: J.-J. Drayton d. 37)*

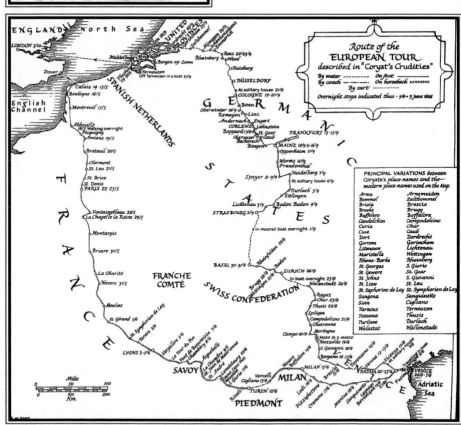

The route of Thomas Coryate's European tour. Michael Strachan, *The Life and Adventures of Thomas Coryate* (1962). *(With kind permission, Estate of Michael Strachan)*

Tourists watching mountebanks in St Mark's Square, Venice. An Englishman is shown, lower right. Giacomo Franco, *Habiti d'huomeni et donne Venetiane* (*c.* 1609). *(Bodleian Library: Antiq. d. I. 5)*

Thomas Coryate meeting a Venetian courtesan. *Coryats Crudities.* *(Bodleian Library: J.-J. Drayton e. 83)*

The Clock Tower of Strasbourg Cathedral. *Coryats Crudities. (Bodleian Library: J.-J. Drayton e. 83)*

The Great Tun of Heidelberg, with added drawing, by William Hole, of Coryate standing on the top. *Coryats Crudities. (Bodleian Library: J.-J. Drayton e. 83)*

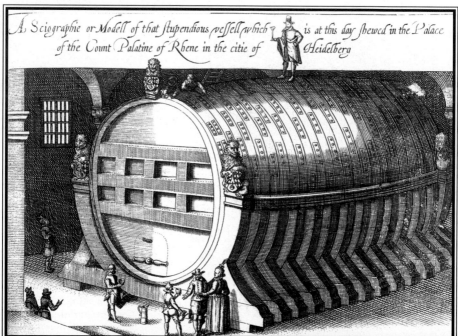

Punishment on the wheel. The man is being beaten to death. Jacques Callot, *Fructus Belli: Les Misères et les malheurs de la guerre* (1633). *(Ashmolean Museum, Oxford)*

The Martyrdom of St Ursula and 11,000 Virgins, Cologne, early sixteenth century, which could have been seen by Coryate. The saint supports her bridegroom as he is killed. Almost directly behind her can be seen the flying buttresses of the unfinished cathedral, and in the right background is the church of St Gereon. *(V&A Picture Library)*

The ass bearing the image of Isis (detail).
Andrea Alciati, *Emblemata* (1591).
(Bodleian Library: Vet. B 1 f. 112)

Left: Thomas Coryate's letter to Sir
Michael Hicks (1610). *(British Library)*

A battle with Barbary corsairs, by Hendrik Cornelisz Vroom (1615). The foreground galley, flying the Turkish flag, is sinking, so drowning the slave oarsmen. *(National Maritime Museum, Greenwich)*

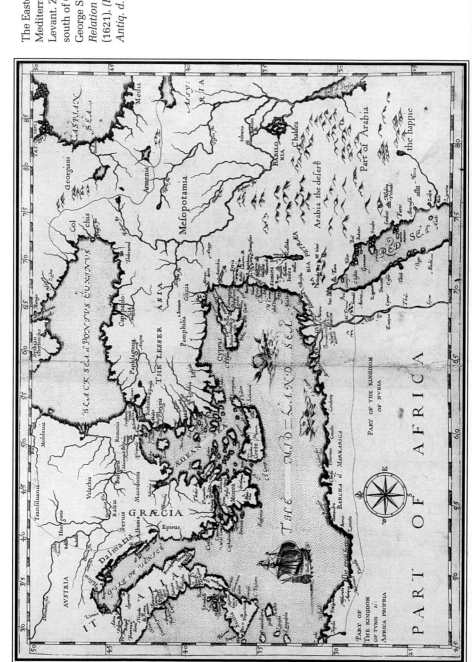

The Eastern Mediterranean and the Levant. Zante is just south of Cephalonia. George Sandys, *A Relation of a Journey* (1621). *(Bodleian Library: Antiq. d. E. 1615. I)*

marry him if he would execute the matter, & to bestow the Kingdome of Lombardy upon him. Whereupon Hemichildus being tempted with this faire offer, murdered Alboinus, as he was asleepe in his bedde. And so by this meanes he obtained indeede the marriage of the Queene, but not the possession of the Kingdome. For being constrayned to flie away presently after he had committed this bloody assassination, he came with his wife Rosamund to Ravenna to the Court of Longinus before named, where after they had remayned a little while, Longinus falling in love with the Queene, perswaded her, to the end he might the sooner enjoy her in marriage, to poyson her new husband Helmichildus. The Queene shortly after delivered her husband a poysoned cup as he came one day out of a bath, which when he had greedily dranke, and now perceived the violent effect of the poyson, he compels Rosamund to drinke the rest; so that she died presently with her husband.

To quote a fabled Victorian review of a performance of *Antony and Cleopatra*: 'How different from the home life of our own dear Queen.'

Verona city walls received high praise, 'the fayrest of all the Italian cities that I saw . . . of a marveilous heigth, in some places forty foot high, according to my estimation', with deep, broad trenches, constantly improved in expectation of attacks from the Spanish-governed Duchy of Milan. Coryate did the rounds of the churches, monasteries and gardens, but his main interest as a classics scholar was in the Roman amphitheatre, which he described at considerable length, 'for indeede it is such an admirable Fabricke that it draweth all strangers into admiration thereof', despite its semi-ruinous state. He describes the great walls and the three rows of arches, each containing three more rows of arches, 'built one above another, and raised to a wonderfull heigth, at the least one hundred and fifty foot high', formerly equipped with red marble pillars. The lowest arcades were reduced to being used as stables, and 'partly for tipling houses for poore folkes to sell wine in, and other necessaries'. He was able to inspect the rooms where the animals were kept that the prisoners had to fight:

for according to the auncient custome of the Romans certaine enormous malefactors that had committed some capital crimes, being condemned to fight for their lives with wilde beasts, were in this place and such other (whereof Rome had many, as the Circus maximus, &c. . . .) if fortune favoured them so well that they slew those beasts, then both their lives were saved, and also they had some reward bestowed upon them, which was commonly called brabium, in token of their victory. But if they were slaine by the beasts, it was esteemed as a just recompense for their wicked deserts.

The English traveller Peter Mundy wrote that 'those that were condemned to fight with wild beasts Were exhibited in the Mornings. The horror [of the contests] was such, as weomen were forbidden to behold them.' Now the central area '(made in the forme of an egge, sharpe at the ends, and broade at the sides, very like to a pond that I have seene in one of Sir Francis Carewes gardens in Middlesex) . . . in length nine & thirty pearches [a perch is 16½ feet], in breadth two and twenty halfe. For I did exactly observe the length and breadth of it.)' was used for jousting tournaments and similar harmless amusements.

At the end, Tom also saw

a very mournefull shew performed by Monkes in Verona. For I saw eighteene couples of them accompany a corse of one of their Fraternitie to Church, being attired with blacke buckram vailes, and marked with the signe of the starre on the left side of their breasts, girt with a blacke girdle, their heads covered with a blacke hood that came all over their shoulders and hid all their face. Before their eyes were made two holes to looke out: each of them carryed a burning candle in his hand of virgin wax, and some of them three candles, and there was put into every candle two peeces of their little tin money called gazets.

Coryate stayed in Verona from Friday morning to 1 p.m. on Sunday 14 August, reaching Desensan (modern Desenzano) about 22 miles away at about 8 p.m., a pace of about 3 miles an hour. Here he was near Lake Garda, oftentimes very rough and boisterous, insomuch that at some times of the yeare it is very dangerous for passengers to passe that way. The cause of which roughnesse is ascribed unto the high cliffes that inclose it on both sides, and interclude [close off] the windes, who having not the liberty there as in the open sea, doe extremely tosse up and downe the waters. It yeeldeth golden sands like those of Tagus by Lisbone, and Pactolus by Sardis in Lydia [of which he had only read, in classical texts]. Also it aboundeth with fish, especially Carpes, Troutes, and Eeles.

The next afternoon he reached Brescia. 'I heard that there are some notable antiquities and inscriptions in this city, but I must intreat thee (gentle Reader) to pardon me although I doe not communicate them to thee. For I made so short aboad in the Citie, that I could not observe halfe so much as I would have done if I had remained there but one whole day.' Moryson had time to notice that the manners and customs of the people of this 'fruitfull area' with 'mines of Iron and Brasse [?]' were more relaxed and 'French' than elsewhere in Venetia, 'and the very weomen receive and give salutations [kisses in greeting], and converse with the French liberty, without any offence to their husbands, which other Italians would never indure'; Peter Mundy noticed many people with goitres, such as Coryate had seen in Aiguebelle. For all Coryate's short stay (he was off at 8 a.m. next day), he managed a considerable amount – a few inscriptions, pacing out the dimensions of the 'sumptuous' Palace court, and noting various pictures, armour and 'goodly' pillars and arches, and the buildings' broad overhanging pentices, as in Verona, and the streets' open arcades ('garnished with faire pillars') as in Mantua and Padua.

His religious researches were, as usual, interesting but frustrating. In the Cathedral was supposed to be

the Crosse that was presented unto the Emperor Constantine in the south part of heaven, about the going down of the sun, at what time he marched with his army towards Rome, to joyne battell with Maxentius [AD 312]. In which Crosse these characters were plainly seene: In hoc signo Constantine vinces [With this sign, Constantine, thou shalt conquer]. The Brixians doe call this Crosse whereof they soe much boast, Oroflamma, which signifieth the golden Flame, &c. and they affirme that it representeth the colour of heaven. Albeit I hold this tradition to be a meere, yea, a grosse figment (for what wise man that hath his wit in his head and not in his heele, will beleeve that this should be the very same heavenly Crosse?) seeing we reade that Constantine himselfe could not have the same, but in steede thereof made another Crosse the next day after of gold and precious stone, which was borne before him in steede of a standard (Euseb. de vita Constant. lib.I).

Coryate sounds distinctly exasperated; he tried to see the cross, but was refused, 'because it is shewed but at certayne times'. Likewise at the Dominicans' church he was told that there was a bone of one of Mary Magdalen's arms there, but again he could not see it, 'because', as the gentle reader will have guessed, 'it is shewed but at certayne times'.

While he was in Brescia there was a dedication of a new image of the Virgin Mary, which he saw performed in

a certaine little Chappel with many superstitious rites. For they attired the image with a great many several roabes, as of sattin, taffata, lawne, &c., and there was a great multitude of little waxen idols brought to the Chappell, whereof some were only armes, some thighes, some presented all the parts of a mans body: although these toyes were no novelties unto me. For I saw many of them before that time in divers Italian Cities. Yet I had a marvailous itching desire to finger one of them, only to this end, to bring it home into England, to shew it to my friends as a token of their idolatry; but I saw there was some difficulty in the matter. Howbeit I gave the venture upon it in this manner. I stood at one corner of the Chappel while many women were at their divine oraizons prostrate before the image, and very secretly conveighed my fingers into a little basket (nobody taking notice thereof) where the images were laid; and so purloyned one of them out, and brought him home into England. Which had it been at that time perceived, perhaps it might have cost me the lying in the Inquisition longer then I would willingly have endured it.

This moral decline continued for some time, as, walking the 30 miles on to Bergamo through the abundant vineyards that effectively formed 'one spacious lane . . . about eighteene miles in length', he frequently helped himself to 'rich grapes, passing faire and sweet . . . which the Italians like very good fellowes did winke at, shewing themselves more kinde unto me then the Germans did afterward in Germany'.

Bergamo also got its Scaliger verses, notes on history and transcription of monuments; here he told off 'certaine Italian Gentlemen' for allowing busts of Julius Caesar and Trajan to be placed sacrilegiously on the northern front of the cathedral (it is not clear what these men could have done about it), which he otherwise found 'passing faire, and worthy to be noted by an industrious traveller'. Nearby was an 'exceeding sumptuous' monument to Bartolomeo Colleoni, whose statue he had admired in Venice; here too Colleoni was on horseback, in gilded armour, with helmet, crest and banners, and with his coat of arms, which, of course, Coryate interpreted as three testicles, believing that nature had given Colleoni 'three stones, one more then other men have, as I have said before'.

Whilst the Bergamese dialect was apparently considered the coarsest in the country, Coryate was impressed by the formality and circumlocution of the residents when talking Latin to him. Furthermore, he noticed the difference in pronunciation of Latin by Italians and most other continentals from that used by the English, 'whereupon having observed such a generall consent amongst them in the pronunciation . . . I have thought good to imitate these nations herein, and to abandon my old English pronunciation . . . as being utterly dissonant from the sound of all other Nations; and having determined (God willing) to retayne the same till my dying day'. It is not obvious why God should wish to prevent him from doing this.

He found the city overwhelmed by the crowds that had come in, Italians from far and near, as well as Germans and Swiss, for the week-long feast of St Bartholomew, 'the greatest faire that ever I saw in my life, except that of Frankford in Germany . . . exceeding plenty of all manner of commodities being there sold'. Unfortunately for Coryate, this meant that all the inns were full, with no lodging to be obtained at any price. 'So that I was faine to lye upon straw in one of their stables at the horse feete, according to a picture that I have made of it in the frontispiece of my booke.' People in England later found this very ridiculous, but things might have been worse: Moryson relates how he had bought a stallion in Padua, and at Verona the stableman deliberately put it in with the mares, 'that the rascall might make himselfe sport with his covering of the mares, which for that time I knew not, but after manifestly found' by the stallion's subsequent friskiness when passing mares; it could have been a lively night for Tom. However,

> (notwithstanding my repose upon so uncouth a pallate [pallet]) I slept in utrumque aurem, even as securely as upon a bedde of downe, because of my long journey the day before. And it was long before I could obtayne this favour, which was at last granted me by the meanes of an honest Italian Priest who had beene a traveller. Unto whom I was not a little beholding for some curtesies that I received at his hands in Bergomo. He promised to revisit me the next morning, to the end to shew me the antiquities of the City. But he was prevented, to my great griefe, by the villany of a certaine bloud-thirsty Italian, who for an old grudge he bare to him, shot him through the body in his lodging with a pewternell [petronel, a large pistol or carbine].

He also received help – possibly life-saving – from a Dominican friar (Coryate must surely have started to moderate a little his views on the Catholic clergy), who warned him to avoid going by the shore of Lake Como, where there was a castle garrisoned by Spaniards who would, he was sure, 'lay their Inquisition upon me, as soone as they would perceive that I was an Englishman, and so consequently torture me with extreme cruelty, if they saw me constant in the profession of my religion, till they might compell me to abjure it, which if I would not doe by the violence of their punishments, then at the last they would put me to death, and excarcinate [torture, flay] me in a very bitter and terrible manner'. This was a real danger: as Tom would have known, as recently as 18 May, a Mr Lichefield, tutor to young Lord Wentworth, had been arrested in Bologna by Dominican friars and imprisoned by the Inquisition. As it happened, Lichefield quickly went over to the Church of Rome, and became a Jesuit priest. On the other hand, William Lithgow, a fierce Protestant, was arrested, imprisoned and tortured by the Inquisition in Malaga in 1620, when he was racked, flogged, beaten, hanged by the arms, forced to swallow water until his body swelled, half-throttled and threatened with burning at the stake; he survived, partially crippled.

So, on 18 August, Tom set off northwards up the Valle Brembana, through the villages of San Giovanni and Mezzoldo. 'Most of this valley is an ascent leading to the Alpes. At the entrance it is something pleasant way, but after I had passed some sixteene miles it was very laboursome and painefull to travell, as well in regard of the steepnesse, as of the extreme hard stones wherewith the greatest part of the way is pitched.' There was some good news; en route, he was told that a thirty-strong gang of bandits, who lived by 'rifling and spoyling of travellers' and whom he might well have encountered, had just been captured (and presumably taken off for execution by one of the ingenious methods that the Italian judicial systems provided). In Mezzoldo he had the good fortune to fall in with an English-speaking former servant of the international financier, Sir Horatio Palavicino. Sir Horatio (who died in 1600) was an Anglo-Italian who had been Collector of Papal Taxes for Queen Mary until her death, when he shrewdly abjured Roman Catholicism and appropriated the money to set up what was to become a Europe-wide business, involving lending money to Protestant governments, including those of England and the Netherlands, and providing information and secret agents; the servant must have had some entertaining gossip to pass on to entertain Coryate.

Onwards and upwards trudged Excelsior Tom, at barely one mile an hour, up the steep and stony tracks and precipitous mountainsides, up to the windy Passo di San Marco, 5,500ft

above sea level, where there was a little inn, declaring itself
174 miles from Venice and marking the boundary of the State
of Venice. Over the door was the golden winged lion, with a
Latin inscription recording the improvement and reopening of
the road in 1594. That this notice can still be read today is due
to Coryate, whose conscientious transcription was traced and
copied by the Italian authorities during the twentieth century,
when it was realised that the original was gone. After the
Latin, as written out by Coryate, comes the Italian:

> Epigrafa posta sulla casa nel 1596 rilevata nel
> 1609 dall' Inglese Tomaso Coryate 'My Observations
> of Bergamo' che percorse la strada priula nel
> viaggio di ritorno in patria.

It is wonderful – if extraordinary – that there is one corner of a
remote foreign field (or mountain inn) that is for ever Coryate.
There, at any rate, Tomaso stepped out of Italy, and across into
the Grisons country.

The Grisons, also known as the Gray Confederacy,
comprised a group of small, practically independent republics
between Italy and Switzerland, mountainous, rugged, not
generally very wealthy, the people passing freely from one
country to another via the high passes. The Valtellina valley
through which Coryate now descended was famous for its
wines, which were exported, not on carts but packed on
horseback or muleback, in order to negotiate the extremely
narrow, winding mountain tracks. Here English Coryate was
interested to see thousands of sheep grazing, belonging,
however, not to local residents but to the people of Bergamo,
who herded them to and fro annually. 'Also I noted marveilous
abundance of little trip-frogges in that part of this valley
Telina, where I travelled. I never saw the hundredth part of
them in so short a space in all my Life. Most of their
meadowes being so full of them, that I could not step five or
six steps but I should finde a little frogge; a thing that I much
wondered at.'

From here Tom and his new companion could see the Spanish castle of which he had been warned, and the 'noble' Lake Como by which the castle stood. That night there was a severe thunderstorm, with such heavy rain that the roads were flooded and impassable, so that they had to proceed by boat to the next village, and then, with a sigh of relief, to the town of Chiavenna. 'This towne ministred some occasion of comfort unto me, because it was the first Protestant [particularly Calvinist] town that I entred since I went out of Italy, yet not wholly Protestant. For some part of it embraceth Popery, and heareth daily masse. . . . This towne is rich, and inhabited with many wealthy merchants; also it hath great store of goodly vineyards growing about it.' It was also the home town of his new friend, who speeded him on his way 'with a cup of excellent wine', which he would have appreciated on account of the very rough tracks he had to follow – 'very offensive to foote travellers. For they are pitched with very sharpe and rough stones that will very much punish and grate a mans feete.' If Coryate complained, they must have been bad indeed. Despite that, on he went, noticing the houses made mostly of pine logs, and the children gathering horse-dung by the wayside, for the cottage gardens.

At his inn in Candolchin (modern Campodolcino) a priest attempted to cheer him up, remarking that, though 'the fare of some places in the country was hard, and the ways bad' (Tom could not have been looking a happy wanderer), nevertheless he travelled in 'as honest a country as any in all Christendome. For had I a thousand crowns about me, I might more securely travell with it in their country without company or weapon, then in any nation whatsoever: affirming that he never heard in all his life of any man robbed in that country.' Silently speculating whether this was due to the natives' natural virtue or the terrifying severity of their laws ('The Justice of the land', wrote Moryson, 'is so severe as they have no theeves nor Robbers among them'), Coryate merely concluded drily that he had never heard of such rare honesty before in all his life, 'in any people whatsoever before or since Christ'.

After he had left Italian-speaking Campodolcino, he climbed continually for 8 miles over the Splügen Pass, and then six miles down again into Splügen, German speaking and wholly Protestant. Some dangers at least were now past. At this point of transfer from Italian to German, one might note some comments and improper jokes reported by Moryson about the German language ('an Imperious and rude kynde of speech') and German pronunciation of Italian.

They have many abuses in pronuntiation as F for V . . . thus a German in Italy, when he would have said, Io ho Veduto, sayd, Io ho fututo il Papa con tutti i Cardinali, instead of I have seene, sayd I have (with leave be it spoken) buggered the Pope, with all the Cardinalls. So they pronounce the letter R lightly, or not at all, which in Italy made a foule mistaking betweene a Curtezan and a German, who saying to her Non importa, was understood as if he had changed the R into T whereupon shee offered him an Italian Cortesy, abhorred by all the nations on this syde the Alpes, and more spetially by the modest Germans. Likewise the Italians observe them to pronounce B insteede of P, remembering a like mistaking of a German at Padoa who telling some Italians that he came from the Portello (that is the gate house) was understood by them as if he had sayd he came from the Bordello (that is the Stewes).

From Splügen, sobersides Tom went on through the upper valley of the Rhine, which flowed very fast, producing 'steep cataracts' raising 'a certaine reaking mist to a great heigth'. Here he saw many old, ruined castles built on high hills, and little cottages set on mountain tops. The houses had very small windows ('I observed this country to bee colder by halfe then Italie'), with wooden walls and roof tiles; the people still drank wine rather than beer, while the size of their trenchers seemed worth mentioning: 'for the most part at the least an inch thicke, and as large in compasse as a cheese of my country of Somersetshire that will cost a shilling.' That big.

At this point in the book, extraordinarily, Coryate abandoned his narrative, and inserted a lengthy oration by one Herman

Kirchner, praising travel in Germany; not many people have read this. A few pages later, in the afternoon of 23 August, Coryate arrived in Curia (now Chur), an ancient city set amidst rich orchards ('their trees being so exceedingly laden, that the boughes were even ready to breake through the weight of the fruite'), capital of the Grisons and a busy market centre. Here he visited the Cathedral ('many images, superstitious pictures, and Papisticall vanities') and the Council House, which provoked some history writing; however, with rare impatience, he concludes: 'He that will be further instructed in the popular government of the Grisons, let him reade a book by that learned Josias Simlerus of Zurich [Josias Simler, *De Republica Helvetiorum*, 1575].' Coryate had had enough of the Gray Confederacy: the next day he arrived in Switzerland.

Through the Mountains

On the way to the town of Walastat (modern Wallenstadt) Coryate saw farmworkers busy on the hay harvest, two months later than in England, but then realised it was almost certainly their second harvest of the year; here, on the evening of 25 August, he recorded with satisfaction that he had his first Rhenish wine (which had an excellent reputation). From here he was able to take a boat, pausing overnight at 'a solitary house by the water side', where he dined well, paying with a Spanish shilling. Early next morning (4 a.m.) he arrived at the great Protestant city of Zurich, 'set in a faire plaine of corne and pasture, lying upon the Rhine, having on all sides woody Mountaines in sight, and neere the City . . . most pleasant fields planted with vines', as Moryson reported.

Tom may have had a letter of introduction to 'that glittering lampe of learning', the Protestant minister Rudolph Hospinian, noted for his monumental and no doubt impartial study, *An History of the Errors of Popery*, who arranged for a young man, Mark Bueler, to act as a guide round Zurich. Through him he met Henry Bullinger, a successor to the famous religious reformer Ulrich Zwingli, and 'a very vigilant preacher of this Citie, and a painefull labourer in the Lords Vineyard', who showed him his library, especially 'one most execrable booke written by an Italian, one Joannes Casa Bishop of Beneventum in Italy, in praise of that unnaturall sinne of Sodomy . . . kept . . . as a monument of the abhominable impurity of a papistical Bishop'. (In Job's words, 'Oh that mine adversary had written a book!')

Bueler took Coryate round the city, showing him the great
defensive walls and carefully sited towers, for the city had
endured 'many bitter brunts . . . having beene tossed to and fro
from one Lord to another, as if shee had beene Dame Fortunes
tennis ball', though it now enjoyed 'great peace and a very
halcedonian [halcyon, peaceful] time with the rest of the
Helveticall Cities under that happie league of union', as PR
man Bueler recited at dictation speed. Tom particularly enjoyed
looking at the great lake with its watermills and large quantities
of fish, as well as a smaller lake famed for its abundance of
frogs (one of his minor interests, it seems). He was taken round
the churches, the 'fayrest' being that dedicated to the martyred
Saints Felix and Regula: beheaded near one of the city bridges,
'they carried their heads in their hands after they were strooken
off from their bodies, to the place where they desired to be
buried. How true or false this is', Tom declined to say. Here,
once again, he was grieved at the inadequate memorialization
of notable men: 'for none of them had any more then a flat
stone laid upon them without Epitaph, or any maner of
inscription to preserve them from oblivion.'

The fourth church had a large armoury (actually, it was
quite common, in England as well, for churches to provide a
storeroom for a few arms). Apropos of arms and the church in
Zurich, Moryson relates how 'the Citizens have a custome that
when they goe forth against the enemy, they place the
Ministers or Pastors in the front, or where they may partake
the danger, and there is a place two miles from the city,
towards Lucerna, where Zwinglius, a famous Preacher and
Reformer of Religion was killed in the field [at Kappel, in
1531]'. Coryate was able to inspect the armoury thanks to
Gaspar Waser, a noted philologist, 'a great professor of
eloquence, a singular linguist . . . he spake seven languages,
being very skilfull in the Hebrew and Greeke tongues, and a
famous traveller', a man very much after Coryate's own heart.
Apart from a large stock of the usual modern weapons –
'culverins, demiculverins, demicannons, sakers, basiliskes
[large cannon, usually of brass, throwing a 200 lb. shot], &c.' –

the armoury also contained various ancient trophies and weapons, including, apparently, arrows, shields and banners used by the Swiss against the Romans, Roman ensigns and, most remarkably, the sword worn by William Tell.

The legend of William Tell was accepted as historical fact in Switzerland, though it was hardly known elsewhere. The version that Coryate set out for his readers, based partly on Sebastian Münster's *Cosmographie* (1544) and partly on what he was told in Zurich, is the earliest telling of the story in English:

When as the Germane Emperours being the Lords of the principall Cities of Helvetia constituted forraine Prefects and rulers about three hundred yeares since as their deputies over three townes, especially above the rest, namely Sylvania, otherwise called Underwald, Urania, commonly called Uri, and Swice, it hapned that the Prefect of the towne of Swice behaved himself very insolently, abusing his authority by immoderate tyrannising over the people. For amongst other enormous outrages that he committed, this was one. He commanded one of his servants to compell all travellers that passed such a way, to doe reverence to his hat that was hanged on a staffe in the high way. The people unwilling to offend the Magistrate, did their obeysance unto the hat. But one amongst the rest, even this foresaid William Tell, being a man of stout courage, refused to doe as the rest did. Whereupon he was brought before the Magistrate, who being grievously incensed against him for his contumacie, injoyned him this pennance: That he should shoote an arrow out of a crosse-bowe at an apple set upon his sonnes head that was a little child, whom he caused to be tied to a tree for the same purpose, so that if he had fayled to strike the apple, he must needs have shot through his sonne. This he commanded him because this Tell was esteemed a cunning archer. At the first he refused to doe it: But at last because he saw there was an inevitable necessity imposed upon him, he performed the matter greatly against his will, and that with most happy successe. For God himselfe directing the arrow, he shot him so cunningly, that he strooke off the apple from the childs head without any hurt at all to the child. And whereas he had another arrow left besides that which he shot at his sonne, the Prefect asked him what he meant to do with that arrowe: he

made him this bould and resolute answere. If I had slaine my child
with the first, I would have shot thee through with the second. The
magistrate hearing that, commanded him to be apprehended, and
carried away in a barke. And when he was come betwixt the towne
of Urania and a certaine village called Brun, having by good
fortune escaped out of the boate, he ranne away with all possible
expedition over the difficult places of the mountaines, where there
was no common way, and so came to a place neere to the which he
knew the tyrant would passe, where he lay in ambush in a secret
corner of the wood till he came that way, and then shot him
through with his other arrow. It hapned that this Tell did weare the
foresaid sword about him when he atchieved these worthy actes,
in regard whereof the Switzers have ever since that time hanged
up the same in their Armory for a most remarkable monument,
though me thinks it had beene much better to have reserved the
arrow with which he shot through the tyrant, then the sword he
wore then. This noble exploit was the first originall of the
Helveticall confederation. For . . . in the end all the Cities of
Helvetia combined themselves together in a league of unity . . . As
for the name of Switzers, it grew upon this foresaid occasion, even
because the above mentioned William Tell the first author of this
league was borne in the towne of Swice. For before this time all
the inhabitants of the country were called Helvetians.

Moving around the city (where at last he got his very worn
shoes repaired, according to a later note), Coryate saw the
military exercise ground (Moryson thought the Swiss 'military
by nature' and 'given to the military life') and archery butts.
The men, from the age of 10 to 100 (he wrote) all wore round
breeches with codpieces, while the women had 'a very strange
and phantasticall fashion with their haire': pigtails. Just
outside the city he saw the punishment ground,

made in the forme of a pit, neere unto the which there standeth a
little Chappell, wherein some Clergie man doeth minister ghostly
counsell unto the offendour before he goeth to execution. In that
Chappell I saw wheeles [a curiously bald statement: perhaps he
wondered whether a church was a suitable location for
instruments of torture]. If they should happen to tremble so much

that they cannot stand upright (as sometimes offendours doe [says worldly Coryate]) they are punished in the Chappell . . . The punishments that are inflicted upon offendours are divers, in number five, whereof the first is beheading, which punishment they only do sustaine that are incestuous men or high-way robbers. The second is the Gallowes, upon the which those are executed that commit Burghlarie or burne houses. The third is the water, which incestuous women doe suffer, being drowned therein. The fourth is the fire wherewith Witches, Sorcerers, and Hereticks are punished, and after their bodies are burnt their ashes are cast into the River Sylla aforesaid. The fifth and last punishment is wheeling, which is onely for murderers.

There were also two prisons, one built in one of the city wall towers and reserved for lesser offenders, the other in a tower built out in the water, kept for capital offenders and debtors (the future banking capital of Europe seems never to have liked bad payers).

Coryate spent only one night in Zurich, at The Two Storks, where he ate well, if relatively expensively, his meal costing 'six battes, that is, fifteene pence English'. The beds he found very strange, 'for every man hath a light downe or very soft feather bedde laid upon him which keepeth him very warme, and is nothing offensive for the burden. For it is exceeding light, and serveth for the coverled of the bedde.' Moryson was less enthusiastic about these early duvets: 'This kind of lodging were not incommodious in Winter, if a man did lie alone, but since by the high way they force men to have bedfellows, one side lies open to the cold . . . But in Summer time this kind of lodging is unpleasant, keeping a man in a continual sweat from head to foote . . . I would advise the passenger to weare his own linnen breeches, for their sheets are seldom or never cleane.' When Montaigne was in Switzerland some twenty years earlier, he complained that there were 'never any curtains for the beds, and always three or four beds to a room, right next to one another; no fireplace, and you get warm only in the common rooms and dining rooms . . . lucky is the man who gets a white sheet, and it is their style never to cover the pillow with a case; and they rarely offer any other covering than that of a feather quilt, and that very dirty'.

Coryate concluded his account of Zurich with a celebration of all the scholars and learned writers that the city had produced, surpassing in quantity (but not, he insisted, in quality) the output of Oxford and Cambridge, before copying out the Latin and Greek letters he sent to Waser, Hospinian, Bullinger and Bueler, and the two replies he received, from Waser and Bueler.

On Saturday 27 August he left Zurich, seen on his way by Bueler (who 'bedewed his cheekes with teares' on parting), taking a boat from Maristella, 9 miles away, and once again spending the night in 'a solitary house'. Eight miles beyond Zurich he passed a chapel containing a large pile of human bones and skulls, reputedly the remains of a battle between Burgundian and Swiss soldiers; early on Sunday morning, he arrived in Baden.

Wandering uncertainly about the city, he was surprised to see heads of boars nailed to the doors of several houses, apparently a widespread custom among boar-hunting Germans at the time. In a chapel of the Cathedral he saw yet another great heap of bones and skulls: 'I never saw so many dead mens bones laid together in all my life before. For the number of them was so great, that I thinke at the day of judgement at the least ten thousand soules will challenge [claim] them. Surely for what cause they heape together these bones (I confesse) I know not.' (The building may simply have been an ossuary, to deal with the problem of an overcrowded graveyard, common in old towns.) His next, more pressing problem was that he could not find the famous hot sulphur baths, that Hospinian of Zurich had particularly advised him to visit, as he could not speak the local language, and the ordinary people could not understand him. In the event, he walked 5 miles out of town to the neighbouring monastery of Köningsfelden, where a kind scholar understood his Latin and walked back with him to the baths.

There were some sixty bath-houses for the better-off visitors,
served by good inns with names such as The Bear, The Ox and
The Sun, as well as two public baths for the poorer people.
Many of these visitors 'were Gentlemen of great worth that
repaired thither . . . partly for infirmities sake, and partly for
meere pleasure and recreation. Most of the private baths are
but little, but very delicate and pleasant places, being divided
asunder by certaine convenient partitions wherein are
contrived divers windowes, to the end that those in the bathes
may have recourse to each other, and mutually drinke
together' from ingenious floating tables. Moryson observed
that 'Men, Weomen, Monkes, and Nunnes, sit all together in
the same water, parted with boords, but so as they may
mutually speake and touch . . . The waters are so cleare as a
penny may be seene in the bottome, and because melancholy
must be avoided, they recreate themselves with many sports
while they sit in the water.' Coryate was shocked to see

Men and women bathing themselves together naked from the
middle upward in one bathe: whereof some of the women were
wives (as I was told) and the men partly bachelers and partly
married men, but not the husbands of the same women. Yet their
husbands have bene at that time at Hinderhove [the location of
the baths], and some of them in the very place, standing by the
bathe in their cloathes, and beholding their wives not onely
talking and familiarly discoursing with other men, but also
sporting after a very pleasant and merry manner . . . Yet all this
while the husband may not be jealous . . . For mine own part
were I a married man, and meant to spend some little time here
with my wife for solace and recreation sake, truly I should
hardly be perswaded to suffer her to bath herselfe naked in one
and the selfe same bath with one only bacheler or married man
with her, because if she was faire, and had an attractive
countenance, she might perhaps cornifie me . . . Here also I saw
many passing faire yong Ladies and Gentlewomen naked in the
bathes with their wooers and favorites in the same . . . Many of
these yong Ladies had the haire of their head very curiously
plaited in locks, & they wore certaine pretty garlands upon their

heads made of fragrant and odoriferous flowers. A spectacle exceeding amorous.

A learned man with whom Coryate got into conversation told him that the baths were very effective in treating a variety of illnesses, and in particular were 'of admirable efficacie to cure the sterilitie of women, and make those that are barren very fruitfull bearers of children. A matter verified and certainly confirmed by the experience of many women.' It seems very likely.

That evening he revisited the abbey at Köningsfelden, where he wrote out a lot of history and inscriptions, before going on to the town of Brugg at 8 o'clock, 'something applauding my selfe in a manner, and congratulating my owne good fortune & successe' in having seen the town of Baden, the baths and the abbey, despite the unfortunate start to the day. The next evening he got to Rheinfelden (managing 20 miles in thirteen hours), a Catholic town with a great gallows on three pillars and a wheel for executions; and the day after, 30 August, arrived at Basel.

His account of the city begins with notes on speculations as to the origins of the name of the city: 'Basilea quasi Pasilea, that is, a place of passage' or from 'the Greeke word Basileia which signifieth a kingdome'. Moryson had heard that it might derive from a knight killing a basilisk (a particularly nasty medieval monster, with the head, wings and feet of a cock and the body and tail of a serpent; to meet its eyes was fatal, and a knight could approach it safely only if he held a crystal ball before his face to deflect the deadly gaze). Pressing on, Tom remarked on the pleasant situation of the city, with wheatfields and vineyards on one side of the Rhine, and hills on the other; 'also the ayre is esteemed as sweet and comfortable as in any City of the whole world, as a certaine English Gentleman told me'. The wooden bridge linking the two parts of the city was 'a very base and meane thing, being compacted together of many rough plankes and uneven pieces of timber that hang something loose'; it was explained to him that the loose planking was a defensive measure against attack from the Duke of Savoy, to enable the rapid – and cheap – dismantling of the bridge. Both parts of the city had battlemented walls; the private houses, four storeys high, he thought beautiful. He was very enthusiastic about the cathedral, with its roof of multi-coloured tiles set out in a chequered pattern, 'the most beautiful Protestant Church that ever I saw, saving our two in London of Pauls and Westminster, which doe very little excell this in beauty (though something in greatnesse) if any thing at all'. Indeed, he was confident that

> one goodly prayer pronounced in this Church by a penitent and contrite-hearted Christian in the holy Congregation of the citizens to the omnipotent Jehovah through the only mediation of his sonne Jesus Christe, is of more efficacy, and doth sooner penetrate into the eares of the Lord, then a centurie yea a whole myriad of Ave Maries mumbled out upon beads in that superstitious manner as I have often seene at the glittering Altars of the Popish Churches.

In this former Popish church he was able to indulge in an orgy of epitaph-transcribing (fourteen, in full, in Latin), including that of the great Catholic humanist Erasmus.

For once Coryate was able to visit the university, in particular the theological school adjoining the cathedral choir. 'It is a very decent and comely place, but inferiour to our Divinity Schoole of Oxford' (which is, after all, rather spectacular). Here he attended a divinity lecture, somewhat sparsely attended; the lecturer, in a very odd hat, made a point of repeating 'every principall sentence of note', a convenience for slow note-takers. Fynes Moryson, a former Cambridge University academic, wrote that

> the students of Germany have little learning from private reading, but take the most part thereof upon trust (or hearsay) from the lectures of those grave professors who dictate their lectures with a slow and tretable [clear, distinct] voyce, which they write out word by word, their many penns sounding like a great shower of

rayne, and if the Professor utter anything so hastily that the Students cannot write it, they knocke upon the Deskes till he repeate it more tretably.

In the city the men wore great codpieces and ruff bands (strips of cloth hanging down), like the men of Zurich, and strange hats

in the forme of a cap, very long crowned, whereof some are made of felt, and some of a kinde of stuffe not unlike to shagge [a worsted or silk cloth with a velvet nap] in outward view. It hath no brimmes at all, but a high flappe turned up behind, which reacheth almost to the toppe of the hat, being lesser and lesser towards the toppe. This fashion is so common in the Citie, that not onely all the men generally doe weare it both Citizens and Academicks (in so much that [the lecturer] wore the same in the Divinity schoole) but also the women whatsoever, both yong and old. Moreover their women, especially maides, doe weare two such plaited rowles of haire over their shoulders wherein are twisted ribbons of divers colours at the endes, as the women of Zurich. I observed many women of this Citie to be as beautifull and faire as any I saw in all my travels: but I will not attribute so much to them as to compare them with our English women, whome I justly preferre, and that without any partialitie of affection, before any women that I saw in my travels, for an elegant and most attractive natural beautie.

He stayed one night in Basel; at his inn, the food was good and remarkable for the variety of dishes, but expensive, 'no lesse then eight battes a meale, which are twenty pence of our money. They use to sitte long at supper, even an houre and a halfe at the least, or almost two houres.' Moryson also remarked on this: 'They drincke stoutly, and though they eate slowly yet by setting long at table Commonly eate to satiety, which two thinges use to provoke venerye, yet no doubt their Chastity is admirable. Perhaps this fullnes chookes their spirittes, and makes them dull, and so less inclyned to venerye.' Here too Coryate encountered the well-known German enthusiasm for drinking. Moryson (among many) commented on the 'National vice of drunckenness in such excesse (espetially among the Saxons), as it staynes all their nationall vertues . . . with them it is no shame especially in the lower partes of Germany from Nuremberg to the Northerne Sea, if they drincke till they vomitt, and make water under the table, and till they sleepe'. Coryate, however, was amongst Swiss Germans, and matters were somewhat better:

> The first noble carowsing that I saw in Germany was at mine Inne in Basil. Where I saw the Germanes drink helter-skelter very sociably, exempting my selfe from their liquid impositions as well as I could. It is their custome whensoever they drink to another, to see their glasses filled up incontinent (for therein they most commonly drinke [pewter and earthenware mugs were still commonly used, but considered poor style: as Falstaff said, 'Glasses, glasses is the only drinking']) and then they deliver it into the hand of him to whom they drinke, esteeming him a very curteous man that doth pledge the whole, according to the old verse:
>
> Germanus mihi frater eris si pocula siccas.
> [German, thou shalt be my brother if thou drainest the cup.]
>
> But on the contrary side, they deeme that man for a very rusticall and unsociable peasant, utterly unworthy of their company, that will not with reciprocall turnes mutually retaliate [which seems an appropriate word] a health. And they verifie the olde speeche . . . eyther drinke or be gon. For though they will not offer any villainie or injury unto him that refuseth to pledge him the whole (which I have often seene in England to my great griefe) yet they will so little regard him, that they will scarce vouchsafe to converse with him.

One gets the impression of a difficult evening for sociable but temperate and economical Coryate. He went on, however, to defend Germans from the general charge of drunkenness: 'that vice reigneth no more there (that I could perceive) then in other countries. For I saw no man drunke in any place of Germany, though I was in many goodly Cities, and in much notable company.' In fact, he went on to the counter-attack:

I would God the imputation of that vice could not be almost as truly cast upon mine owne nation as upon Germany. Besides I observed that they impose not such an inevitable necessity of drinking a whole health, especially those of a greater size, as many of our English gallants doe, a custome (in my opinion) most barbarous, and fitter to be used among the rude Scythians and Gothes then civill Christians: yet so frequently practised in England, that I have often most heartily wished it were clean abolished out of our land, as being no small blemish to so renowned and well governed a Kingdome as England is.

Hamlet, a few years earlier, ostensibly speaking of Danes, reproved a drinking 'custom More honour'd in the breach than the observance . . . heavy-headed revel east and west'. The vigour of Coryate's phrasing suggests memories of tiresome evenings spent with the literary boozers and 'gallants' in the taverns of London.

Early in the morning of 1 September, Coryate (none the worse, one hopes, for any unaccustomed drinking the night before) took a boat down the fast-flowing Rhine (Moryson reports that the strength of the current forced the watermen of Basel to sell their boats downstream at Strasbourg, having no reasonable hope of getting them back upstream); despite the speed of the river, he had to spend the night on board, lying on a heap of straw,

> having for my coverled the cold open aire which did not a little punish me: yet I comforted myselfe with the recordation of that old verse

> Dulcia non meruit qui non gustavit amara,

> that I did not deserve the sweet junkats of my little experience without some bitter pills and hard brunts of adverse fortune.

And so, after this cold comfort, philosophical Tom disembarked on a river quay in Strasbourg, early in a chilly autumn morning, no doubt in need of a good, warming breakfast.

SEVEN

Down the Two-Horned River

For most of the way from now on, Coryate's journey would be determined by the course of the Rhine, which he felt required a little disquisition all to itself, tracing its 'original spring from a certaine Mountaine of the Rheticall Alpes called Adula but a little way distant from the citie of Curia above mentioned, which yeeldeth two severall fountaines; wherehence rise two rivers that meete together in one about five miles above the said Curia, whereof one is called the first Rhene, the other the second . . . Virgil calleth this river bicornis . . . because it hath in a manner hornes, and those in number two, whose names are Lecca and Wahalis. In which respect other Poets also as well as he termed it bicornis.'

Coryate concludes his discussion of the Rhine by reporting

one more strange property then any river in the whole world that I could either heare or reade of in any history whatever sacred or prophane, that whensoever any infants were cast into his channell (a thing that hath sometimes hapned) if they were begotten out of lawfull wedlocke, the river as a just revenger of the mothers polluted bedde would presently swallow it up in his swift streame, but if he found them to be begotten in the honest and chaste couple of marriage, he would gently and quietly conveigh them upon the toppe of the water, and restore them into the trembling handes of the wofull mother, yeelding safety unto the silly [innocent] babe as a most true testimony of the mothers impolluted chastity.

Moryson also reports this belief, but without Coryate's imaginative engagement (and apparent credulity). The two writers' difference is also suggested by Moryson's expatiating on the German character ('All writers commend the Germans or high Dutch for Modesty, Integrity, Constancy, Placability, Equity, and for gravity, but somewhat inclining to the vice of Dullnes . . . All the Germans have one Nationall vice of drunckennes . . . Otherwise, the men (as the women) are modest in speeches, and hold it great immodesty to make water in the streetes, and in some places the magistrate will punish any unshamefastnes in that kynde'), and word-man Coryate speculating on the origins of the names Teutonia, Alemannia and Germany. 'Teutonia some will have to be so called quasi Tuisconia from Tuisco the sonne of the Patriarch Noah by his wife Arezia . . . Others derive it from one Teutanes . . . who was the Lord of this country after the death of King Tuisco.' As for Alemannia, 'some write that it taketh his denomination from Alemannus the surname of Hercules, who (as that ancient Chaldaean author Borosus writeth) did heretofore reigne in this country'. Others derived it from two German words, 'All' and 'man', 'because the auncient Alemannes were very couragious and valiant men, yea they were All men . . . so the Aleman quasi All man, he is all valour, every part of him is viril, manly and couragious, no jot effeminate', whilst yet others derived it from 'a Dutch word which signifieth a promiscuous multitude'. The third name, Germania, he derived from the Latin *germanus* meaning those born from the same parents, 'because the auncient Germans did with such a brotherly affection share dangers and fortunes of warre'.

As for Strasbourg itself, Coryate commended 'the loftinesse of the building, the multitude of their houses, the beauty and spaciousness of their streets and the cleane keeping thereof, the great frequency of people, their strong walles made of hard stone and adorned with stately battlements, divers towers, strong bulwarkes, faire gates, mighty and deep trenches that are moated round about it' (it is noticeable how all these cities are prepared for war); this summary catalogue suggests his eagerness to get on to his two main objects of interest, the Cathedral tower and clock.

The tower, begun in 1277 and twenty-five years in the
building, 'the exquisitest peece of work for a Tower that ever I
saw, as wel for the heigth, as for the rare curiosity of the
architecture', he considered one of the principal wonders of
Christendom, not unreasonably, as it was then, and until the
construction of the Eiffel Tower, the tallest building in Europe:
he was told it was 574ft high, though in fact it measures 465ft,
high enough. The famous clock, 'the Phoenix of al the clocks
of Christendom', excelled all other clocks, he wrote, 'as a fayre
yong Lady of the age of eighteen yeares that hath beene very
elegantly brought up in the trimming of her beauty, doth a
homely and course trull of the Countrie'. Where did this
extraordinary, improbable and far-fetched image come from,
setting clock towers against an ordinary country girl (perhaps
in Somerset) and a vision of a beautiful young gentlewoman,
perhaps from the Court, some unobtainable impossible? Years
later in India, he was reported as repeating orations in praise
of the young and beautiful Lady Frances, married to the Earl of
Hertford, who had been Lord Lieutenant of Somerset in 1602
and 1608, when Tom might have met her (his father had been
chaplain to a predecessor of the Earl). As they said in those
days, 'Thought is free.'

Construction of the clock began in 1571; apart from merely
telling the time, it showed the eclipses of the sun and moon
for a 32-year period. Above various statues (of Urania, muse of
astronomy, an unknown king and Copernicus) was a figure of a
cock, which crowed at eleven in the morning and three in the
afternoon, 'yeelding as shrill and loud a voice as a naturall
cocke, yea and such a kind of sound (which maketh it the
more admirable) as counterfeyteth very neere the true voyce of
that bird'. Below that he observed 'the greatest astronomicall
globe that ever I saw, which is supported with an artificial
Pellican wounding his breast with his beake, wherewith they
typically represent Christ, who was wounded for the salvation
and redemption of the worlde'; by this was an elaborate globe,
and another orb with a hand pointing out four hours. Beside
this were two angels, one striking a brazen serpent with a

mace, every hour, and a death's head or skeleton ('Notable objects tending to mortification'). Golden lions and Latin inscriptions filled more space, before 'a great company of mathematicall conceits which do decipher some of the most abstruse & secret mysteries of the noble science of Astronomy'. Another orb showed a half-moon and stars; seven brass bells were ranged for 'certaine artificial men' to come out and strike them every quarter of an hour 'with a very delightfull and pleasant grace'. Coryate did his best to record everything, but he had only half an hour to examine it all, as the sexton wanted to lock up and go home.

So off he had to go, looking round the city (containing 'one of the fairest shambles that I saw in all my travels'), noticing that the women here also wore their hair in plaits, as in Basel, but that no one wore those strange, tall caps, but very broad caps, of cloth, fur or black velvet. The next morning he was off again, crossing the narrow, loosely planked bridge (again for defensive purposes) over the Rhine, 'a thousand four score and six paces long. For I paced it.' At this point Coryate had a little grumble about the difficulty of calculating distances, the word 'mile' meaning several different lengths – a Swiss mile being equivalent to five English miles, a middle German mile corresponding to four English miles, and a Netherlandish mile to three English miles. After spending the night in the (Protestant, he noted) town of Litenawe (modern Lichtenau) – 'about sixteen English miles distant from Strasbourg' – he at last arrived in the city of Baden (another 'sixteene miles', 'English' being understood), but not without misadventures.

The first of these was getting lost in 'woods and vast deserts, glancing sometimes by meere chance upon some poore hamlet', where he 'found the waies to be so exceeding intricate, that after I had wandered almost three miles about the wood alone by my selfe, at length to my great discontent I returned to a village where I had beene about two houre before'. For some time he was in 'a kind of irremeable [admitting no return] labyrinth', until 'an honest clowne [peasant]' was able to put him on his way. Later on things picked up for a while, when he called in at a Franciscan monastery, where he was given 'a profound draught of good Rhenish wine, which gave great refection to my barkinge stomach. A courtesie that I neither craved nor expected.' Before that, however, he had a nasty scare.

Tramping alone and uncertainly through the Black Forest, Tom saw coming towards him two more 'clownes commonly called Boores, who because they went in ragged cloathes, strooke no small terrour into mee; and by so much the more I was afraid of them, by how much the more I found them armed with weapons, my selfe being altogether unarmed, having no weapon at all about me but onely a knife'. There was no evidence that these ragged peasants were robbers; sensible men did not walk through these lonely woods unarmed. On the other hand, robberies were common (Moryson was robbed in similar circumstances, in Metz; although he had hidden his money in his quilted doublet, the robbers took that, his sword, cloak, shirt and hat. He was not left destitute, however: he had also hidden sixteen French crowns in a box of stinking ointment for treating scabs, and another six in balls of thread that had needles sticking out). Tom rose to the occasion:

Whereupon fearing least they would eyther have cut my throate, or have robbed me of my gold that was quilted in my jerkin, or have stripped me of my clothes, which they would have found a poore bootie. For my clothes being but a thread-bare fustian case were so meane (my cloake onely excepted) that the Boores could not have made an ordinary [cheap tavern] supper with the money for which they should have sold them; fearing (I say) some ensuing danger, I undertooke such a politike and subtile action as I never did before in all my life. For a little before I mette them, I put off my hat very curteously unto them, holding it a pretty while in my hand, and very humbly (like a Mendicant Frier) begged some money of them (as I have something declared in the front of my book) in a language that they did but poorely understand, even the Latin, expressing my minde unto them by such gestures and signes, that they well knew what I craved of them: and so by this begging insinuation I both preserved my selfe secure and free from the violence of the clownes, and withall obtained that of them which I neither wanted nor expected. For they gave me so much of their tinne money called fennies (as poore as they were) as paid for halfe my supper that night at Baden, even foure pence halfe-penny.

It does not sound as though he splashed out in celebration. Anyway, so much for the bloodthirsty rogues: poor, ragged but generous peasants.

The most notable features of this second Baden (or lower Baden, as it was known) were, of course, the hot springs and large number of baths. The water was so hot that Coryate feared it would scald his hand if he held it in during a count of twenty; reputedly, one could quickly boil an egg in the water, which could also scald off the feathers from a bird or the skin off a pig. The springs in turn fed an extremely large number of (not quite so hot) baths attached to various inns; at Coryate's inn, 'The Golden Lion', there were sixty-five baths crammed into narrow rooms. The water, to which might be added brimstone, salt or alum were, as he read and wrote, reputed helpful in cases of asthma, moist eyes, cramp, 'coldnesse of the stomacke', liver and spleen pains; dropsy; 'griping of the bowels, the stone, the sterility of women: It appeaseth the paine of a womans wombe, keepeth off the white menstruous matter, asswageth the swelling of the thighes, cureth the itch and blisters or whelkes rising in any part of the body; and to be short, it is said to be of greater efficacie for curing of the gowte then any other bathes whatsoever.' For all that, these baths do not sound as much fun as those of 'higher' Baden.

Plodding on from Baden on Monday 5 September, he got to Turlowe (modern Durlach) that evening, passing through rich cornfields, one of which was so large that it was, he guessed, six times as large 'as the best corne field of that famous mannour of Martock in Somersetshire neere to the parish of Odcombe where I was borne'. Near Ettlingen he also saw 'marveilous abundance' of fruit, especially pears, as well as an extraordinary great quantity of cabbages, coleworts, turnips, and radishes, which are sowen in their open fields . . . Moreover I perceived that because God hath so plentifully blessed them with these commodities, that they are not such niggards of them as to watch them in the field, to the end to preserve them from strangers, but rather they give free leave to any passengers to trespasse them, by going boldly into their ground, and taking a convenient quantity of these things for their own use. For their turnips and radishes are so toothsome and pleasing to the palate, that I have often seene many a poore traveller with a farthing loaf in his hand (for bread is so cheape in many places of Germany, especially in some of the higher parts, that a man can buy a convenient loafe for two of their little coynes called fennies that value but little more then an English farthing) goe into their common fields, and take so many turnips and radishes out of a plot, that he hath made an indifferent meale to satisfie nature, & asswage hunger for one poore farthing, though his meale in an Inne or victualling house might perhaps cost him twenty times as much, how thrifty soever he were.

One thrifty 'poore traveller' writes here with some fervour, with later experience in mind. Meanwhile, Tom was pleased to see 'a wonderful great company of frogges in most places of this territory, especially in their Lakes. So that a man can hardly walke by any lake but he shall see great abundance of frogs leape into the water out of the bankes wherein they shrowd themselves.' On the other hand, he 'could see no Snaile in all Germanie but red, like those that I saw a little on this side the Alpes in Savoy, as I have before written'. Tom was able to see more of the lesser wild life on his way than one might nowadays, both because he was quiet and slow, and because much of it has been casually killed off in recent years.

Durlach, when he got there, was 'very prety', but Tom had difficulty in getting into the walled town, the halberdiers guarding the town gates requiring him (in true jobsworth fashion) 'to send certaine testimonies that I had about me to the Prefect of the Princes Court, whom I found afterward to be a very courteous and affable Gentleman, and one that used me very graciously'. Likewise he was not allowed to view the Prince's 'very magnificent and beautifull Palace', despite the Prince being away hunting with friends at his other castle in Mühlberg. ('Neere Heidelberg', Moryson relates, 'we passed a great wood of Oakes, full of great heards of red Deare, which lay still by the way, and would not stirre for our cries, or feare of our Coach Wheeles, but seemed to know their priviledge, all hunting [except by the nobility] being forbidden upon high penalties'.) The next day Coryate saw the castle ('a building of great strength and magnificence') in the distance, as he passed large numbers of haymakers in the meadows, engaged on their second harvest of the year. After a night in another 'solitary house' he tramped into 'the noble City of Heidelberg about noone [on 7 September], being almost wet to the skinne with a vehement shower of raine' – which would not have done the hay harvest much good.

After the usual verses by Scaliger, Coryate thought it worth spending some lines praising the fertility of the surrounding countryside: 'store of wheate of the finest sort, barlie, coleworts, cabbages, turnips, and radishes . . . plenty of fat bullocks, and sheepe . . . vineyards and chest-nut trees, & much frequented with Deere, Goates, and Kids. Neare the City great store of Hearnes [herons] doe nestle themselves in the woods upon the hils.'

After the bucolics, onomastics: futile speculations as to the origins of the name of the city.

> Some derive this word Heidelberg from Heydelber, which doth signifie black-berries, such as doe grow upon brambles, because in former times there were more of them growing about this city then in any other part of the country. Some from Heydelbeern, that is, myrtle trees, which doe yet grow plentifully upon the hilles about the City . . . Againe there are others that draw the name from the Dutch word Heyden, that signifieth a Nation, because this was ever well inhabited with people . . . Moreover there are some that affirme it is called Heidelberg quasi Adelberg, that is, a noble City, in regard of the nobility, the elegancie, and sweetnesse of the situation thereof.

At which point Coryate gave up and left it to 'the learned censure of the judicious reader': clearly, this was a game anyone could play, words melding and mutating irrespective of actuality.

In the city, his first concern was with the Palatine library (the city was the capital of the Palatinate), the keeper of which was a scholar of international reputation, Jan Gruter, with whom Coryate was able to converse in Latin, noting his 'most elegant and true Ciceronian phrase . . . graced with a facill & expedite deliverie'. Gruter personally conducted him to the library, housed in two large rooms built over the roof of the Church of the Holy Ghost, claiming to have at least a hundred more manuscripts than in the Bodleian Library catalogue, which of course chauvinist Coryate could not accept: 'Howbeit Mr Gruterus will pardon me I hope if I preferre one Librarie of my owne nation before the Palatine, even that of our renowned University of Oxford, whereof . . . Mr James is a keeper. For indeede I beleeve it containeth a few more books (though not many) then this of Heidelberg.' Unfortunately, no sooner had the tour begun than two young princes of Anhalt 'came suddenly into the roome upon me, being usherd by their golden-chained Gentlemen. Whereupon I was constrained to withdraw my selfe speedily out of the Librarie, all the attendance being given unto the Princes.' He had no more luck in the adjoining chapel where the monuments of local aristocrats were contained, the door being locked and key-holder Gruter dancing attendance upon the princes. Coryate was very disappointed at not being able to copy out so many epitaphs, but then found in the church a splendid inscribed monument to Philip, Count Palatine of the Rhine, famed for liberating Vienna from the Turks, and triumphantly, if irreverently, 'apprehended it with my pen while the Preacher was in his pulpit: for I doubted least if I had differed it till the end of the sermon, the dores might have bene sodainly shut, & so I should have bin defeated of the opportunity'. *Amor* (of epitaphs) *vincit omnia*.

Heartened by this success, Coryate now set off for the Castle, the Prince's Palace, knowing from experience how difficult it was to gain access to princes' courts in Germany. However, he had already had a word with Gruter, telling him of his acquaintance (at least) with Sir Henry Wotton, who had studied in Heidelberg in 1589–90 and become friendly with one Master Lingelsheim, former tutor to the Prince, and now a senior court official: armed with 'a token' from Gruter, Tom went to Lingelsheim's house, was received courteously and sent off with one of his men to the Prefect of the Court, who in turn granted him admittance. After all that, physical access was difficult enough, the building being set high on a hill with 'a very tedious & difficult ascent by a steepe and stonie way'. Had he been there before 1537 he would have had to climb to the very top, to the original palace, which was destroyed by lightning 'striking casually a heape of Gunpowder that was kept in a certaine roome of the Palace, which no sooner tooke fire, but immediately in the very twinckling of an eye it burnt up the whole building, and scattered the stones (a most lamentable spectacle to behold) farre asunder, some downe to the present Palace where the Prince now dwelleth, and some to the Citie, to the great detriment of both places' – much the sort of effect Guy Fawkes was supposed to have had in mind. The new Castle was very splendid, the part built by Prince Frederick – completed only the year before – coming in for particular praise: 'rare sumptuousnesse . . . faire statues . . . I must needes confesse that I attribute more unto it . . . then to the Front of any Palace whatsoever I saw in France, Italie or Germanie.'

The next thing that Tom was shown, however, caused him even greater enthusiasm:

> the most remarkable and famous thing of that kinde that I saw in my whole journey, yea so memorable a matter, that I thinke there was never the like fabrick . . . in all the world, and I doubt whether posterity will ever frame so monstrously strange a thing: it was nothing but a vessel full of wine [the Great Tun of Heidelberg] . . . such a stupendious masse (to give it the same epitheton that I have done before to the beauty of St Marks streete in Venice) that I am perswaded it will affect the gravest and constantest man in the world with wonder . . . so I hope it will not be unpleasant unto thee

to reade a ful description of all the particular circumstances thereof: and for thy better satisfaction I have inserted a true figure thereof in this place (though but in a small forme) according to a certaine patterne that I brought with me from the City of Franckford, where I saw the first type thereof sold. Also I have an imaginary kinde of representation of my selfe upon the toppe of the same, in that manner as I stood there with a cup of Rhenish wine in my hand.

He then got into something of a tangle working out quantities, translating German fuders, omes and firtles into English hogsheads and pottles, before measuring the length (27ft) and height in the centre (18ft), and concluding with a warning to the gentle reader: 'I advise thee (I say) if thou dost happen to ascend to the toppe thereof to taste of the wine, that in any case thou dost drinke moderately, and not so much as the sociable Germans will persuade thee unto. For if thou shouldest chance to over-swill thy selfe with wine, peradventure such a giddinesse wil benumme thy braine, that thou wilt scarce finde the direct way downe from the steepe ladder without a very dangerous precipitation.' *Experientia docet*. Normally a very moderate drinker, Tom was, he admits, 'exhilarated . . . with two sound draughts of Rhenish wine'. He had intended to visit the university as well, but somehow did not get round to it.

The next morning (9 a.m., a late start for him), on Thursday 8 September, he set off westwards, making his way with great difficulty through 'the manifold turnings and windings of the way' through the woods (a supposedly 12-mile journey taking eight hours), before being ferried over the Rhine to reach Speyer. Set at the conflux of the Rhine and Speyer, the ancient city had battlemented walls with extremely tall towers, broad streets and 'sumptuous buildings' with fronts 'very curiously painted' and gable ends rising in battlemented form, like those at Heidelberg. The Cathedral, remarkable for its four lofty turrets, 'a pretty kinde of forme not unlike to a cradle', contained the monuments of eight German emperors and two empresses, whom he carefully listed; unable to spend enough time transcribing, one general epitaph had to serve for them all.

He was not to be defeated altogether, however: dismissing
the 'hypercriticall carpers' who might accuse him of triviality,
he included a description of a 'sumptuous pulpit . . .
wonderfull gorgeously gilt . . . and decked with many
[religious] sentences', which he copied out over nearly four
pages. Nearly five pages were devoted to writing out Bernard
of Clairvaux's epistle urging the Second Crusade of 1146, and
more to transcribing his praises of the image of the Virgin
Mary that were inlaid on the floor of the Cathedral. 'It is
reported that the image did utter a voyce at that time to Saint
Bernard . . . But the answere that Saint Bernard made to the
image I meane to conceale till some other edition of my booke
after my future travels (if God shall mercifully prolong my life
to accomplish some other outlandish voyage) and that for
certaine reasons of no meane importance which I will not
discover to the world.'

At the end, Coryate recorded how 'Attila King of the Hunnes
after he marched out of Hungary and Austria with his huge
Armie to conquer Germany, greatly wasted this city of Spira,
ransacking it after a most cruell and mercilesse manner with
fire and sword, as he did other of the German cities that I have
already described, and others also that I shall hereafter
describe'. He was not to know of the devastation that such
cities were soon to suffer during the Thirty Years War, and
later in the century, and 300 years later.

After two nights in Speyer, he left on Saturday 10
September, passing through the 'new town' of Frankenthal,
built entirely during the previous half-century by Dutch
refugees expelled by the Spanish, and reached 'the beautiful
city' of Worms that evening. On the way, he got into trouble:

Which was this. I stept aside into a vineyard in the open field that
was but a little distant from the high waie, to the end to taste of their
grapes wherewith I might something asswage my thirst: hoping I
might as freely have done it there, as I did often times before in
many places of Lombardie without any controulment. There I pulled
two little clusters of them, and so returned into my way againe

travelling securely [confidently. As Ben Jonson wrote, 'Man may
securely sin: but safely, never'] and jovially towardes Wormes,
whose lofty Towers I saw neere at hand. But there came a German
Boore upon me (for so are the Clownes of the country commonly
called) with a halbert in his hand, & in a great fury pulled off very
violently my hat from my head (as I have expressed in the
frontispiece of my booke) looked very fiercely upon me with eyes
sparkling fire in a manner, and with his Alamanne wordes which I
understood not, swaggered most insolently with me, holding up his
halbert in that threatening manner at me, that I continually expected
a blow, and was in deadly feare lest he would have made me a prey
for the wormes before I should ever put my foote in the gallant City
of Worms. For it was in vaine for me to make any violent resistance,
because I had no more weapon then a weake staffe, that I brought
with me out of Italy. Although I understood not his speeches, yet I
gathered by his angry gestures that the onely cause of his quarrel
was for that he saw me come forth of a vineyard (which belike was
his maisters) with a bunch of grapes in my hand. All this while that
he threatned me with these menacing termes I stood before him
almost as mute as a Seriphian frogge, or an Acanthian grashopper
[Erasmus discusses these taciturn creatures in his *Adagia*], scarce
opening my mouth once unto him, because I thought that as I did
not understand him, so likewise on the other side he did not
understand me. At length with my tongue I began to re-encounter
him, tooke heart on grace, and so discharged a whole volley of
Greeke and Latin shot upon him, supposing that it would bee an
occasion to pacifie him somewhat if he did but thereby conceive
that I had a little learning.

A little learning proved to be a dangerous thing, as 'the
implacable Clowne' became all the more enraged. Fortunately,
some men from the city passed by, one of whom spoke Latin
('There is not a man among the German sorte who cannot
speake Lattin', claimed Moryson, with pardonable
exaggeration) and offered to act as a mediator.

But first he told me that I had committed a penal trespasse in
presuming to gather grapes in a vineyard without leave, affirming
that the Germanes are so exceeding sparing of their grapes that

they are wont to fine any of their owne countreymen that they catch in their vineyards without leave, either with purse or body; much more a stranger. Notwithstanding he promised to do his endeavour to get my hat againe, because this would be a warning for me, and for that he conceived that I was a good fellow. And so at last with much adoe this controversie was compounded betwixt the cullian and my selfe, my hat being restored unto me for a small price of redemption, which was twelve of their little coynes called fennies, which countervaile twenty pence of our English money. But I would counsel thee gentle reader whatsoever thou art that meanest to travell into Germany, to beware by my example of going into any of their vineyards without leave.

With considerable relief and his hat, but without the grapes, he walked on, arriving in the city at about 6 p.m. The religion here was mixed, as at Speyer, 'partly Protestant of the Lutheran religion, and partly Papisticall. Unto the Papistes belongeth the Cathedrall Church, as that of Spira, because the Bishop of the City is a Papist. But the Protestant faction is both the greater in number, and the stronger in power.' (The first English translation of the New Testament, by the master of English prose William Tyndale, was printed here in 1525.) The cathedral received only perfunctory attention, his main interest being in the Bishop's Palace (where Luther defended himself before Charles V and the Electors, at the famous Diet of Worms in 1521), particularly the façade ('the most sumptuous front of any Bishops Palace that ever I saw'); this was decorated with twelve prophecies, taken to predict the coming of Christ, attributed to the ancient Greek Sibyls, 'a thing so notably memorable that I saw not the like before, and doe doubt whether I shall ever see the like againe . . . so I hope it will be very pleasant to the learned reader to reade so rare a matter'. The first was attributed to the Delphic oracle, reputedly living 1525 BC: 'Nascetur Propheta absque coitu ex Virgine, eum cognosces proprium Dominum tuum, ipse verus erit Dei filius' (A prophet shall be born of a virgin, without coitus, him thou knowest to be thine own lord, the same will be the true son of God). Further inscriptions and statues on the

Senate House were recorded, and several pages of history copied from Münster's *Cosmographie*, and after noon on the Sunday Coryate set out for Mainz. On the way he acquired

> such a notable companion as I never had before in all my life. For he was both learned and unlearned. Learned because being but a wood-cleaver (for he told me that he was the Jesuits wood-cleaver of Mentz) he was able to speake Latin. A matter as rare in one of that sordid facultie as to see a white Crowe or a blacke Swanne. Again he was unlearned, because the Latin which he did speake was such incongruall [incongruous, incorrect; not recorded in the *OED*] and disjoynted stuffe, such antiprisicianisticall [ungrammatical; not recorded in the *OED*] eloquence, that I thinke were grave Cato alive (who . . . never or very seldome laughed) he should have more cause to laugh if he should heare this fellow deliver his minde in Latin, then when he saw an Asse eate thistles.

It did not occur to Coryate that this man had not had the benefit of an expensive education, with Latin beaten into him at the equivalent of Winchester College.

The Cathedral at Mainz ('very sumptuous') contained several monuments with elaborate carvings and irresistible epitaphs for transcribing. Coryate also visited the Jesuit College ('a convenient faire house, but much inferiour to the majestie of divers Colledges in our famous Universities of Oxford and Cambridge, to whome I attribute so much for the statelinesse of their building, that I preferre some of them by many degrees before any Colledges that I saw in my travells'), where he was treated kindly by the Principal, Nicolas Serarius, who showed him the Library and a book he had recently written about the antiquities of Mainz ('I would to God hee would cease to write so virulently against our Protestants, especially poore Martin Luther, whom he hath most bitterly exagitated [inveighed against]'). Probably on advice from Serarius, Coryate later visited a stone column known as the Acorn Stone, set on a hill to the south of the city, supposed to have been erected by the Emperor Drusus, 'a thing very worthy the observation both for the worthinesse of the founder, the nobility of the worke, and the mention of it in ancient authors'. The city itself provoked a great deal of history writing, listing emperors, archbishops (the first, Boniface, an Englishman, 'his name first was Winifride'), and famous people who had died there. 'One thing that is very memorable I will not omit in the discourse of this famous city of Mentz, that it gave the first vitall light to that learned and Rhetoricall Shee-Pope Joane, where after shee had sate two yeares in the Popedome, immediately after Leo the fourth [ninth century], she died in child-birth.' Also worth recording – indeed, celebrating – was 'that most incomparably excellent art of printing . . . was first invented in this city . . . by a Gentleman or rather Knight of this city one Joannes Cuttenbergius [Gutenberg, *c.* 1410–68] in the yeare of our Lord one thousand foure hundred and forty [and who produced the first printed Bible in 1455]', which led to an exordium on the wonderful virtues of printing, without which 'the true studies of all disciplines both divine & humane would have suffered a kind of shipwrack, and have bene halfe extinct before this age wherein we breathe'. With this in mind, it was particularly appropriate that the next place he visited – diverting eastward from his steady northward, homeward progress – was Frankfurt, the traditional centre of the book trade in Europe (to this day).

The first part of the journey there involved a boat trip along the River Main, which unfortunately led him to include an especially painful example of bookish wit, or pedantic ingenuity, by the writer Melancthon (Philip Schwarzerd, who, with Luther, produced the first German translation of the New Testament), playing 'in a very conceited and wittie veine upon the five letters of the name of the river Moenus, which according to a pretty kind of hieroglyphicall manner he hath so finely contrived, that the five letters (but as they are the elements of the Greeke alphabet, not as Latine characters) doe expresse the full number of the daies of the yeare'. Coryate thought Melancthon's verses would be 'very acceptable to the learned reader. The learned reader I say, but not to the unlearned. For indeed he must have both learning and a good

capacity that shall rightly conceive the meaning of them.'
Coryate was thrilled: 'For mine own part I will boldly say they
do expresse the most ingenious conceit that ever I read in my
life. In so much that the first time I saw them, I did even hugge
them with a great applause.' In the four lines of Greek verse,
the wit depends on the fact that, like the Romans, the Greeks
used letters for numbers. Thus, M indicated 40, E equalled 5,
N was 50, O was 70, and Σ stood for 200, the total being 365:
rapture among the learned.

To move on: his 'liquid journey' up river to the great fair was
in a boat carrying 'a strange miscellany of people of sundry
nations at that time, whose languages were (I think) a quarter
as much confounded as theirs were in ancient times at that
famous confusion of Babel. For in this barke there were some
few of every principall nation of Christendome travelling
towards Frankford Mart that began the day before.' They
admired a rich pastoral landscape and 'sumptuous' palaces,
but, just outside the city, also 'observed a most rufull spectacle
that strooke a certaine horrour into me, and so I thinke did
into the hearts of most other relenting travellers that passed
that way: the bodies of sixteene men hanging upon a great
stonie gallowes hard by the high way side'; for once, he did
not describe the gallows as 'faire'.

Divided in two by the river, Frankfurt displayed impressive
stone walls, 'beautified with a great company of towers, strong
bulwarks, and faire gatehouses' ('upon the east side is the gate
Heilegthore, where is the Jewes streete, who are permitted to
dwell in this famous Mart-towne, and sucke the blood of
Christians by extortion', wrote Moryson, with unexpected and
uncharacteristic venom). 'There are three things which make
this citie famous over all Europe. The one the election of the
King of the Romanes [the heir presumptive to the Holy Roman
Emperor], the other the two noble fayres kept heere twise a
yeare', for two weeks in March and September. Frankfurt fair
had been famous since the Middle Ages, and was responsible
for a considerable proportion of the city's wealth. Henri
Estienne, who wrote an *Encomium of the Frankfort Fair* in

1574, wrote of the large number of visitors 'as varied in garb and feature as in the tongues they speake'; a census of 'strangers' (from out of town or from other countries) staying at just one inn, the Nurnberger Hof, during fair times between 1587 and 1620, showed an average of 125 guests a year. Estienne claimed that the fair possessed as much merchandise as there were stars in the sky, and was 'an epitome of all the emporiums in the world'; it sold nearly everything – horses and hams; swords and guns; gold, silver, bronze and iron work; paintings, prints and pottery; Bohemian and Venetian glass, Saxony silver, Strasbourg clocks; Rhenish and Alsace wines; Italian wines, olive oil and Eastern spices; sausages and tarts (human and otherwise); and books. 'The riches I observed at this Mart', wrote Coryate, 'were most infinite, especially in one place called Under den Roemer, where the Goldsmiths kept their shoppes, which made the most glorious shew that ever I saw in my life, especially some of the citie of Norimberg. . . . The wealth that I sawe here was incredible, so great that it was impossible for a man to conceive it in his minde that hath not first seene it with his bodilie eies.' One of the best displays was by 'one Thomas Sackfield, a Dorsetshire man, once a servant of my father', who had gone abroad and done well, so that 'his glittering shewe of ware in Franckford did farre excell all the Dutchmen, French, Italians or whomsoever else'. What turned out to be a less satisfying coincidence was meeting his 'thrise-honourable countryman' (and, Tom claimed, his cousin), the Earl of Essex (whom he had just missed in Lyons), 'after he had travelled in divers places of France, Switzerland, and some parts of high Germany'; the bareness and brevity of the sentence suggest the warmth and length of the meeting.

After this I went to the Bookesellers Streete where I saw such an infinite abundance of bookes that I greatly admired [wondered at] it. For this streete farre excelleth Paules Churchyard in London, Saint James streete in Paris, the Merceria of Venice, and all whatsoever else that I sawe in my travels. In so much that it seemeth to be a very epitome of all the principall Libraries of

Europe. Neither is that streete famous for selling bookes only, and that of all manner of artes and disciplines whatsoever, but also for printing of them. For this city hath so flourished within these fewe yeares in the art of printing, that it is not inferiour in that respect to any city in Christendome.

The book fair was famous throughout Europe: first established in 1485, its first sale catalogue appeared in 1564. It was also the centre of the German book-publishing trade. Scholars and intellectuals came from all over Europe – 'For here all may enjoy the living voice of many honoured persons, who gather here from many different academies,' wrote Estienne. 'Here very often right in the shops of the booksellers you can hear them discussing philosophy no less seriously than once the Socrateses and the Platos.' Casaubon, whom Coryate visited in Paris, came in 1590; Sir Henry Wotton visited five times between 1589 and 1612. (Unfortunately, severe censorship by the Jesuit-controlled Imperial Book Commission, the wars in the Netherlands and later the Thirty Years War caused a decline in trade, and the book fair ceased trading in 1749; however, in 1949 it was revived, to regain much of its former glory.)

The Church of St Bartholomew was also doing a good trade, selling 'excellent pictures, inventions of curiosity, whereof most were religious, and such as tended to mortification'; presumably it was not here that Coryate bought his print of the Great Tun of Heidelberg. (Elsewhere in the city, reported Moryson, was

a house of old belonging to the Teutonike order of Knights, which by old priviledge is to this day a Sanctuary for banckrupts and manslaiers, so they be not wilful and malicious murtherers, but they enjoy this priviledge onely for fourteene daies, so as when the time is neere out, or upon any opportunity during the time, they use to steale out, and returning after an houre, begin anew to reckon againe the fourteene daies. A little before my comming thither, a certain bankrupt of Colen [Cologne] entered the same for a debt of twenty thousand Guldens.)

Coryate's account of his time in Frankfurt concludes with what was to prove a curious coincidence: 'I received a special kindnesse in this City of an English Gentleman . . . even Mr Thomas Row the eldest sonne of Sir Henry Row, that was Lord Mayor of London about two yeares since. Truly this Gentleman did me such a singular courtesie [what? what?], that he hath perpetually obliged me unto him all the dayes of my life.' Years later in India, Coryate was treated kindly by the new ambassador, 'a very generous and worthy English knight, a deare friend of mine', Sir Thomas Roe, cousin of this Thomas Row.

Having spent two whole days in Frankfurt, Coryate returned by land to Mainz on the 16th; he had intended to have a look next day at a nearby palace, but 'certayne Gentlemen of Colen craved my company in a boat downe the Rhene towards Colen' (probably to make up the numbers for a lower individual rate), so off they all went, arriving in the town of Boppard in the evening of the next day. Going down the Rhine, Coryate noticed that there were many more towns and castles on the left bank than on the right, and was told that this was a consequence of the Romans having fortified the left bank whilst not risking any building on the far side, for fear of attack by the Germans. In any case, there were eleven riverside towns between Mainz and Cologne, each imposing a customs tariff on passing traffic:

> All passengers whatsoever they are, noble or ignoble, must arrive in each of these places, and stay a while till the boatman hath paid custome for his passage. To the passenger it is no charge at all, but onely to the maister of the boate. If any should dare in a resolute and wilfull humour to passe by any of these places, and not pay the stinted amount of money, the Publicans [tax-gatherers] that sit at the receipt of custome, will presently discharge (as I heard) a peece of Ordnance at them, and make them an example to all after-commers.

The first town they had to stop at was Bingen, famous for three things, he reported. The first was for the death of the Emperor Drusus, either slain by the Germans while sitting on his horse, or killed by falling off his horse; the horse had something to do with

it, anyway. The second was for being the residence of the famous
mystic St Hildegard (a friend of Bernard of Clairvaux):

> Truly there are very admirable matters written of this woman by
> the historians. For it is reported that she was often rapt in the
> middest of her sleepe with certaine enthusiasmes, that is, divine
> inspirations, whereby she learned the Latin tongue after a
> miraculous manner without any teacher. A thing that will seeme
> unto many readers a mere paradoxe, but certainly for my owne
> part I beleeve it to be true. For I receive it from the authority of a
> very grave writer, Sebastian Munster.

The third feature of Bingen was a tower set on an island, about
which Münster had a good story, which Coryate wrote out as a
notable example of divine justice.

> It hapned in the yeare 914 that there was an exceeding famine in
> Germany, at what time Otho surnamed the Great was Emperor, and
> one Hatto once Abbot of Fulda was Archbishop of Mentz . . . This
> Hatto in the time of this great famine before mentioned, when he
> saw the poore people of the country exceedingly oppressed with
> famine, assembled a great company of them together into a barne,
> and like a most accursed & mercilesse caitiffe burnt up those poore
> innocent soules, that were so farre from doubting any such matter,
> that they rather hoped to have received some comfort and reliefe at
> his hands. The reason that moved the Prelate to commit that
> execrable impiety, was because he thought that the famine would
> the sooner cease, if those unprofitable beggars that consumed more
> bread then they were worthy to eate, were dispatched out of the
> world. For he said that these poore folkes were like to mice, that
> were good for nothing but to devoure corne. But Almighty God the
> just revenger of the poore folks quarrel did not long suffer this
> hainous tyranny, this most detestable fact unpunished. For he
> mustred up an army of mice against the Archbishop, and sent them
> to persecute him as his furious Alastors [relentless avenging
> deities], so that they afflicted him both day and night, and would
> not suffer him to take his rest in any place. Whereupon the Prelate
> thinking that he should be secure from the injury of mice if he were
> in a certaine tower that standeth in the Rhene neere to the towne,

betooke himself unto the said tower as to a safe refuge and sanctuary from his enemies, and locked himselfe in. But the innumerable troupes of mice continually chaced him very eagerly, and swumme unto him upon the top of the water to execute the just judgement of God, and so at last he was most miserably devoured by those silly creatures; who pursued him with such bitter hostility, that it is recorded they scraped & gnawed off his very name from the walles and tapestry wherein it was written, after they had so cruelly devoured his bodie. Wherefore the tower in which he was eaten up by the mice is shewed to this day for a perpetuall monument to al succeeding ages of the barbarous and inhumane tyranny of that impious prelate, being situate in a little greene Iland in the middest of the Rhene neere to this town of Bing, and is commonly called in the Germane tongue the Mowse turn [tower].

Down river from Bingen, as far as Bonn, Coryate noticed steep, rocky mountains rising on both sides of the river, with towers, castles and citadels, belonging to the neighbouring combative princes. Of more immediate concern, however, was

a very strange custome observed amongst the Germanes as they passe in their boates between Mentz and Colen, and so likewise betwixt Colen and the lower parts of the Netherlands. Every man whatsoever be he poore or rich, shall labour hard when it commeth to his turne, except he doth either by friendship or some small summe of money redeeme his labour [be he rich . . .]. For their custome is that the passengers must exercise themselves with oares and rowing alternis vicibus, a couple together. So that the master of the boate (who me thinkes in honestie ought either to doe it himselfe, or to procure some others to do it for him) never roweth but when his turn commeth. This exercise both for recreation and health sake I confesse is very convenient for man. But to be tied unto it by way of a strict necessity when one payeth well for his passage, was a thing that did not a little distaste my humour.

Grumble, grumble – not unreasonably; but, having to watch his pfennigs, Coryate had no real choice. Down they went, past Bacchara, 'famous in Germanie for her generose wines', and Protestant, like Cuve; then Wesel, 'Popish':

Much is this towne spoken off for the martyrdome of a yong child
in the same called Wernerus, of the age of seven yeares, in the
yeare 1287. For it is written that the same Wernerus was in the
same yeare upon the thirteenth day of May most cruelly martyred
by the barbarous Jewes, in this manner. They tied him to a certaine
wooden pillar in a low vault under the ground, and whipped him
so bitterly, that the poore innocent child died with it. After they
had thus handled him they conveighed away his corps, and buried
it under a certaine hedge where brambles and thornes grew, But
being afterward casually [by chance] found out by some of the
townesfolke of Wesel, it was therehence translated to a place
called Bavaricum, where they built a church to almighty God in
memory of that punie Martyr, & it is called by the name of
Wernerus Church to this day. As for the wooden pillar whereunto
they tyed him when they scourged him to death, it was afterward
removed to an hospitall Church of Wesel neare to the Rhene,
where they erected it at the toppe of the high Altar, and is there
shewed to this day as a monument of that Jewish cruelty —

or of the kind of random child murder not unknown
nowadays. In most versions of this widespread story, the body
is associated with various miracles, often leading to
sanctification; but Wesel seems to have missed out.

After Wesel they arrived at another custom town, St Gewere
[St Goar], where there was a violent current, dangerous to
boats, 'by meanes of the manifold anfracts [twistings] and
intricate windings thereof'. There turned out to be more to be
done at St Goar then to pay customs dues, for Coryate at least;
as a newcomer to the town, he had to go through a traditional
initiation ritual.

A little within the towne gate there hangeth an yron collar fastened
in the wall with one linke, which is made fit to be put upon a
mans necke without any manner of hurt to the party that weareth
it, and they use first to conveigh it over the head, and so to the
necke. This collar doth every stranger and freshman the first time
that he passeth that way (according to an auncient custome
observed amongst them) put upon his necke (at the least as the
Gentlemen told me that went in my boate) which hee must weare

so long standing till he hath redeemed himselfe with a competent measure of wine. And at the drinking of it there is as much jovialty and merriment as heart can conceive for the incorporating of a fresh novice into the fraternitie of boone companions. And from thenceforth he is free from all such manner of exactions as long as he liveth. That this is true I know by mine own experience. For I was contented for novelty sake to be their prisoner a little while by wearing of the foresaid collar. This custome doth carry some kind of affinity with certaine sociable ceremonies that wee have in a place of England which are performed by that most reverend Lord Ball of Bagshot in Hamptshire, who doth with many and indeed more solemne rites invest his Brothers of his unhallowed Chappell of Basingstone (as all our men of the westerne parts of England do know by dear expense to the smart of their purses [including Tom?]) then these mery Burgomaisters of Saint Gerewe use to do.

In any event, 'after much Mercuriall and Joviall conversation' they got back on board again, and reached Boppard at eight that night. Here Coryate was able only to jot down some history (Richard I besieged it, Henry VII mortgaged it), as they shot off downstream at six the next morning. Lahnstein, Coblenz, Engers, Andernach and Linz flashed by ('I observed a fayre wooden bridge . . . I observed that this city is invironed with strong walles . . . they shewed me a very faire Monastery . . . I saw a very strong and impregnable Castell . . .'), and then, at last, after some 30 miles, Oberwinter, where they spent the night. 'In this place we solaced ourselves after our tedious labour of rowing as merily as we could', by drinking and telling stories. Nevertheless, at three in the morning they were off again, and reached Cologne at about 10 o'clock.

A sombre, even savage note dominates the latter part of Coryate's 'Observations of some parts of high Germanie', commenting on the consequences of years of war and disorder:

I observed in a great many places, on both sides of the Rhene, more gallowes and wheeles betwixt Mentz and Colen, then ever I saw in so short a space in all my life, especially within a few miles of Colen, by reason that the rusticall Corydons of the country, which are commonly called the Boores and the Free-booters (a name that is given unto the lewd murdering villaines of the country that live by robbery and spoyling of travellers, being called Free booters because they have their booties and prey from passengers free, paying nothing for them except they are taken) do commit many notorious robberies neere the Rhene, who are such cruell and bloody horseleaches (the very Hyenae and Lycanthropi [crazed wolf-men] of Germany) that they seldom robbe any man but forthwith they cut his throat. And some of them doe afterward escape, by reason of the woodes neere at hand in which they shelter themselves free from danger. Yet others are sometimes taken, and most cruelly excarnificated and tortured upon these wheeles . . . For I sawe the bones of many of them lie uppon the wheele, a dolefull spectacle for any relenting Christian to beholde. And uppon those gallowes in divers places I saw murderers hang, partly in chaines, and partly without chaines. A punishment too good for these Cyclopicall Anthrophagi, these Caniball man-eaters.

Fortunately for Coryate's spirits, a few miles before Cologne they arrived at the 'fayre towne' of Bonn.

Here the Archbishop hath a Palace situated hard by the Rhene, a most magnificent and princely building, but much inferiour to divers Palaces both of our King James, and of many Noblemen of England. Which I therefore adde because one of my company that advised me to behold it well, told mee it was a Palace of so great magnificence, that he thought all my country of England could not yeeld the like. But surely his opinion was very false and erroneous. For besides many other English Palaces that do surpasse that of the Archbishop of Colen, there is one in mine owne country of Somersetshire, even the magnificent house of my most worthy and right Worshipful neighbour and Maecoenas Sir Edward Philippes now master of the Rolles (whome I name honoris causa) in the towne of Montacute, so stately adorned with the statues of the nine Worthies, that may bee at the least equally ranked with this of Bonna, if not something preferred before it.

With this patriotic panegyric, the party at last arrived on 19 September at the great city of Cologne, finding it *en fête* for the Feast of St Michael the Archangel.

To the Hollow Land

Like many others, Coryate seems to have regarded Cologne as the transition point to the Netherlands, with which the city had long been involved, both commercially and politically. Inevitably it got caught up in the Dutch War of Independence against Spanish rule; it also had its own War of Cologne, when the Catholic Archbishop Elector of Cologne, Gebhard Truchsess, wanted to marry the Countess Agnes von Mansfeld. In order to do this, he became a Protestant; unfortunately, he attempted to take the rest of the city with him; he was promptly deposed, and a Catholic archbishop appointed in his place. In the ensuing war, the Spanish naturally supported the Catholics, whilst Truchsess was backed by the Dutch and English; while that war was now (theoretically) concluded, the whole surrounding area was still subject to the ravages of the freebooters of whom Coryate had so bitterly complained. He remarked how the nearby city on the Rhine, Remagen (much later to be taken by the American Army and then Hollywood), 'some ten years since was miserably ransacked by . . . so great a troupe as consisted of almost three thousand persons. The towne itself they defaced not, but only took away their goods, to the utter impoverishment of the inhabitants.'

Not surprisingly, Cologne had 'stone walls . . . raised to a stately heigth, and distinguished with a great company of turrets which doe especially garnish the citie', presenting 'afar off a passing beautifull shew unto them that approch towards the City upon the river'. Coryate's response to these fortifications appears merely aesthetic: the last city sieges in England were before his time – and the brutal batterings of the Civil War were well in the future, and hardly imaginable. The city's walls encompassed such a large area that one could hardly walk round it in less than four hours, 'which if it be true, it containeth in circuit at least eight of our English miles . . . The buildings of the City both publique and private are very faire, and many of their private houses I observed to be of a notable heigth, even foure stories high, whereof some are built altogether with stone, and some with timber'. He was very impressed by the Hay Market,

> the fairest that I saw in my whole voyage, saving that of St Marks street in Venice. For it is two hundred and fourescore paces long, and fourescore and foure broade. For indeede I meated [measured] them both. . . . Surely the beauty of this market place is such by reason of so many magnificent houses including it, that I thinke if a clowne [country-dweller] that never saw any faire shewes in his life should suddenly arrive there, he would be halfe amazed with the majestie of the place.

In the Second World War, an estimated 85 per cent of the city was destroyed.

The Senate House or *Rathaus* earned unusually high praise: 'Certainly the outward workmanship of it is a thing of such gorgeous magnificence and admirable state that I preferre it both for the front, and for most of the outward worke, before any Senate house that ever I saw either in my owne country, or abroad: only the Praetorium of Padua excepted.' Coryate had always liked statues and carved images, and was intrigued by a relief carving of a man fighting a lion:

> A passing memorable historie . . . as worthy the reading as any thing I have written in my whole booke. It hapned about the yeare of our Lord 1260 that there was great dissention betwixt the Archbishop of Colen and the City: at what time it chanced also that two of the Canons of the Cathedrall Church that favored the Bishops faction, had a certaine Lyons whelpe, which they fed and

brought up for the honour of the Bishop. [It is perhaps worth remarking that it had long been a status symbol to own a menagerie of exotic animals. Tom had seen the ostriches at Fontainebleau, and possibly the lions in the Tower of London, where James I took a particular interest in breeding the lion cubs, even designing a nipple for a feeding bottle. London's lions seem to have been milder – or better instructed in the Bible – than those of Cologne: when, in 1604, a live lamb was lowered into their cage, it was reported, 'they very gently looked upon him and smelled him without any further hurt. Then the lamb was softly drawn up again'.]

Now whereas the said Canons bare a great spite and malice to the Consul of the city whose name was Hermannus Gryn, they invited him one day very kindly to dinner under colour of friendship, and when he came to their home, shewed him this young Lyon, whome they kept hungry without meate some two or three daies before, and so forced him unawares and fearing no such matter, to approach neerer to the Lyons denne then it was fitte for him. Presently after this the Canons conveighed themselves out of the roome, and having shut the dore waited without, still expecting when the Lyon would devoure the man. But the Consul being a man of a notable courage and stout spirit, when he saw that he was by the treachery of these lewd Prelates brought to these extremes, either to be devoured by that mercilesse and fierce beast, or to fight manfully for his life, did put on a valiant resolution, verifying that speech of Virgil,

Audentes fortuna juvat
[Fortune favours the brave]

Clapped his cloake about his left hand which he boldly thrust into the Lions mouth as he came gaping towards him, & with his right hand slue him, & so finally by this meanes escaped free from danger. Afterward he sent Officers for the two Canons with commandement to apprehend them, and to see them incontinently hanged. Which was accordingly performed.

Coryate concluded that he had never read or heard of anything like this, before listing 'Sampson, Daniel the Prophet, King David, Bonaiah one of Davids three Worthies, Captaine

Lysmachus in the time of Alexander the Great, and one of our
English Kinges Richard the first surnamed Cor de Lyon', which
rather spoiled the effect.

The story of hostility between Archbishop and City reflected
the lengthy history of conflict between church and city in
Cologne; the effects were manifest in the Cathedral, begun in
the thirteenth century and still incomplete for lack of funding,
its towers mere stumps in comparison with their intended
height (it was not completed until 1880). Nevertheless, it
contained much to see after Tom's own heart. The chief object
was the monument dedicated to the Three Kings, or Magi,
which he examined with particular care. 'Therefore both the
description of the sepulcher where the bones lie [they arrived
in Cologne in 1164], and the history I present unto thee for a
noveltie . . . Blame me not if I am something tedious. For this
being the most renowned monument of Christendome may not
be briefly past over with a few words.' He was anxious lest
strict Protestants should disapprove, and conceded that there
might be 'some vaine and frivolous things contained', but felt
that it should be reported.

The chapel containing the great reliquary was at the east end
of the cathedral, accessible for only two hours a day, and
enclosed in a painted iron cage with 'a great multitude of
golden starres, in token that a starre conducted them to Christ'.
Raised 6ft above the floor, the shrine was 'pure bright shining
brasse' with 'many exquisite devices' and 'wonderfull
abundance of precious Stones', with a silver gilt image of the
Virgin and Child, ten golden goblets, 'a marvellous rich crosse
of massie gold adorned with a great multitude of precious
stones', and an image of the three kings presenting their gifts.
'One of the Kings is presented like a blacke Moore with a
golden crowne upon his head. The other two uncovered.'
There were also lengthy Latin inscriptions outlining the
legend of the Magi, which Coryate of course transcribed in full
over several pages, before providing his own translation,
professing himself as not 'a scholler' but only 'a friend and
lover of the Muses'. It being better to be brief than tedious (as

the Duke of Clarence's murderer remarked before tipping him
into the malmsey barrel), a shortened version is provided here,
as 'a novelty to every reader that hath not seene the same':

1. The Magi, which first of all the Gentiles adored the infancy of
    our saviour Christ in Bethleem the thirteenth day after his
    nativity, were three in number. And (if we beleeve Epiphanius)
    they derived their pedigree from Abraham, descending from
    his sonnes which he begat upon his handmaid Cethira . . .

2. The first . . . is said to be Melchior [they acquired names in the
    sixth century], an olde man with a long beard and haire. He
    offered Golde to the King our Lord.

    The second, whose name was Gaspar, a beardlesse young
    man and ruddie, honoured God with Frankensence, as being an
    oblation beseeming God.

    The third, called Balthasar, being tawny and fully bearded,
    by Myrrhe signified that the Sonne of man should die. But in
    that one of them is wont to be painted black, and as an
    Æthiopian, (as it appeareth by many & those very ancient
    pictures amongst us) hereupon it seemeth to be grounded, both
    that Beda affirmeth that the third was tawnie, as also that in the
    72 Psalme it is sung in the Church upon the Kinges day, The
    Æthiopians shall fall downe before him.

3. That they were not of any obscure place or degree, but princes,
    yea kings, which doth greatly illustrate the glory of Christ, it is
    a part of piety to beleeve. For it is agreeable both to the figure
    of the old law which went before in Solomon, & to the
    Prophecies of the Prophets, especially of David and Esay
    [Isaiah]; whereof the one saith, The Kings of Tarsis and of the
    Iles shall bring gifts. The other saith: And nations shall walke
    in thy light, and Kinges in the brightnesse of thy rising up . . .
    Neither doth this make at all to the matter, that the Evangelist
    hath not called them Kings, but Magi. For that was done to
    great purpose, in regard that Christes glory and our religion
    seemed to bee established rather by the testimony of Magi or
    Wisemen, then by the power of Kings.

4. As concerning their profession, albeit there are some that by
    the name of Magi doe understand wicked persons, and those
    that practise magicke artes: yet the opinion of them ought to

prevaile more with us that thinke they were wise Astrologers, who by the Mathematicke art (as Cyprian speaketh) knew the force and course of the Planets, and by certaine rules of experience observed the nature of the Elements, and the offices of the Starres . . .

5. That they came out of Arabia Felix (as Justin Martyr, Tertullian, Cyprian, and Epiphanius have written) it seemeth very probable. Both because Arabia, in respect of Judea, is situate towards the East (according to the testimony of Tacitus) and also because it yeeldeth plenty of gold, frankensence, and myrrhe. Finally for that this opinion doth agree with the Prophecie of Esay: All they of Saba [Sheba] (which is Arabia, as Hieron [Jerome] doth witnesse . . .) shall come, and bring gold and frankencence . . .

6. Also the Queene of Saba, whome authors do write to have bene of the stocke and familie of these Magi, bestowed the like giftes, namely golde and spices (unto which shee added precious stones) upon King Solomon as being a figure and type of Christe . . .

7. After Christs ascension they were more fully instructed by St Thomas the Apostle in the faith of Christ, and also baptised, yea (which is more) they were ordained Pastors and Doctors, or Bishops of the people amongst whom they lived . . .

8. After that in their old age they had departed out of this life, their bodies being brought first to Constantinople by the meanes of the Empresse Helena, then to Milan by Eustorgius, Bishop of that Citie, at last in the yeare after the incarnation of Christ 1164 being translated therehence to this city . . .

After all this, and the copying of other inscriptions, one of the Cathedral canons invited Coryate to his house and dinner. Fortified, he moved on to more churches and relics. The first was that of St Ursula, whose legend he related. 'There was in Brittaine a most Christian King called Dionet [or Deonotus, not that it matters, as neither of them existed] who was the father of this Lady Ursula, the fame of whose vertues extended it selfe so farre that a certaine King (his name I can not mention) hearing of the same, resolved to marry her to his onely sonne.' However, Deonotus was unhappy that his daughter should not marry a

Christian, and refused consent, until a divine revelation made him agree, with the condition that the young man

> should be baptized, and that he should give unto his daughter eleven thousand Virgins [presumably readily available in those days], to the end that she might convert them to the Christian religion; which being granted [four and twenty virgins came down from Inverness], and she having converted them all to the faith, a little after sailed into France with a prosperous wind, and from thence to Colen, where she with her husband and all her company of Virgins suffered martyrdome for the faith of Christ in the yeare 238, being all put to the mercilesse dint of the sword by certain Barbarians and heathenish Moores that did at this time inhabit this Citie of Colen. The bones of them being afterward gathered together were brought unto this place, and laid in this Church.

As they were, in large numbers: the skull (asserted to be that) of St Ursula, in a covering of gold, was placed on the top of the high altar (but displayed only on special days). The bones and skulls of other virginal martyrs were piled in great heaps in three places around the church, as well as in the main body (so to speak). 'At one end of the Church there is a certaine frame made in the forme of a cupboord that containeth their skuls onely' displayed behind glass. 'Againe all the upper part of the quire round about are filled up with their bones, the skuls being placed under them, whereof most have little black taffata cases that are distinguished with little spangels, which yeeld a shew like twinkling starres in the firmament.'

(A modern account indicates that Ursula – derived from a pagan Swabian goddess, Hörsel – and her companions were supposed to have been killed in AD 237 by Huns returning from a defeat in Chalons that actually occurred in AD 451(!). The legend seems to have been formulated in the tenth century, when an inscription reading XI MM VV (eleven martyred virgins) was misinterpreted as XI Millia Virginium (11,000 virgins). In the twelfth century, a site in Cologne was excavated, turning up large numbers of bones – probably from Roman times – which were taken to be those of Ursula and her

chaste companions. There was a brief difficulty when the
bones of men and children were uncovered, but fortunately St
Elizabeth of Schönau had a vision that revealed that these
were the remains of Ursula's companions, including her
betrothed, Pope Cyriacus and a number of dukes and bishops
with their attendants.)

Coryate was unwilling to condemn the 'Colonians' for
superstition; he was, however, rather uneasy about the rival

> Church of the Maccabees, in which they report the Bones of that
> holy mother of the Maccabees and her seven sons doe lye, that
> were with such horrible and exquisite tortures punished by King
> Antiochus before the incarnation of Christ, as it appeareth at large
> in the seventh chapter of the second booke of the Maccabees [in
> the Apocrypha], where it is mentioned that the seven sonnes
> together with their mother had their tongues and the utmost parts
> of their bodies cut off by the commandement of King Antiochus,
> their skinne pulled over their heads with their haire, and lastly
> were fryed in a frying pan, only because they would eat no swines
> flesh. Certainly this monument is very memorable, and worthy to
> be seene by a curious traveller, if a man were sure that these were
> the bones of them. For truly for my owne part I will confesse, I
> love to see these kind of things as much as any man living,
> especially when I am perswaded that there is no delusion. But
> indeed there is so great uncertainty in these Papisticall reliques,
> that a man cannot tell which are true, and which are false.

For all that, he wrote down descriptions of inscriptions
associated with images of the mother and her sons being
boiled in a cauldron, and of the monument behind the altar
reputed to contain their skulls and bones.

Then it was on to the Church of St Gereon, who was martyred
by the Emperor Diocletian, with many tombs of the saint and
the Thebans martyred with him, as well as of various Moors
martyred with St Gregory; in the choir there were more bones
and skulls of martyrs cased in glass, with black cloths, and in
the middle 'the head of a blacke Moore', representing St
Gregory. Almost sated with martyrs and miracles and

memorials, Coryate nevertheless reported on one last 'notable thing', a picture of 'our famous English Jesuite Henry Garnet, publikely exposed to sale'. Coryate did not relate the story of Garnet, who was executed in 1606 on suspicion of being implicated in the Gunpowder Plot. A young Catholic named Wilkinson witnessed the execution, when Garnet was hanged, drawn and quartered in the usual way: a drop of blood splashed onto a basket of straw, an ear of corn fell out, and was picked up by Wilkinson as a sacred souvenir. A few days later, looking at it again, he saw on one of the husks a pattern forming a tiny image that looked like a face – obviously Garnet's. Word got around; there were stories of a miracle, and of miraculous cures; people converted (or returned) to the Catholic faith on the strength of 'Garnet's Straw'; the Archbishop of Canterbury instituted an enquiry. The wonderful straw with Garnet's image became well known throughout Catholic Europe, where pictures of it were widely available. This time, of course, Coryate knew what to think: 'the truth of it is such that it may be well ranked amongst the merry tales of Poggius the Florentine [an early collection of comic anti-clerical stories].'

'Thus much of Colen.'

Two days later, on 21 September, Coryate took a boat down the Rhine, in the company of four Englishmen, three returning from the Frankfurt fair, the fourth from studying at the university in München, together with a young German who had been with him all the way from Mainz. After a night at 'a solitary house' they passed Düsseldorf, and then Duisberg, where the famous map-maker, Gerard Mercator, was buried. Going by river not only speeded travel; it was also considerably safer than walking alone, as Coryate had had cause to realise, not only by his fright in the woods but by the sight of so many hanging bodies of executed robbers. Downstream from Duisburg he also 'observed the lamentable tokens of the Belgicke warres, three Churches very miserably battered and sacked, which was done by the [Dutch] soldiers of the Grave [Graf, Prince] Maurice [son of William the Silent]'. The war between Spain and the Dutch had been going on since 1568, destructively but otherwise not unsuccessfully for the Netherlanders (the confederacy of the United Provinces was set up in 1579), prohibitively expensively for the Spanish. Peace negotiations were also protracted, the armistice of 1607 having to be extended to 1608; talks at The Hague eventually broke down late in August, when the Spanish representatives were informed that, unless the independence of the United Provinces was acknowledged by the end of September, war would start again.

On 22 September Coryate and his companions arrived in the war zone at the fortified town of Rheinberg, occupied by a Spanish garrison. Here, their

> whole companie was stayed from passing any farther by certaine officers for the space of two houres, to our great terror and amazement, in so much that we could not be suffered to depart till we had been all convened before the Governor of the towne, who was a Spanish Gentleman, a man that used us more graciously then we expected. For after a few termes of examination he gently dismissed us. Here I saw one of their towers most grievously battered with shot, and many of their other buildings, which was done about a dozen yeares since by the Grave Maurices souldiers.

His Spanish informants presumably did not mention the more recent damage done by the Spanish general Spinola's forces, when they had taken the town two years before. Here also Coryate

> heard most tragicall newes of two Englishmen in this towne. For it was reported unto me, that whereas two of them went into the field to fight [a duel], the one being slaine by the other, he that killed his fellow was condemned by the Governor to receive this punishment; to be shot to death by a dozen of his countreymen. And to be first tyed to a post or some such thing with a paper pinned upon his breast, having a blacke marke in the middle. So this was accordingly performed. But the offendour was so stout-hearted a fellow, that his countreymen were constrained to discharge two or three volleys of shot at him before they could dispatch him.

Their delay at Rheinberg proved doubly inconvenient: when they arrived at Rees at about seven that evening, they found that the gates of the town were locked, and they were refused entry. It seemed that there was nothing for it but to spend what had become a cold, wet night on one of the boats moored at the quay, taking 'a hard lodging there all night upon the bare boordes'. The time seemed unlikely to fly by: 'No sooner were we in the ship but I beganne to cheare my companie as well as I could with consolatorie termes, and pronounced a few verses and fragments of verses out of Virgil, tending to an exhortation to patience in calamities.' Fortunately the Burgomaster of the town took pity on them and, having first sent two soldiers with muskets to question them, let them in, 'to our infinite comfort. For we were all most miserably weather-beaten and very cold, especially I for mine own part, who was almost ready to give up the ghost through cold. But when we came to our inne we were exceedingly refreshed with all things convenient for the comforting of distressed travellers' – except for uninterrupted sleep, as 'all the night a certaine fellow walked about the towne, and once every houre winded a horne'. They had to spend the next day in Rees, 'by reason that the weather was so boysterous, and the Rhene so furious, that there was no travelling upon the river without great danger'. Coryate passed the time admiring the brick houses, pacing out the length and breadth of the marketplace, and inspecting the church ('a wonderfull multitude of Papisticall images & pictures, amongst the rest the images of St Christopher and St George of Cappadocia killing the dragon, and another of that royall Virgin the King of Ægypts daughter, whom he freed from the serpent'). In the graveyard he saw stone crosses inscribed with the names and dates of death of the deceased, 'a custome much observed in many places of the Netherlands', a remark suggesting that he was not familiar with this practice in Somerset.

Early in the morning of the 24th they got away, reaching Emmerich at 9 a.m., where 'refection of [the] body' – eating – allowed no time for sightseeing. At noon, they were off again;

along the way they passed a famous fortress 'called Skinkel-sconce [Schenkenschanz: Schenk's Fort] . . . esteemed the strongest sconce of all Europe . . . and standeth in a certaine little Island which was converted to such an impregnable fortification by the rare invention of a certaine Dutchman whose name was Skinkel'. Schenk had been one of the most notorious, savage and successful freebooters of the recent wars, terrorizing the population for miles around until his death in 1589.

That afternoon Coryate landed in Nijmegen in Gelderland, a busy, Protestant city, 'much given to traffique [commercial activity] and inhabited by many wealthy Merchants', set amidst flat, fertile country noted for corn and for rich pastureland used for fattening cattle. The city was theoretically subject to Spain, but was garrisoned by 3,000 Netherland soldiers. Here Coryate inserted a discussion of Dutch and German eating and drinking habits:

> It is their custome in the Innes to place some few peeces of browne bread hard by the guests trencher, and a little white loaf or two. In many places also at the beginning of dinner or supper they bring some martlemasse [salt] beefe . . . and a good pestle of bacon to the table . . . One of their customes I much misliked, that they sit exceeding long at their meales, at the least an howre and halfe. . . . In most places between Colen and the farther end of the Netherlands . . . I observed that they usually drinke beere & not Rhenish wine, as in the higher parts of Germany. . . . This custome I also observed amongst those of Cleveland, Gelderland, and Holland, that whensoever one drinketh to another, he shaketh his fellow by the hand, and whensoever the men of the country come into an Inne to drinke, they use to take a tinnen tankard full of beere in their hands, and sit by it an howre together, yea sometimes two whole houres before they will let their tankards go out of their hands.

Fynes Moryson also commented on the long sitting at meals, as well as heavy drinking, and complained about being pestered by inn servants for tips, or drinckgelt, that is drincking mony (as if mony were no use but for drincking). And these, being at first free guifts, are nowe challenged of right. The servants in Inns, though they doe a passenger no service, but only at table, not so much as pulling off his bootes, and be so rude, as if he call to have any thinge reached him, they will readily answer he hath as many handes and feete as they, and may reach it himselfe, and though they give him foule sheetes to his bedd, yet they will challenge of him this drincking mony as theire due. Yea if he goe away and forgett to give it, they will followe him to exact it.

The next morning Coryate and his companions went down the river Waal, on both sides of which were

a great company of little castels or Forts not above halfe an English mile distant asunder, which they call Ridouts [redoubts: small outlying fortifications], wherein presidiarie [garrison] souldiers do lie for the defence of the country, fifty persons or thereabout in each . . . I heard that this was the occasion of building these Ridouts: because the enemie was wont heretofore to invade the States territories in the night time, and to take some Gentleman or special man prisoner, and to keepe him captive till he ransomed himselfe with a great summe of money. Hereupon for the security of the country, the States thought good to erect these little Ridouts.

In fact, the river had effectively become the front line, defended on both banks by both sides. He also saw, in the 'farthest frontier towne westward of Gelderland, Bommel (modern Zaltbommel) . . . a great bullet sticke in the Tower of their Church, even about the toppe, which was shot by the enemy in the yeare 1574, which figures (1574) are subscribed in such great characters under the bullet, that a man may very plainly discerne them afarre off'. In the evening he reached Gorcom (modern Gorinchem) in Holland, and at this point in his narrative he inserted a brief disquisition on the country and people:

This country was heretofore called Batavia, and the inhabitants Batavi, which are mentioned by Caesar and Tacitus. They were

in times past accounted a very sottish & foolish people . . . But
in this age they deserve not to be so esteemed. For they are as
ingenious both for al manuary arts, and also for the ingenuous
[liberal, intellectual] disciplines as any people whatsoever in all
Christendome: which a man that liveth amongst them may
easily perceive.

Moryson was also of the opinion that there was more to the
Dutch than appeared, or had been:

> For witt, they seeme a very simple people . . . But howsoever they
> seeme, no doubt the men are indeede most Crafty espetially in
> traffique, eating up all nations therein, by frugality, industry, and
> Subtilety . . . They are a just people, and will not Cozen a Chylde,
> or a stranger, in changing a peece of gold, no in the price or quality
> of thinges they buy . . . In manners they were of old rude, and are
> so to this day in some measure, and the Hollanders have of old
> beene vulgarly called Plumpe, that is blunt or rude. Yet since their
> last long warr in which they have intertayned English and French
> Soldyers and leaders, they are much refined in manners.

The name of Batavia was in general use, Coryate wrote, until a
great flood in AD 860, that 'did so scowre and wash the very
bowels of the earth' that it made the land hollow, so that the
name was changed to Holland, 'which is so called quasi
hollow land, or quasi Hol-land. For hol in the Flemish tongue
doth signifie as much as our word hole'.

Though he stayed in Gorinchem only one night, he was
charmed by the little town, his description evoking the quietly
luminous townscapes by Vermeer and Pieter de Hooch – warm
red-brown bricks, clean-swept courtyards, order:

> The sweetnesse of the situation, the elegancy of their buildings,
> the beauty of their streets, and all things whatsoever in this town,
> did wonderfully delight me, in so much that as soone as I entred
> into one of the longer streets, me thought I was suddenly arrived in
> the Thessalian Tempe, or the Antiochan Daphne . . . And I
> observed some of their streets to be passing beautifull, both for
> breadth and length. And they are much graced by the fayre bricke

pavier. For every streete is very delicately paved with bricke,
which is composed after that artificiall manner that a man may
walke there presently after an exceeding shower of raine [such as
that on 25 September?], and never wet his shooes. The buildings
are all of brick, of a goodly heigth, and an excellent uniformity in
most of the streets, the toppes rising with battlements. I observed
that these kinde of prety buildings are of just correspondency on
both sides of the streets, which doe minister notable beauty to the
towne. Their market place is very spacious and neatly paved with
bricke like to the streets. At one side whereof there is a faire Stadt-
house adorned with a beautifull turret, from the toppe of which I
heard it credibly reported by a Gentleman of good note, a man may
plainly perceive in a faire day two and twenty goodly walled
townes, together with many faire villages and Gentlemens Palaces
in the country. At their docke or key which is neare to one of their
bridges, I observed a great company of prety ships and barkes also.

The next morning he sailed for Dordrecht; on the way he
saw evidence of the great inundation of 1421, when the sea
and rivers combined to submerge many towns and drown
thousands of people:

I never read of the like in Christendom since the generall
cataclysme in the time of the Patriarch Noah. For they
overwhelmed sixteene faire Townes: some write there were no
lesse then three-score and ten of them drowned. And they
swallowed up at the least a hundred thousand persons with al
their goods, cattels, and whatsoever else . . . I saw many Churches
halfe drowned, all the upper part of the tower appearing very
plainly above the water . . . utterly defaced with the mercilesse
furie of the angry God Neptune . . . Moreover I saw a faire Castell
drowned a little on this side Dort, which in former times belonged
to a noble man of the country. It was seated in a faire towne, which
hapned to be so overwhelmed with water at the same time . . . that
there remayneth not the least stone thereof to be seene, saving only
a part of the foresaid Castell.

Dordrecht itself, 'a very famous, opulent and flourishing
towne', became an island, which did not prevent its success as

an entrepôt and trading centre: 'For traffique I have heard that this towne doth more flourish then any town of all Holland, saving famous Amsterdam. And the Merchants of the towne are said to be very wealthy. For heere is the principle Staple of Holland for all manner of Wines, especially the noble Rhenish Wine, from whence it is afterward transported into divers remote regions, as to England, &c.'

Dordrecht was memorable for one thing especially, in that it was called 'the Mayden City of Holland', partly because it was supposed to have been founded by a virgin ('For a monument whereof they have pictured a beautifull Virgin in lively colours according to the full proportion of her body, over the gate neare to the haven at the first entrance into the towne'), and also because of a favour from God shared only with Venice: 'For it was never conquered, though all the circumjacent Cities and townes of the whole territorie of Holland have at some time or other been expugned by the hostile force.' For all that, both Prince Maurice on the one side, and the Spanish general Spinola on the other, had resided in the city, either at the Doole Palace or at the Peacock Inn, on the way to and from peace negotiations at the Hague.

The buildings and streets were of brick, like those at Gorinchem. Coryate visited the Mint, and noted the inscriptions painted on the façade, of some interest in the context of the recent wars, including 'Paci semper est consulendum' (Peace is always advisable), 'Pecunia mater belli' (Money is the mother of war), 'Omnia pecunia effici possunt' (Everything can be done with money) and 'Pecunia vincere speciosum non est' (It is no good thing to conquer by money). The city was wholly Protestant, and guarded with five companies of soldiers, including one English, 'For the Leager (this is the name of the States armie which doth use in the time of warres to lie abroad in the fieldes) was dissolved when I was in Holland, by reason that there was a truce betwixt the Archduke and the States, and it was distributed into many severall companies that were planted abroad in divers cities and townes for the common safety of the country.'

Tom had intended to divert from his homeward progress to visit a monastery near Leiden, but was prevented by 'a certaine sinister chance' or 'disastrous impediment' (unspecified and probably exaggerated). Nevertheless, he wrote out the story that had drawn his attention, beseeching the pardon of the courteous reader for reporting matters beyond the limits of his travels. He had hoped to see a monument erected to the memory of a Countess Margarite, who 'hapned to be delivered of three hundred sixty five children at one burden about three hundred and fourteene yeares since, even just as many as there are daies in the yeare. All which, after they were baptized by one Guido, Suffragan of Utrecht, the males by the name of Johns, & the females by the name of Elizabeths, died that very day that they came into the world: and were buried all together in one monument in the Church of the Monastery of Laudun, which is to this day shewed (as I have heard many worthy travellers report) . . .'. Coryate admitted that 'This strange history will seeme incredible (I suppose) to al readers. But', he insisted, 'it is so absolutely and undoubtedly true as nothing in the world more'. Confirmation of this 'miraculous and stupendious' event was provided by another, explanatory story. A poor woman who had had twins came begging to the Countess, who

scornefully rejected her, affirming that it was not possible shee should have those two children by one man. The poore soule being much vexed in spirit through these injurious words of the Lady, pronounced such a bitter imprecation upon her, that she wished that God would shew a miracle upon the Lady, as well for a due revenge upon her that had so slandered her, as for the testifying of her unspotted honesty & chastity; she wished, I say, that God would shew this miracle, that the Lady might bring forth as many children at one burden as there are daies in the yeere; which indeed came to passe, according as I have before mentioned. For the Ladie in the fortieth yeare of her age was delivered of just so many upon a Saturday about nine of the clocke in the morning, in the yeare of our Lord 1276.

The exactitude regarding time in the last sentence is no doubt intended, as in *The Mikado*, 'to lend verisimilitude to an otherwise bald and unconvincing narrative'.

Coryate sailed from Dordrecht at about noon on 27 September, spending the night 'in a hard lodging of my barke upon the water'. On the way he saw more drowned churches, and peasants labouring to build a dike with earth and straw. The next evening (9 miles covered in eleven hours, presumably struggling against the wind) the boat arrived at Arnemuiden, in those days a busy harbour, 'For there al the Ships that come from Dort do arrive, as in a safe station, & therehence many a great fleete doth often launch forth into the Ocean Sea.' On the 29th, Michaelmas Day, he passed through Middelburg, having no time to inspect the place, but calling in at 'the house of our English Merchants, which is a faire building, having delicate gardens and walkes belonging to it' (Middelburg had long been important in the cloth trade between England and the Netherlands: Chaucer's Merchant 'wolde the see were kept for any thing | Betwixe Middelburgh and Orewelle'), presumably on business, perhaps connected with his impending passage back to England. Soon after, he was in Flushing.

'The towne is not great: yet very faire, and beautified with many stately buildings, that are made all of bricke, according to the rest of the Zelandish and Hollandish cities.' Here he saw a great many storks nesting on the rooftops; Moryson also commented,

The Germans Cherish Storkes, which builde theire nests upon the tops of houses, yea themselves builde large nests of wood upon the topes of theire Senate houses and of their publike and private houses, to invite them to breede there. These Birdes only abyde with them in Sommer (except some fewe which are tame, and have theire winges Clipt) and when they goe away towardes winter, they say that they use to leave one of theire young ones, as for the Rent of theire nests, and kill another as for a sacrifice.

A busy trading city, Flushing was 'inhabited with many rich Merchants that have within these fewe yeares very much inriched themselves by the art of navigation', as Coryate observed. Their success derived from the wars. Commerce had declined in the Spanish provinces during these years, especially in Antwerp: the mouth of the Scheldt, Antwerp's outlet, was controlled by Flushing, itself held by the English.

> Their haven is very strong, and it is a notable harbour of goodly ships. For I can say more of Flushing then of any other haven towne that I saw in my travels: that their haven contained such an exceeding multitude of ships, as I could not see the like in Venice it selfe, the Arsenall only excepted. For I heard that all those that I saw at Flushing were in number at the least two hundred.

The English soldiers in the town were commanded by Sir William Browne, who treated him with 'very special courtesie', as did the Protestant minister, Mr Pots, which earned them his special thanks, and mention in his book, in this, 'the full period and finall conclusion to my outlandish observations'. On Saturday 1 October (the day on which war was to be resumed if the Spanish Commissioners failed to satisfy the States' demands) Coryate sailed away at about 4 p.m., arriving at the Custom House in London twenty-four hours later, having enjoyed 'a very pleasant and prosperous gale of wind all the way between Flushing and London'.

Coryate omitted – it probably never occurred to him – to provide any concluding general reflections on the advantages or disadvantages of travel in the Continent, or on the various peoples and cultures that he had encountered. He was not a reflective or analytic man; but he was an enthusiastic and curious observer. He had been on a long, and at times demanding, journey – been there, done that, got the fleabites – so he measured his achievement by simply adding up the distance he had travelled (mostly on foot, with one pair of shoes) from Odcombe to Venice and back, estimating the total at 1,975 miles. Sir Roger Ascham had written how

> All travellers do gladly report great prayse of Ulysses,
> For that he knew mens maners, and sawe many Cities,

and Coryate concluded his account by listing the number of
cities that he also had seen in his epic journey:

> The Cities that I saw in the space of these five
> Moneths, are five and forty. Whereof in
> France five. In Savoy one. In Italie
> thirteene. In Rhetia one. In Hel-
> vetia three. In some parts of
> high Germanie fifteene. In
> the Netherlands
> seven.
> FINIS.

And that was that.

NINE

Home and Away: Prose, Verse and Worse

Back in England, Coryate (as he wrote in a Latin letter to his new continental acquaintance, Gaspar Waser) spent a few days in London with welcoming friends, recovering and no doubt doing some celebrating, before going down to Odcombe. Here he must have had something of a shock: on 2 October, while he was in mid-Channel on his way back, his mother, after nineteen months' widowhood, had married one John Salmon (about whom nothing is known). Had Tom been aware that this was in the offing, five months before – and, if so, had that had anything to do with his departure? It does seem remarkable that Widow Gertrude had hurried to the altar during her son's relatively brief absence. Hamlet was deeply disturbed by his mother Gertrude's remarriage, with mutterings about cold baked meats; there is no record of Tom's reaction to his Gertrude's remarriage – but his later letters to her were addressed to Mrs Coryate, and he was ostentatiously forgetful of her new husband.

It is not known how long Mr and Mrs Salmon remained in Odcombe, before moving to Yeovil, but Tom was busy there for some time. Among the first things he did was to give thanks for his safe return at Odcombe Church, to which, remarkably, he donated the tattered clothes and worn-out shoes in which he had made his journey (and which remained there on display until early in the eighteenth century); they figure in the upper right corner of the frontispiece of his *Crudities*. The mixture of swagger and self-mockery is characteristic: if people were inclined not to take him seriously, he gave them cause. The metaphor of the book's title, *Coryats Crudities* [crudités, raw vegetables] *Hastily gobled up in five Moneths travells . . . Newly digested in the hungry aire of ODCOMBE . . . now dispersed to the nourishment of the travelling Members of this Kingdome*, suggestive of verbal manure, at best (and some people, in effect, accused him of logorrhoea), together with the undignified episodes displayed in the frontispiece, promised amusement but served fatally to undermine the nature of his achievement and the seriousness of the book. The hanging-up of his clothes inevitably associated him with the clown, Will Kemp, who, after his celebrated and successful dance-journey from London had hung up his shoes in Norwich Town Hall. In one of the poems prefatory to Coryate's book, John Strangways wrote,

> Kemp yet doth live, and only lives for this
> Much famous, that he did dance the Morris
> From London unto Norwich. But thou much more
> Doest merit praise . . .

– but Kemp and he were now linked together. The tattered, lousy state of his clothes, emphasized in the artist William Hole's drawing, also provoked some mockery. Thomas Farnaby was less severe than some:

> In briefe from Venice he to Flussing hobled
> With no more shirts than backs, shoes seldom cobled.
> Which shirt, which shoes, with hat of mickle price,   [little]
> His fustian case, shelter for heards of lice . . .
>   [clothes of coarse material]
> Hang Monuments of eviternall glory, at
> Odcombe, to th'honour of Thomas Coryate.

It seems clear that many of those who wrote verses for his book got no further than the frontispiece, which encouraged a derisory response.

However he may have felt about his mother's remarriage, he was certainly disappointed in another matter on his return.

Joseph Starre, the Yeovil linen-draper with whom he had had
a 'travel-insurance' contract or bond, and from whom he was
now expecting 200 marks, declined to pay (possibly on the
grounds that Coryate had not been away long enough to put
himself at risk and so deserve the money, or for Starre usefully
to invest the deposit). Coryate promptly sued him in the
Common Law Court; the action seemed a straightforward one.
Starre, however, turned to the Court of Chancery, which was
less strictly tied to the letter of the law and invoked the
principle of equity, asking that Coryate's action be not allowed
to proceed, and for the bond to be qualified or even annulled.
Coryate appeared for himself before the Master of the Rolls in
May 1609, making one of his characteristic extravagant
orations; part of this he proudly printed in his follow-up book
to the *Crudities*, *Coryats Crambe*, omitting the legal arguments
but parading the rhetoric that his friends enjoyed (it retains
some entertainment value):

My antagonist, my craftie and versute [cunning] adversarie Joseph
Starre, hath composed such a Bill as no Christian whatsoever
(except he hath a very cauteriate [de-sensitised] conscience, or
hath been brought up amongst the inhumane Garamants, the
barbarous Getes, the uncivill Gothes or Tartars) would doe the like.
For it is nothing else but a *cinnus*, a rabble, a rhapsodie, a
miscellanie of diabolicall falsehoods . . . He coacervateth [heaps
together] and conglomerateth a meere farrago of lyes. Also he
traduceth me about the smalnesse or commonnesse of my Voyage,
as having beene out of England but five moneths. Can he justly call
this a smal and common Voyage to passe almost two thousand
miles by land? to expose ones body to such a world of imminent
dangers both by Sea and Land as I did? to passe those stupendious
mountaines of the snowie Alpes? to dispatch my journey with
such a dispendious [costly] disadvantage to my estate? and after
the consummation of my travels to be thus opposed by a
Vilipendious [contemptible] Linnen Draper? to walke above the
clouds over hils that are at least seven miles high? For indede so
high is the mountain Senys [Mt Cenis] I passed over, which
disterminateth Savoy and Piemont: the danger whereof is such, that

if in some places the traveller should but trip aside in certaine narrow wayes that are scarce a yard broade, he is precipitated into a very Stygian *Barathrum* [abyss] or Tartarean lake six times deeper than Pauls tower is high. Continually to stand in feare of the Alpine cut-throates called the Bandits? Being entred into Italy, to passe through that carnificina [slaughterhouse], that excruciating and excarnificating [agonising and butcherly] torture of the Spanish Inquisition, which is more cruel than Phalaris his brasen Bull, or the exquisitest torturs that the Sicilian tyrants were wont to inflict upon offendors? These dangers and many more I was exposed unto, and like to bee circumcised in Venice amongst the Jewes for maintaining the cause of my Saviour and Redeemer against their refractorie obstinacie, as that Honourable and completly accomplished Knight Sir Henry Wotton, our Kings Leager [resident] Ambassador in Venice, that was an eye witnes of the conflict between them and me, can testifie. At last being as desirous to see my native countrey as Ulysses after his ten yeares travels was to see his Ithaca, which is so deare unto me that I preferre the very smoake of England before the fire of Italy, I walked alone afoote with one onely paire of shooes through many fierie and warlike nations betwixt Venice and Flushing in Zealand, having my throate like to bee cut neere the Citie of Worms in Germanie, and my body to bee turned into wormes meate onely for pulling a poore cluster of Grapes in a Vineyard. These perils beeing considerd I hope your Lordship wil say I have as hardly gotten my money as poor laborious Brickmakers eight pence a day for making Brick.

Whether the judge was impressed by this account of heroic achievement, or the case was indeed very straightforward, he found in Coryate's favour; despite this, Starre could not pay. It turned out, however, that Starre had some sort of guarantor, so he and Coryate together appealed that this guarantor, Richard Rowe, should pay. Rowe in turn appealed to the Chancery Court, which agreed to refer the matter to a Chancery Master. After that, we have no further information as to what happened next; it seems likely that some settlement was reached, as Christopher Brooke, in one of the *Crudities* poems, remarks how printing the book used up Coryate's money: 'The Presse hath spent the three for one you got | At your returne.'

While this was going on, Coryate was busy working on his book. He called himself the Odcombian leg-stretcher, but seems to have been no mean pen-pusher: five months' travel was written up (some 200,000 words) in about five months. Apart from his own notes and memories, he employed various other sources. François Schott's *Itinerarium Italiae* provided material on some Italian towns, notably Cremona and Mantua, and he acknowledged borrowings from Sebastian Münster's *Cosmographie* in writing about Switzerland and Germany, whilst L. Guicciardini's *Descrittione di Tutti I Paesi Bassi* was useful for the Netherlands. All these provided factual and background material, but the life of the book lay in his own observations and reports on his experiences. A basic pattern, deployed whenever possible in dealing with each city, was to include Latin verses by Julius Caesar Scaliger, before providing potted history and a general description, with careful accounts of the main buildings, with measurements and transcriptions of epitaphs and inscriptions, together with more or less credible popular local legends. The analysis of courts and legal and financial systems that Francis Bacon recommended was not his forte: as he said, he had little time, was no 'statist' and his linguistic powers were as yet limited. Whilst he occasionally deploys his fancy style, with Latinate neologisms and coinages, mostly he writes in a clear, brisk, plain style, marred by an over-dependence on a limited range of adjectives – 'certain', 'fair', 'goodly', 'sumptuous'. The book was unusual in its time, and not everyone knew what to make of this mixture of genres (John Donne complained, "Tis no one thing'). A cornucopian volume, its tourist-guide accounts of cities and buildings, its pocket histories, its serio-comic reports on personal experiences and its curious stories inset in Renaissance romance fashion all served to amplify a traditional epic quest, of the lone adventurer challenging and escaping Circe in the heart of the Bower of Bliss, before an arduous but successful return.

Apart from his main text, there was other material that required inclusion. The dedication to his patron, the Prince of

Wales, was fortunately not written in his facetious-pedantic style, but expresses the hope that what Coryate (regrettably) calls his 'Silly [presumably meaning simple] Observations' might encourage 'many noble and generose yong Gallants that follow your Highnesse Court' to travel abroad – which he knew Henry approved of and tried to encourage. He admits to a disproportionately long stay in Venice, 'the Queene of the Christiane world, that Diamond set in the ring of the Adriatique gulfe, and the most resplendent mirrour of Europe', and rejects a possible criticism that this was 'Crambe bis cocta [twice-cooked cabbage] as it is in the proverb', because Venice had been described before, on the grounds that he has given far more detailed information than was available before. He proposes further travels, in Germany and Italy, Greece, Constantinople and the Holy Land, and 'other sacred places mentioned in the Scriptures', and signs off as 'Thomas Coryate, Peregrine [pilgrim, traveller] of Odcombe'.

The 'Epistle to the Reader' is remarkable for his relatively lyrical encomium on travel:

> Of all the pleasures in the world travell is (in my opinion) the sweetest and most delightfull. For what can be more pleasant then to see passing variety of beautifull Cities, Kings and Princes Courts, gorgeous Palaces, impregnable Castles and Fortresses, Towers piercing in a manner up to the cloudes, fertill territories replenished with a very Cornucopia of all manner of commodities as it were with the horn of Amalthea, tending both to pleasure and profit, that the heart of man can wish for.

(Did Shakespeare remember these words in Prospero's farewell, in *The Tempest* in 1611, to 'this vision, | The cloud-capped towers, the gorgeous palaces, | The solemn temples'?) It is the man-made world and its achievements that Coryate responds to, or is aware of responding to: palaces and fortresses; even the landscape is judged in terms of its 'commodities'. In this respect he is not uncharacteristic of his time, though some of his contemporaries were capable of responding to the beauties of the natural world. One might cite

Sir Walter Raleigh in his *Description of Guiana*: 'I never saw a
more beautiful country . . . the deer crossing in every path, the
birds towards the evening singing on every tree with a
thousand several tunes, cranes and herons of white, crimson
and carnation perching in the river's side . . .' But while
Raleigh was seeking to encourage possible future colonists,
Coryate's pleasure was in sightseeing for its own sake,
responding to the wonderful variety of human activity. 'Yea
such is the exuberancie and superfluity of these exotic
pleasures, that for my owne part I will most truly affirme, I
reaped more entire and sweet comfort in five moneths travels
of those seven countries mentioned in the front of my booke,
then I did all the dayes of my life before in England, which
contayned two and thirty yeares.'

He goes on to acknowledge a criticism by one reader, 'as it
were laid in my dish as a choaking peare, that for the short
time that I was abroade I observed more solid matter then any
English man did in the like space this long time. For I copied
out more inscriptions and epitaphes (said a certaine Knight
that shall passe namelesse) that are written upon solid pieces
of stone, then any judicious traveller would have done in
many yeares. For which cause he branded me with the note of
a tombe-stone traveller.' One wonders how sensible it was of
Coryate to pass on a good phrase and joke at his own expense,
even one by a knight. 'Whereas it had beene much more
laudable (said he) to have observed the governement of
common-weales, and affaires of state.' Coryate, however, was
no Philip Sidney, of important family, with leisure, money and
letters of introduction to the great and good of Europe; not
being 'a statesman', as he said, 'matters of policie are
impertinent unto me', and he hardly had time or opportunity
for such matters; in any case, as a keen Latinist, he liked the
style, the 'sweet elegancies', of the inscriptions he copied.
What he did not – could not – say was that it was not just a
matter of aesthetics: frequently he was distressed at the
inadequate commemoration of the dead. His devoted
repetitions of these stony namings and commendations were

his contribution to the persistent human struggle against loss of identity by time's obliteration, and utter oblivion. Concluding with promises of memorable things in his next travel book, he signed off as 'Thy benevolent itinerating friend . . . The Odcombian Legge-Stretcher'.

Late spring or summer saw Coryate up in London, to use his court and literary contacts to get the book published. The person he would have spent most time discussing the book with was Ben Jonson, a friend and dominant figure of the London literary world, also with connections with Prince Henry and the Court. Jonson wrote a lively 'character' of Coryate for his book, that gives a good sense of an amiably bumptious figure, bustling about, full of himself and his book and what it might do for him:

He is an Engine, wholly consisting of extremes, a Head, Fingers, and Toes. For what his industrious Toes have trod, his ready Fingers have written, his subtle Head dictating. He was set a-going for Venice the fourteenth of May, anno 1608 and returned home (of himself) the third of October following, being wound up for five moneths, or thereabouts: his paises [weights] two for one [does this imply that his reimbursement by Starre/Rowe was only two for one?]. . . . He hath ever since the first designe of printing hereof, bene à Deliciis to the Court; but served there in his own cloathes [that is, not in livery, as one of Henry's servants], and at his own costs . . . when he should have been taken up for the place . . . hee conditioned to have no office of charge or neerenesse cast upon him, as a Remora [sucker-fish, or drag] of his future travaile; for to that he is irrecoverably addicted. The word Travaile affects him in a Waine-ox, or a Packe-horse . . . The mere superscription of a letter from Zurich sets him up like a top: Basil or Heidelberg makes him spinne. And at seeing the word Frankford, or Venice, though but on the title of a Booke, he is readie to breake doublet, cracke elbowes, and overflowe the roome with his murmure . . . He is a great and bold Carpenter of words, or (to expresse him in one like his owne) a Logodaedale: which voyce, when he heares, 'tis doubtfull whether he will more love at the first, or envy after, that it was not his owne. All his Phrase is the same with his manners and haviour, such as if they were studied to make Mourners mery . . . He is alwaies Tongue-Major of the company, and if ever perpetuall motion be to be hoped for, it is from thence. He will aske, How you doe? Where have you bene? How is it? If yow have travelled? How yow like his booke? with, what newes? and be guilty of a thousand such curteous impertinences in an howre, rather than want [lack] the humanity of vexing you. To conclude this ample Traveller in some bounds, you shall best know him by this: he is frequent at all sorts of free tables, where though he might sit as a Guest, he will rather be served in as a Dish, and is loth to have any thinge of himselfe kept cold against the next day.

Jonson also wrote an eulogistic poem for him, and verses annotating the frontispiece, as did Tom's friend Laurence Whitaker; the verses printed here are a conflation of both writers' words:

A. First, th'Author here glutteth Sea, Haddocke and Whiting
    With spuing, and after the world with his writing.

B. Though our Author for's Venerie felt no whips smart,
    Yet see here he rides in a Picardie cart.
                             [lechers had to ride in carts]

C. This Horse pictur'd showes, that our Tatter-de-mallian
    Did ride the French Hackneyes, and lye with th'Italian.
                             [horses, whores]

D. Here up the Alpes (not so plaine as to Dunstable)
    Hee's carried like a Cripple, from Constable to Constable.

E. A Punke here pelts him with egs. How so?   [whore]
    For he did but kisse her, and so let her go.

F. Religiously here he bids, row from the stewes,
    He will expiate this sinne with converting the Jewes.

G. Thy Cortizane clipt thee, 'ware Tom, I advise thee,
    And flie from the Jewes, lest they circumcise thee.

H. He longs for sweet grapes, but going to steale 'em,
    He findeth sour graspes and gripes from a Dutch Skelum.
                             (A Rascal)

I. Old Hat here, torne Hose, with Shoes full of gravell,
    And louse-dropping Case, are the Armes of his travell.

K. This picture unlike him*, showes hee's not come home as
    He went, but chang'd, and turn'd travelling Thomas.
                    (*But you differ in opinion (Mr Laurence) from all my
                                                        other friendes)

L. Here France, and Italy both to him shed
    Their hornes, and Germany pukes on his head.

M. And here he disdain'd not in a forraine land,
    To lie at Livory, while the Horses did stand.

N. But here, neither trusting his hands, nor his legs,
    Beeing in feare to be rob'd, he most learnedly begs.

One wonders whether Jonson had anything to do with the
selection of incidents illustrated in the frontispiece, which
present Coryate as a comic figure. He probably had something
to do with engaging the artist, William Hole, an illustrator
starting what was to be a distinguished career; Hole had
recently drawn some new maps for Camden's *Britannia*, and
later illustrated George Chapman's translation of Homer,
Michael Drayton's *Polyolbion* (with a fine portrait of Prince
Henry), Raleigh's *History of the World* and the title page of Ben
Jonson's *Works* (1616). Hole's frontispiece and picture of
Coryate with the Venetian courtesan show a rather lumpy-
browed, bearded, solemn face, not much like the description
provided by Thomas Fuller (who never saw Coryate) in his
Worthies: 'He carried folly (which the charitable called
merriment) in his very face. The shape of his head had no
promising form, being like a sugar loaf inverted, with the little
end before, as composed of fancy and memory, without any
common sense.' Coryate's friend, Laurence Whitaker, in his
verses on the frontispiece, said that the picture was 'unlike
him', but Coryate claimed that all his other friends disagreed.
Hole's portraits are generally thought to be good likenesses.

Coryate suggests (following true modest author convention)
that he was encouraged to publish by his friends, who, apart
from Jonson, included Lionel Cranfield, a successful
businessman, who had become a member of the Levant
Company in 1605 (which probably came in handy when Coryate
later sailed to the Levant), and Laurence Whitaker, secretary to

Coryate's patron, Sir Edward Phelips of Montacute. It is possible that none of the London printer/booksellers wanted to take on such an unusual book by such an unusual character; in the event, Coryate decided to publish by himself. To increase general interest and sales, he decided to get his well-known literary friends to provide eulogistic verses at the beginning of the book (quite a common practice at the time); however, it went wrong. Influenced by the amusing frontispiece, which clearly was printed and circulated separately from the text, many of the verses – often uninvited – that arrived were not merely ironic in their praise, but derisive. Coryate attempted to stem the flood, as he explained in his introduction, but matters had got out of hand, with Prince Henry joining in the fun. Having received so many more than he wanted, Coryate resolved, as he wrote,

> to put above a thousand of them into an Index purgatorius, and to detain them from the presse. Whereupon the Princes Highnesse (who hath most graciously deigned to be the Hyperaspist [Coryate's coinage: protective shield] and Maecenas of my book . . . gave me . . . strict and expresse commandement to print all those verses . . . many of them are disposed to glance at me with their free and mery jests, for which I desire thee (Courteous Reader) to suspend thy censure of me till thou hast read over my whole booke.

When the book appeared, there were contributions by some forty-eight writers (with more latecomers printed in *Coryats Crambe*). Most were of limited literary merit, written in English, Welsh, Greek, Latin, French, Italian, Spanish, macaronic (a mixture of languages) and in invented languages, 'Antipodean' and 'Utopian', mostly in doggerel couplets, but also shaped like an egg and set to music. Coryate did his best, sorting them out so that the first thirteen were those composed by knights (the first, over a Greek pseudonym, was probably by Sir Edward Phelips); the next thirteen were by people he felt to be on friendly terms with, including John Donne, Richard Martin, Laurence Whitaker, Hugh Holland, Christopher Brooke, John Hoskyns,

Lionel Cranfield and Inigo Jones; the next group included some able writers, including Richard Corbet, Thomas Campion and Michael Drayton, whose poem, before moving into social satire, began courteously, with a side-swipe at the book's versifiers:

> Many there be that write before thy Booke,
> For whom (except here) who would ever looke?
> Thrice happy are all we that had the Grace
> To have our names set in this living place.

The writing generally is indeed of variable quality; one extravagant piece, with a running 'food' metaphor, by the pseudonymous Glareanus Vadianus, is in its way unforgettable. He begins by describing Coryate as

> March-pane of Mirth, the Genova paste of love,   [marzipan]
>   The Graces gallipot*, Musicks fiddle-sticke,
>   The spout of sport, and follies turtle Dove . . .
>   (*It is a vessel into which womens teares blended with loves
>   sighes are distilled . . .)

before going on to ask

> How should I sing thy worth in fitting layes,
>   With starveling verses of an hide bound Muse,
>   And crowne thy head with mistletoe for bayes,
>   Unless thy knapsacke did new thoughts infuse? . . .

Coryate never mentions having a knapsack, and Hole does not draw him wearing one, only a cloak; it would seem sensible, even essential, to have one. Vadianus goes on to suggest Coryate's rhetorical powers:

> For Tom's a cap-stone, and a turne-spit jacke,
>   A skrewed engine Mathematicall,
>   To draw up words that make the welkin Cracke
>   Out of a wit strangly dogmaticall . . .

Tom is the padlocke of all secrecie,
> [shuts out reserve or restraint]

Whose tongue the tell-tale of whats done and more,
Vents out the barmy broth of surquedrie,
> [pours out the ferment of excess]

By thirteene to the dozen, thirtie to the skore.

Tom's a Bologna sawcidge lovely fat,
Stuft with the flesh of a Westphalian sow . . .
> [full of tasty material]

Tom is a twinne, and yet an Odde, and both,
Twinne shoes, odde shirt, and both by combination . . .
> ['Tom' is Hebrew for twin; he is odd – i.e. single,
> odd and from Odcombe]

In general, the writers content themselves with versifying the incidents that Hole had depicted, with prurient sniggers about Coryate's presumed near-circumcision by the Jews and encounter with the Venetian courtesan. One will serve for many, as Hugh Holland works out an analogy that would have pleased Coryate:

Ulysses was a merry Greeke they say,
So Tom is, and the Greeker of the tway.
Ulysses left at home an aged Syre,
And Tom an aged mother by the fyre.
Ulysses was an Islander I trow,
How then? I pray you is not Coryate so?
Perhaps Ulysses did in wit excell,
Our Coryate though doth of more learning smell.
Ulysses had a ship of no great bulke,
And Coryate went to Calais in a hulke.
Ulysses in the Trojan horse was hid,
The Heidelbergian barrell Tom bestrid.
Good harnesse did Ulysses guarde and grace,
Where Coryate nought had but a fustian case.
Ulysses hardly from his Circe sluncke,
As hardly Tom from his Venetian Puncke.

By land Ulysses in a Chariot rode,
And Coryate in a Cart, the greater lode.
Ulysses with sterne Ajax had to doe,
With the Dutch Boore so had poore Coryate too.
At home left Ulix store of beasts and chattell,
And Coryate home came guarded with more cattell.
Ulysses us'd to drinke the Aethiop wine,
With whitson-ale his cap doth Coryate line.
Just twentie yeares Ulysses with his Greekes
Did wander: Coryate just as many weeks.
Ulysses all that while had but one carvell,   [caravel, ship]
Tom but one pair of shoes, the greater marvel.
Minerva holp Ulysses at a lift,
And Patience Coryate, for there was no shift.
Ulysses heard no Syren sing: nor Coryate
The Jew, least his prepuce might prove excoriate.
Ulysses had a wife to lust unprone,
But Coryate had a chaster, having none.
Ulysses seem'd a beggar all to-torne,
So Coryate did; and was, I dare be sworne.
Ulysses in his travell builded Flushing,
Where Coryate ending, o're the Sea came brushing.
One Homer only sang Ulysses praise,
But Coryate all the Poets of our daies.

(As Touchstone told Rosalind, 'I'll rhyme you so eight years together, dinners, and suppers, and sleeping hours, excepted.') Indeed, Coryate had scooped up a large haul, some of them good catches.

What tends to interest the modern reader are clues as to his manner and looks. Sir Edward Phelips (if he really is Apodemountephilos, 'friend of the sojourner abroad'), tells us of Tom's youth:

The child in time was waxen great,
And all the Sophists he did threat,   [Greek philosophers]
    Their problems to confound;
Grammarians sore did stand in feare
The coynage of his words to heare,

> So uncouth was their sound . . .
> This wandring Squire full oft I heard
> The circle of his beard had squard,
> And skowred every haire . . .
> He had a kind of simple blush
> That kept him still from being flush,
> When Ladies did him wooe:
> Though they did smile, he seem'd to scowle,
> As doth the faire broade-faced fowle
> That sings to whit to whooe . . .

Donne also suggests an embarrassed blush, a lack of confidence under the polysyllabic bravado:

> Goe bashfull man, lest here thou blush to looke
> Upon the progresse of thy glorious booke . . .

Inigo Jones suggests much the same:

> when thou drink'st,
> Thou mak'st a *crab-like face, shak'st head and wink'st.
> (*The modesty of the Author being such, and his temperance
> in drinking, that he sometimes frowneth when a health is
> drunke unto him.)

Coryate's indications of distaste regarding drinking, and drinking of healths, in Germany come to mind. There are frequent suggestions that he was smallish, with a relatively large head and small eyes. Henry Goodyer, remembering some clownish jest involving Tom at Court, tells us,

> Who thinks him light, aske them who had the taske
> To beare him in a trunke unto the maske,

and John Gifford writes that

> he's a spectacle unto all eyes
> That makes great things of small (in wordy wise!)

Lionel Cranfield observes how

> He Greeke and Latin speakes with greater ease
> Then hogs eat akornes, or tame pigeons pease.
> His ferret eyes do plod so on his booke,
> As makes his lookes worse than a testie cooke . . .
> He is not proud, his nature soft and milde,
> His compliments are long, his lookes are wild . . .

John Chapman also remarks that

> His little eyes set in his living head
> See farther than great eyes in one that's dead . . .
> His jests and acts are purely naturall,
>   [spontaneous; and those of a 'natural',
>   or 'simple' person]
> Stuffed full of Greeke and Latin whipt into him,
> Having learning just enough to undoe him.

Michael Drayton, reflecting satirically on their strange, prodigious age,

> Wondring what fruit it to the world would bring,
> At length it brought forth this: O most strange thing,
> And with some throwes, for that the greatest head
>   [throes, birth-pangs]
> Ever is hard'st to be delivered.

Coryate's friend Laurence Whitaker well summed up the effect of what another called 'Typographical Topographical Tom' and his writing:

> But I'le not write thy labours Inventory,
> I'le say but this of thee, and of thy story,
> Thou well describ'st the marvels thou didst see,
> And this thy booke as well describeth thee.

For all the absurdity of the almost innumerable verses, they provided good publicity, and probably helped sales – at first.

Unfortunately, the book was also lumbered with some ill-considered additions: Coryate's translations of two orations on travel, uninteresting correspondence and, at the end, in misplaced acts of filial piety, the writings of George Coryate, his father.

With all this, it was now time to get the book published, and for this Coryate needed official approval, and a licence. He began by persuading the Revd John Seward of Yeovil to write to the Chaplain of the Bishop of London (who was responsible for appointing a licensing panel), but this was not successful, the Chaplain claiming that they were responsible for religious writings. He then wrote to the Archbishop of Canterbury, Richard Bancroft, who, frustratingly, died on 2 October 1610, without issuing a permit. He tried an oration to Prince Henry. Early in November, at a dinner given by Arthur Ingram, a London merchant and friend of Lionel Cranfield, he met Sir Michael Hicks, secretary to the Lord Treasurer, and wrote to him asking for his assistance.

The letter (now in the British Library's copy of the *Crudities*), dated 15 November 1610, is the only example remaining of Coryate's handwriting. He begins by apologising for an inappropriate witticism at the dinner table, provoked by the mischievous 'merry prompting of the joviall blackbearded gentleman that sat next unto me', and promising lifelong gratitude for any help that Hicks might provide, 'in the strictest bonde of true observance till I suffer the fatall dissolution of my bodie and soule'. Having summarised his travels, he relates how

> I was disposed to turne my microcosme (a phrase that a certaine learned gentleman not long since used of me [suggesting that Coryate was a small man]) into eyes, I meane to prie into all thinges of chiefest remarque that were obvious unto my eyes, in every place where I travelled; in soe much that by my incessant industrie and Herculean toyle, I wrote soe many observations in the foresaid countries as have filled very neere 4 quiers of paper.

He explains how he has delivered an oration to Prince Henry, who has promised to accept the dedication, and has tried

writing to the late Archbishop and to the Bishop of London; he
now asks Hicks to intercede with the Lord Treasurer:

> No man of our nation since the incarnation of Christe hath
> observed more for the time in the foresayd countries, which I hope
> you would not hold to be unlikely if you did but know what
> intolerable paynes I tooke in my travells both by day and night,
> scarce affording myselfe 2 howers rest sometimes of the whole 24
> in the citie of Venice by reason of my continuall writing;
> whereupon divers English men that lay in the same house with
> me, observing my extreme watchings, wherewith I did grievously
> excruciat my bodie, instantly desired me to pittie my selfe, and not
> to kill my selfe with my inordinate labours. To conclude, if it shall
> please your Worship to gratifie me in this my earnest supplication,
> you will adde unto me the very spurres of diligence, and give me
> wonderfull encouragement to observe such thinges in my future
> travells as I doubt not but shall be acceptable to the King and
> Queene themselves and all their royall children, as also to the
> greatest peeres and nobles of this kingdome . . .

This passionate appeal he followed up with a formal petition
to Prince Henry, written, not in the plain English of his letter
to Sir Michael Hicks, but in the exaggerated and facetious style
expected of him at that Court:

> For as much as that great *Oecolampadius** (*The Archbishop of
> Canterburie) of England, even that refulgent Lamp of Gods house
> [a translation of oecolampadius, Coryate's coinage], hath lately lost
> his light, the snuffe thereof having fallen downe into the Socket,
> and so consequently is extinct for a time; that Lampe which
> should have given lustre, and lent her light unto my poore
> Hodoeporicall lucubrations [Coryatese for 'travel writings'], as the
> Sunne doth to the Moone, by the eclipse whereof they are now
> dimmed, and lurke in a darknes more than Cimmerian [the
> Cimmerii were reputed to live in pitch darkness]; My thrise-
> humble and thrise-suppliant suite unto your Highnesse is this, that
> you would graciously vouchsafe to cherish and maintaine the
> scintillant embers of my diminutive Lampe, by infusing into them
> the quickning Oyle of your Gracious indulgence; by vertue of

which, my Candle, which is now hid under a Bushell, may gather strength, and bee elevated even to the conspicuous and elevated places of this Kingdome, and disperse abroad her coruscant light to the illuminating of the caliginous [dim] understandings of my travelling Countrimen. Your Highnesse suppliant and humble Petitioner, Thomas Coryate, The Odcombian Traveller.

Something must have worked: on 26 November, *Coryats Crudities* was entered in the Stationers' Register. As Ben Jonson wrote in his welcoming, acrostic verse:

Come forth thou bonnie bouncing booke then, daughter
Of Tom of Odcombe, that odde Joviall author,
Rather his sonne I should have cal'd thee, why?
Yes thou wert borne out of his travelling thigh
As well as from his braines, and claimest thereby
To be his Bacchus as his Pallas: bee
Ever his thighes Male then, and his braines Shee.

(Jonson's rather laboured conceit depends on the myths that Pallas Athene was born from the head of Zeus, and Bacchus from his thigh.) Yet still it was not satisfactory: the book was not well printed, with many misprints. Coryate added a lengthy note, blaming the many errata on the printer, and promising more care for the second edition (which never appeared): 'I must tell thee (Courteous Reader) it grieveth me extremely to shut up my booke with an Index of so many faults as I now present unto thee, which it makes me in a manner blush [!] for shame to behold. But impute it not I intreate thee to my ignorance . . . Most of which ascribe I pray thee (candid Reader) to the negligence of the Corrector, and not to my unskilfulnesse.'

Now it was time for another publicity drive – literally so: as Coryate shuttled about bearing presentation copies to members of the Royal Family at various palaces, he had the heavy copies carried around on the back of a donkey, in a box inscribed ASINUS PORTANS MYSTERIA, a characteristic Coryate scholarly whimsy, referring to a legend illustrated in

Andrea Alciati's well-known collection *Emblemata* (1591), in which an ass carrying an image of the goddess Isis thought that people were worshipping him rather than the sacred image, until he was forcibly corrected by the carter. On the evening of Easter Monday, Coryate showed up at St James's Palace, for a presentation oration to Prince Henry, apparently the 'Most scintillant Phosphorus of our British Trinacria' (Sicily – Trinacria – and Britain being alike, in each having three corners):

> With this May-dew of my *Crude* collections, I have now filled this new-laide Egge-shelle, not doubting of the like effect in your Highnesse, the radiant Sunne of our English Hemisphaere, that the great Phaebean Lampe hath over a naturall Egge-shel produced by a checkling Henne . . . and so by your Gracious irradiation to make it conspicuous and illustrious. Yea (which is more) I wish that by the auspicious obumbration [shading] of your Princely wings, this sencelesse Shell may proove a lively Birde . . . In the meane time receive into your indulgent hand (I most humbly beseech your Highnesse) this tender feathered Red-breast [the Prince's presentation copy was bound in red velvet].

On Tuesday 2 April he was off to the King at Royston, contrasting himself with English merchants, in that his 'farre-fetched lading' and ship were his book, 'swimming in the liquid Ocean' of his brain; the King's favour would be both a pleasant, helpful gale and a 'wel-fenced docke and secure haven of tranquillitie, where she may ride at Anchour on a Halcedonian [halcyon] calme, and shoote off her Ordnance against the Criticall Pirates and malignant Zoiles [carping critics] that scowre the surging Seas of this vaste Universe'. On Friday evening he was with the 'radiant Aurora of Great Brittaines spacious Hemispheare', the Queen, at Greenwich Palace, and on Sunday noon, explaining the title of the book to Princess Elizabeth, at Kew, before heading back to St James's Palace that evening, to the Duke of York (the future Charles I – Prince Henry was to die of typhoid, in November 1612), comparing himself to Caesar and his *Veni, Vidi, Vici*:

I came to Venice, and quickly tooke a survey of the whole modell of the Citie, together with the most remarkable matters thereof; and shortly after my arrival in ENGLAND I overcame my adversaries of the Towne of Evill, in my native Countrey of Somerset, who thought to have suncke mee in a bargaine of Pilchards [pilchard fishing took place off the south-west of England], as the wise men of Gotham once went about to drowne an Eele.

Charles seems to have been quite taken with him, as he was allowed to make him another oration, on 20 May, on his election to the Order of the Garter.

To keep up the publicity and sales momentum, in June Coryate prepared another book, *Coryats Crambe, or his Colwort twice Sodden, and Now served in with other Macaronicke dishes, as the second course to his Crudities*, the 'crambe' and 'colwort' referring to cabbage cooked twice, an unappetising offer of stale news, consisting of some fifty pages of verses delivered too late for inclusion in the *Crudities*, together with his petition to Prince Henry, his orations to the Royal Family, part of his speech in the Court of Chancery, and his description of his Church-Ale performances at Odcombe and Yeovil in 1606. Before this could appear, however, came a bombshell – *The Odcombian Banquet Dished foorth by Thomas the Coriat, and served in by a number of Noble Wits in prayse of his Crudities and Crambe too*: a book not by Coryate at all, but a rip-off, a pirated reprint of the verses in *Crudities*, with some of the preliminary matter, and some Crambe material, but omitting Coryate's own material, declaring it not worth reading. The anonymous editor (if so he may be called) explained:

Know (gentle Reader) that the booke, in prayse whereof all these preceding verses were written, is purposely omitted for thine and thy purses good, partly for the greatnes of the volume, containing 654 pages, each page 36 lines, each line 48 letters, besides Panegyricks, Poems, Epistles, Prefaces, Letters, Orations, fragments, posthumes [swellings, amplifications], with the comma's, colons, ful-points, and other things thereunto appertaining: which being printed of a character legible without spectacles, would have caused the Booke much to exceed that price whereat men in these witty dayes value such stuffe as that.

The mock-eulogistic verses by so many leading figures had aroused a lot of interest: more people wanted to snigger at the varying wit and insults by more or less well-known figures, together with mockery of Coryate's use of the Alciati donkey motto (making Coryate the donkey), than were prepared to pay to read Coryate's own writing. Unfriendly Thomas Fuller later declared 'the porch . . . more worth than the palace, I mean the preface of other men's mock-commending verses'. The *Banquet*, drawing on printed material in the *Crudities* and, presumably from manuscript or early printed sheets from the *Crambe*, came out before Coryate's book, with damaging effect. The printer/publisher, Thomas Thorpe, was skilled in getting hold of unpublished and incomplete material: he had earlier got hold of writing by Marlowe, and was later to print Shakespeare's *Sonnets*.

Coryate did his best to counter-attack, with an addendum defending the *Crudities*:

At the conclusion and upshot of this Booke, let mee a little advertise thee (gentle Reader) of a Booke lately Printed in hugger-mugger, intituled the Odcombian Banquet. And I am the rather induced to make mention of it because it doth not a little concerne my credit to cleere myself of two very scandalous imputations laide upon me by that virulent and rancorous pessant, some base lurking pedanticall tenebricious Lucifuga [light-avoider] that set forth the booke. Whereof the first is the Motto in the first leafe of the booke. ASINUS PORTANS MYSTERIA.

He explains his use of the motto, and how the *Banquet*'s title page 'most sinisterly and malignantly applied it (as all the Readers doe interpret it) to myselfe', before defending his own writing: 'I will boldly affirme for the better justification of my Observations, and by way of opposition against the malicious censure of that hypercriticall Momus [god of ridicule, or foolish critic], that of the sixe hundred fiftie and four pages (for indeede so many are in the booke) he shall find at the least five hundred worthy the reading.' In other words, by his own admission, nearly a quarter of the book was not worth reading.

Coryate's books sold, but not as well as they might have done; he was, however, more widely known, moderately famous. In one of the prefatory poems, his friend Christopher Brooke had suggested that Oxford's Bodleian Library, opened in 1603, should acquire a copy, and Tom duly presented one (no longer in the Library's stock). A letter from Thomas Bodley, on the occasion of Coryate ('the famous Traveller') visiting Oxford, asks that the Librarian should display the book, placing it 'for the time in some such Place in the Library, as he may seem to have magnified the Author and the Book'. Some admired his achievement; some continued to enjoy him much as they had done before; some now knew of him as a target for mockery.

One episode involving Coryate, of particular literary-historical interest, concerns a symposium or drinking party, a 'Convivium Philosophicum', that took place in the Mitre Tavern, off Fleet Street in London, on 2 September, probably in 1611. We know of it from an entry in John Aubrey's *Brief Lives*, for Richard Martin (1570–1618), eventually Recorder of London (another of Coryate's legal-literary acquaintances), of whom Aubrey writes, 'I thinke he dyed of a merry symposiaque', which seems a very good way to go. In any case, there is a humorous poem about a drinking party, a gathering of writers, possibly – but by no means certainly – by John Hoskyns (1561–1638), of whom Aubrey tells us, 'His acquaintance were all the witts then about the towne, e.g., Sir Walter Ralegh . . . John Donne . . . Sir Henry Wotton . . . [his] conversation was exceedingly pleasant . . . a great master of the Latin and Greke languages . . . His verses on the fart in the Parliament House are printed in some of the *Drolleries*.' The poem is in Latin, with nineteen verses, listing the various guests expected at the party, with Latin versions of their names; a contemporary translation exists, attributed to John Reynolds of New College, Oxford (whose portrait in fresco is one of those lining the upper reading room in the Bodleian). It begins,

> Quilibet si sit contentus
> Ut statutus stet conventus
>   Sicut nos promisimus;
> Signum *Mitrae* erit locutus,
> Erit cibus, erit jocus,
>   Optimatatissimus.

The translation reads,

> Whoever is contented
> That a number be convented
>   Enough but not too many;
> The *Miter* is the place decreed,
> For witty jests and cleanly feed,
>   The betterest of any.

The poem lists those attending, including Christopher Brooke, John Donne, Lionel Cranfield, Sir Robert Phelips, Sir Henry Nevill, Richard Connock, John Hoskyns, Richard Martin, Sir Henry Goodyer, John West, Hugh Holland, Inigo Jones and, most of all, Tom Coryate:

> But yet the number is not ri[gh]ted;
> If Coriate bee not invited,
>   The jeast will want a tiller.

> For wittily on him, they say,
> As hammers on an anvil play,
>   Each man his jeast may breake.
> When Coriate is fudled well,
> His tongue begins to talke pel-mel,
>   He shameth nought to speake.

> A boy he was devoid of skill,
> With white-pots and oaten-cakes at will
>   [west-country milk puddings]

Somersetizated.
And is a man with Scots and Angles
With silken scarfs and with spangles
[like a morris-dancer or clown]
Fitly accommodated.

Are you in love with London citty?
Or else with Venice? he will fitt ye;
You have his heart to prize it.
Or love you Greeke — of tongues chiefe,
Or love you Latin? hee'le in briefe
Sir Edward Ratcliffize itt.

This orator of Odcombe towne
Meaning to civilise the clowne,
To parley 'gan to call
The rusticks and the Coridons,
The naturalls and moriones, [simpletons and deluded]
And dis-coxcombde them all.   [instructed them]

To pass the sea, to pass the shore,
And Fleet-street it all Europe o're,
A thing periculous.   [dangerous]
And yet one paire of shoes, they say,
And shirt did serve him all the way,
A thing pediculous.   [lousy]

Whoso him exoutherizeth   [exauthorizes, devalues]
Garretating swaberizeth,   [talks abusively]
And for this injurie
He shall walk as disrespected,
Of good fellows still neglected,
In city and in curie.   [court]

To a fool thus elevated,
Mountebanke-like thus he prated,
Harringuizing rowndly.   [haranguing]
Whosoe will be counted prudent,
Let him be no other student
But to drinke profoundly.

(While Tom should not be criticized, it would be foolish to copy his style of talking; instead, one should drink.) The poem then outlines the characteristic activities of those attending, before concluding:

> Thus every man is busy still,
> Each one practising his skill,
>   None hath enough of gayne.
> But Coriate liveth by his witts,
> He looseth nothinge that he getts,
>   Nor playes the fool in vayne.

The last sentence seems a shrewd observation. Much more is written about Coryate than any of the others; if not the guest of honour, he is expected to provide much of the entertainment.

This dinner at The Mitre links interestingly with one of Coryate's letters from India in 1615, directed to 'the High Seneschall of the Mermaid Club' and what he calls 'the right Worshipfull Fraternitie of Sirenaicall Gentlemen' there, the 'Sirenaics' possibly being admirers of mermaids or sirens, or even the muses (all attractive females). This group, which was presumably very similar in character (and possibly in membership) to the guests at The Mitre, presented him, before he set off on his travels again in 1612, with a comic 'incomparable elegant safe-conduct . . . for the security of my future peregrination, concinnated by the pleasant wit of that inimitable artizan of sweet elegancy, the moytie [portion] of my heart and the quondam Seneschall of the noblest Society, M[aster] L[aurence] W[hitaker]'.

This letter of Coryate's is the only evidence of the famous literary gatherings at the Mermaid Tavern that Shakespeare and Jonson were later supposed to have attended. Aubrey had a note regarding 'Heroes & Witts of that time' meeting at the 'Mermayd in Fryday Street', which Antony à Wood used in his *Athenae Oxonienses*. In a verse letter of 1613, the dramatist Francis Beaumont wrote,

> What things have we seen,
> Done at the Mermaid! heard words that have been
> So nimble, and so full of subtle flame,
> As if that every one from whence they came
> Had meant to put his whole wit in a gest,
> And had resolv'd to live a fool, the rest
> Of his dull life . . .

Unfortunately, Beaumont gave no indication of who had been there; Coryate might have been, but there is no evidence whatsoever, despite Fuller in his *Worthies* evoking 'wit combats' between Shakespeare and Jonson (which he could not have seen), that either of them was there.

Coryate, however, was now very much part of the London literary world, and, as such, open to comment by more and different kinds of people. The most notable of these, as far as Coryate was concerned, turned out to be John Taylor, the 'Water Poet', so called because for some years he had been a Thames waterman, rowing passengers up, down and across the Thames, before he found versifying more comfortable and more profitable. In 1612 he brought out *The Sculler's Travels . . . or Gallimaufry of Sonnets, Satyres*; included was a verse,

> *To Tom Coriat*
> What matters for the place I first came from
> I am no Duncecombe, Coxecomb, Odcomb Tom,
> Nor am I like a wool-pack, cramm'd with Greek,
> Venus in Venice minded to goe seeke;
> And at my backe returne to write a Volume
> In memory of my wits Gargantua colume.
> The choysest wits would never so adore me;
> Nor like so many Lackies run before me,
> But honest Tom, I envy not thy state,
> There's nothing in thee worthy of my hate;
> Yet I confesse thou hast an excellent wit:
> But that an idle Braine doth harbour it.
> Foole thou it at the Court, I on the Thames,
> So farewell Odcomb Tom, God blesse King James.

Feeble stuff; yet this poor jibe may have offended Coryate;
whether or not it did, at any rate, Taylor, in his *The Eighth
Wonder of the World*, claimed

> Sir Thomas much my writing blam'd,
> Because an Epigram therein was written,
> In which he said he was nipt gald and bitten.
> He frets, he fumes, he rages, and exclaimes
> And vowes to rouze me from the River Thames.

Coryate had experienced worse from better wits; indeed, in his
follow-up piece, *Laugh and be fat*, Taylor remarks how

> The broad-fac'd Jests that other men put on you,
> You take for favours well bestow'd upon you.
> In sport they give you many a pleasant cuffe,
> Yet no man's lines but mine you take in snuffe.   [resent]

Class-consciousness seems pretty clearly to be the problem
here, with both of them. Taylor pretends to excuse himself, by
disingenuously interpreting his offending lines innocently:

> The cause, I heare, your fury flameth from,
> I said I was no dunce-combe, coxcombe Tom.
> Whats that to you (good Sir) that you should fume,
> Or rage or chafe, or thinke I durst presume
> To speake, or write, that you are such a one?
> I onely said, that I my selfe was none . . .
> I further said, I envied not your state,
> For you had nothing worthy of my hate.
> In love, your innocence I truly pitty,
> Your plentious want of wit seems wondrous wittie . . .

He concludes, however, with an attempt at a parody of the
socially and educationally superior Coryate, threatening in his
extravagant vein:

Contaminous, pestiferous, preposterous, stygmaticall, Slavonian,
slubberdegullions; since not the externall unvalued trappings,

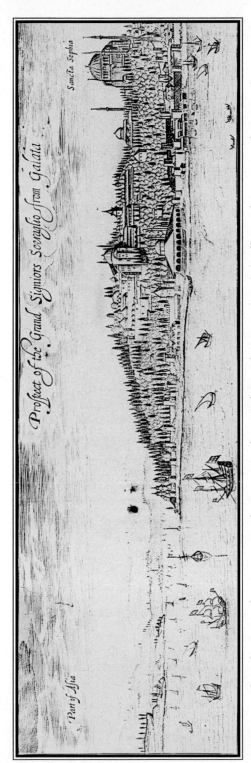

The Sultan's Seraglio, Constantinople. George Sandys, *A Relation of a Journey* (1621). *(Bodleian Library: Antiq. d. E. 1615. I)*

A Dervish.

A Turkish Dellee.

A Turkish Janissary.

All from Nicolas de Nicolay, *Le Navigationi et Viaggi* (1577). *(With permission, the Warden and Fellows, All Souls College, Oxford)*

Turkish punishments. In the background is Santa Sophia. Peter Mundy, *The Travels of Peter Mundy* (1907–36). *(Bodleian Library: G31. B 1. 1/NS 17)*

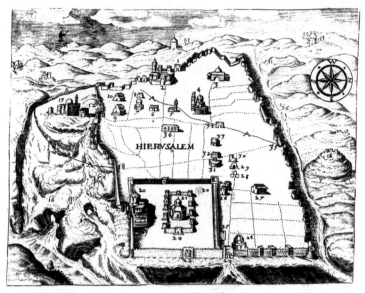

1. *The gate of Ioppa.*
2. *The Castle of the Pisans,*
3. *The Monastery of the Franciscans.*
4. *The Temple of the Sepulcher.*
5. *A Mosque, once a collegiat Church where stood the house of Zebedeus.*
6. *The iron gate.*
7. *The Church of S. Marke where his house stood.*
8. *A Chappell where once stood the house of S. Thomas.*
9. *The Church of S. Iames.*
10. *The Church of the Angels where once stood the pallace of Annas the High Priest.*
11. *The Port of Dauid.*
12. *The Church of S. Sauiour, where stood the pallace of Caiphas.*
13. *A Mosque, once a goodly Temple there standing, where stood the Cœnaculum.*
14. *Where the Iewes would haue taken away the body of the Blessed Virgin.*
15. *Where Peter wept.*
16. *The fountaine Siloe.*
17. *The fountaine of the Blessed Virgin.*
18. *Port sterquiline.*
19. *The Church of the Purification of the Blessed Virgin, now conuerted into a Mosque.*
20. *The court of Solomons Temple.*
21. *A Mosque, where stood the Temple of Solomon.*
22. *The Golden gate.*
23. *The gate of S. Steuen.*
24. *The Church of Anna, now a Mosque.*
25. *The Poole Bethesda.*
26. *Where the pallace of Pilate stood.*
27. *Where stood, as the say, the pallace of Herod.*
28. *Pilats arch.*
29. *The Church of the Blessed Virgins swouning.*
30. *Where they met Simon of Cyrene.*
31. *Where the rich Glutton dwelt.*
32. *Where the Pharisee dwelt.*
33. *Where Veronica dwelt.*
34. *The gate of Iustice.*
35. *Port Ephraim.*
36. *The Bazar.*
37. *The circuite of part of the old City.*

We entred as afore-said at the West gate called the gate of *Ioppa.* On the right hand and adioyning to the wall, there standeth a small ill-fortified Castle: yet the onely fort that belongeth to the City; weakely guarded, and not ouer-well stored with munition; built by the *Pisans* at such time as the Christians inhabited this City. Turning on the left hand, and ascending a part of Mount *Gihon,* we came to the Monastery of the *Franciscans* (being now in number betweene thirty and forty) who in the yeare 1561, thrust out of that which they had on Mount *Sion,* had this place assigned them. But of the founders name I am ignorant: nor is he much wronged by being forgotten: since so meane a building can giue no fame to the builder.

The

Sir Robert Sherley in Persian dress, by Antony Van Dyck. Petworth House, The Egremont Collection *(The National Trust, NTPL/Roy Fox)*

Sir Thomas Roe, Ambassador (1604). Samuel Purchas, *Purchas his Pilgrimes* (1905 edn.) *(Bodleian Library: 2031. d. 10)*

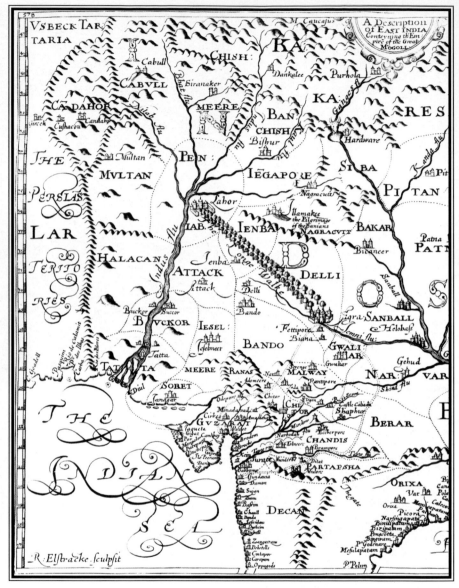

Sir Thomas Roe's map of the Mughal Empire (detail). The tree-lined Lahore–Agra road, the cow's head at Hardwar and the Hindu festival at Jallamakee derive from Coryate's reports. Samuel Purchas, *Purchas his Pilgrimes* (1905 edn.). *(Bodleian Library: 2031 d. 10)*

Title page of *Thomas Coriate, Traveller* (1616). Coryate is shown in full European dress with sword, boots and spurs, incorrectly. *(Bodleian Library: 4º L. Art. (18))*

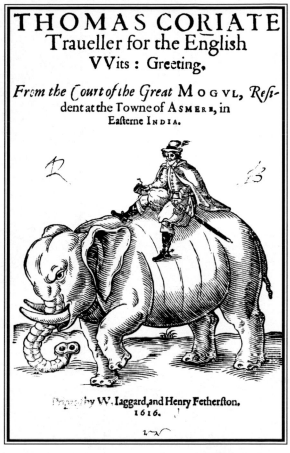

THOMAS CORIATE
Traueller for the English
VVits : Greeting.

From the Court of the Great MOGVL, *Refi-*
dent at the Towne of ASMERE, in
Eafterne INDIA.

Printed by W. Iaggard, and Henry Fetherfton.
1616.

The Emperor Jahangir, his son and woman slave. Taken from separate miniatures painted *c.* 1617 by the celebrated Hindu artist Manohar Das. The inscription is in Jahangir's hand, recording that this was by Manohar, at Mandu, in Jahangir's fiftieth year. A similar portrait of his son Shah Jehan, by Abu'l Hasan, is in the V&A. Samuel Purchas, *Purchas his Pilgrimes* (1905 edn.). *(Bodleian Library: 2031 d. 10)*

Pictures out of the Indian Copies made by the Mogols painter

Sultan Corooan &

his woman Slaue

Selim Shah the Great Mogoll

Frontispiece, Edward Terry,
A Voyage to East-India
(1655). *(Bodleian Library: 8⁰
T 26 Med.)*

In EUROPE, AFRICK, ASIA have I gonne,
One journey more, and then my travei's done.

The English factory in Surat. In the foreground, bullock carts transport goods. At
the back is the chapel, with a ship weathervane, and the garden with a dovecote.
On the right are warehouses, on the left, living quarters with roof terrace. J.A. von
Mandelslo, *Les Voyages célèbres* (1719). *(With kind permission of the Provost and
Fellows of the Queen's College, Oxford)*

caparisons, or accoutrements, that I weare as outward ornaments or invellopings of the more internall beauty of the mind within them . . . could stay the rugged robustious rage that your innated hereditary incivility or inhumanity hath made you to inflict upon me; I vow and sweare . . . that I will execute on you such confounding vengeance, that your offsprings offspring, to the 39th generation, shall ban [curse] with execrations as bitter as coloquintida [a bitter purgative] the day, houre, and baldpated Time of your audacious insolency.

Coryate had had enough, and went so far as to petition the King that Taylor should be punished for abusing him, but, not surprisingly, was brushed off. It appears that Coryate then found that *Laugh and be fat* had not been properly licensed, and appealed to the Wardens of the Stationers' Company, who had the book burned. All that happened was that, of course, Taylor got a licence and reissued the book (no doubt privately thanking Coryate for the publicity). Coryate had now become Taylor's prime butt for mockery; following Coryate's departure for the Levant in October 1612, in May 1613 Taylor brought out *Odcombs Complaint*, a mock elegy on Coryate's supposed death at sea (actually one of his better efforts):

> Hee was the Imp, whilst he on earth surviv'd
> From whom this west-worlds pastimes were deriv'd,
> He was in City, Country, Field and Court,
> The Well of dry brained Jests, the Pump of Sport . . .
> Who now like him in spite of wind and weather
> Will weare one shiftless shirt five months together?
> Who now to do his native country grace,
> Will for a Trophee execute his case?   [hang up his clothes]
> Who now will take the height of every *Gallowes*?
> Or who'll describe the height of every *Alehouse*?
> Each Tower, each Turret, and each lofty steeple,
> Who now (like him) will tel the vulgar people?
> Who now will set aworke so many writers,
> As he hath done in spite of his back biters,
> With Panegericks, Anagrams, Acrosticks,
> T'emblazon him the chiefe among fantasticks?

> Alas, not one, not one alive doth live,
> That to the world can such contentment give . . .

The poem goes on to give an account of Coryate drowning on
the way to Constantinople, the fish that eat him becoming
eloquent in Greek and Latin. August saw the publication of
*The Eighth Wonder of the World, or Coriat's Escape from his
supposed drowning*; word had got back of Coryate's doings,
and Taylor picked up on a mock knighthood conferred on
Coryate at (what he thought was) Troy:

> Here there was double dub'd a doughty knight,
> Rise up Sir Thomas, worship'd may'st thou be
> Of people all (that are as wise as thee).

Later still he got hold of Coryate's last letter, to his mother,
which he published in 1618 with some verses of his own,
more complimentary than offensive. Hearing of Coryate's
death, he wrote kindly of him in the course of his *Praise of
Hempseed* (1620):

> O famous Coriat, hadst thou come againe
> Thou wouldst have told us newes, direct and plaine . . .
> Of cranes, and pigmes, lizzards, buzzards, owles,
> Of some with hornes, of thousand beasts and fowles . . .
> But farewell Thomas, never to returne
> Rest thou in peace within thy forraigne Urne,
> Hempseed did beare thee o'er the raging fome
>   [sails and rigging made of hemp]
> And O I wish that it had brought thee home,
> For if thou hadst come back, as I did hope,
> Thy fellow had not been beneath the cope.   [heavens]
> But we must loose that which we cannot save,
> And freely leave thee whom we cannot have.

All this was yet to come; but by the autumn of 1612, after a
last, farewell oration to friends and neighbours at Odcombe
Cross, Coryate was gone, 'in desire of many marvels over sea',

in Kipling's phrase. He was not seeking wealth: people remarked on his indifference to possessions, and even Thomas Fuller, no admirer, said he cared 'for coin and counters alike; so contented with what was present, that he accounted those men guilty of superfluity who had more suits and shirts than bodies, seldom putting off either till they were ready to go away from him'. Driven by wanderlust, what he sought was 'that last infirmity of noble mind', fame, in his own time and after, as explorer and reporter on the Ottoman Empire, the Holy Land, and beyond, wherever his wandering feet might take him.

In 1585 Sir Richard Grenville ('of *The Revenge*') wrote as Tom might now have done:

> Who seekes the way to win renowne,
> Or flies with wings of high desire,
> Who seekes to wear the lawrell crowne,
> Or hath the minde that would aspire,
> Let him his native soil eschewe,
> Let him go range, and seeke anewe. . . .
>
> To passe the seas some thinke a toile,
> Some thinke it strange abroad to roame;
> Some thinke it a griefe to leave their soile,
> Their parentes, kinfolk, and their home.
> Thinke so who list, I like it not:
> I must abroade to try my lot. . . .
>
> Wherefore who lust may live at home,
> To purchase fame I will go roam.

Sailing to Byzantium

On 20 October 1612 Coryate set off for the last time: it is not clear from Samuel Purchas's edited version of Tom's notes (in *Purchas his Pilgrimes*, part II, book X), which are all we have to go on for his Levantine travels, whether this refers to his leaving Odcombe or London, or setting sail. The sea journey – probably in a small trading vessel of the Levant Company – was not without its perils: the Dunkirk pirates ranged the length of the Channel, and autumn storms could be expected in the Atlantic and the Bay of Biscay. A poem by one R.R., printed in one of Coryate's letters from India, reports on the irrepressible scholar-traveller aboard ship:

> To see him in a Morning Sunne,
> In his rough Lambeskin and bare gowne
>   the Scuttle hole ascending,   [hatchway to the deck]
> Would make a horse his halter breake,
>   [presumably with laughter]
> To heare him vomit forth his Greeke
>   with all the Ship contending.

Coryate, as a word-man, relished sailors' jargon, which he loved to parade:

> With Starboord, Larboorde, Helme, Alee,
> Full, Come no neere, 'tis done, quoth he
>   who at the Helme doth stand.
> War no more, cries an angry Mate,
> Oh Odcombe, these be termes of State,
>   not usuall on the land.

The ship did not make particularly good progress, possibly delayed by bad weather:

> On Christmas day he drunke in jest,
> Conjur'd a storme out of the East,
>   in clambring up the cradle:
>   [a framework or platform on the mast]
> Before, the winde was wondrous faire,
> Now forc't to ride in Gebralter,
>   withouten horse or saddle.

There may have been other dangers:

> Of Drums, Guns, Trumpets, he will tell,
> Of haling Ships, of Pyrats fell . . .

All along the North African coasts were the nests of the Barbary corsair raiders: the states of Morocco, Algiers, Tripoli and Tunis, though theoretically subject to the Turks, operated independently, receiving a considerable portion of their income from their privateers, the corsairs, who seized passing ships and their cargoes, and sold into slavery thousands of sailors and passengers – 'the cage of unclean birds of prey, the habitation of sea-devils . . . the whip of the Christian world, the wall of the Barbarian; terror of Europe . . . scourge of the islands, den of pirates', as Samuel Purchas expressed it. Purchas seems to think of the corsairs as not European, but Christopher Marlowe (in *Tamburlaine I*) knew that quite a few of 'that damned train' were in fact 'straggling runagates' from northern Europe, often from England (particularly after James I's peace policy gave them less to do). One of the most notorious was John Ward, who transferred himself and his English crew and ship to Tunis; in 1607 he captured a large Venetian treasure ship; William Lithgow met him in retirement in 1615. Between 1600 and 1640, over 800 British and Irish trading vessels were taken, and at least 12,000 of their men sold into slavery (usually lifelong) in North Africa and the Ottoman Empire, these being, of course, but a very small proportion of the European numbers overall.

When Coryate and his shipmates passed through in
midwinter, it was the worst time of the year: from May to
October a Turkish fleet of up to sixty galleys patrolled the
Mediterranean, collecting tribute money and restraining
privateering, but during the winter months the corsairs
operated unchecked. Nevertheless, the little ship got through,
and arrived at the island of Zante (modern Zakinthos) in the
Ionian Sea on 13 January.

Being part of the Venetian Empire (though paying a tribute
of falcons – probably light cannon, so-called, rather than
hunting birds – to the Turks, who raided Venetian ships in the
area), Zante normally required a bolleta, or certificate of
health, from travellers – especially from the East; it appears
that the English travellers were excused this. A major reason
for calling here was trade: with its 'commodious haven', as
Fynes Moryson observed, and advantageous position relative
to Greece, Venice and Cyprus, Zante did well as an entrepôt, as
well as an exporter of 'the best oile of the worlde . . . excellent
strong wines . . . [and, especially] currants', as George Sandys
(1578–1644, minor poet and seventh son of the Archbishop of
York) noted a few years later. William Lithgow, typically,
disapproved of 'some Liquorous lips' in England, 'who
forsooth can hardly digest Bread, Pasties, Broth and (verbi
gratia) bag-pudding without these curraunts. And as these
Rascall Greekes becoming proud of late with this lavish
expence, contemne justly this sensuall prodigality, I have
heard them often demaund the English in a filthy derision
what they did with such Leprous stuffe . . . There is no other
Nation save this thus addicted to that miserable Ile.' Indeed,
the young shepherd in *The Winter's Tale* was sent to buy
currants for the sheep-shearers' feast. Certainly the men of
Zante were ruthless businessmen: Sandys tells of an English
sailor pursued on board ship, and killed, for not paying
customs duty on a small bag of currants; fortunately, Coryate
had learned his lesson in Germany, or was warned by the
resident English merchants. Among the sights of Zante were
the women scandalously riding their donkeys astride, which

Coryate had 'never read or heard of amongst any other women' (though it may have been an Italian practice: Moryson 'mett a Dutches carryed in a horse litter to Rome, whose gentlewomen and ladyes of honour rode astride upon ordinary hackney horses, in dobletts and breeches'). He also inspected an unmarked grave, reputed to be that of Cicero; as usual, he was distressed by the lack of commemoration (the tombstone had been removed to Venice).

Coryate, like other visitors generally, remarked on the frequency of earthquakes in the island, and the consequently flat roofs on the low houses. The windows were not glazed, but had wooden lattices, which were often removed in the heat of summer, 'and then, seeing they are Greekes, and merrie Greekes too, they may be very properly said to keepe open house'. Ho ho. The violent earthquakes often drove people out of their houses, 'even out of their naked beds, men in their shirts, women in their smocks, carrying their clothes with them, that they have hastily caught up'. He 'observed a strange custome . . . for whensoever any one of the kindred is married, all the day, all of the consanguinity do hang out of their Windowes certaine Carpets, by which it is generally knowne in the Towne that such a one is married'. The more worldly Sandys has a different account: 'The nuptiall shootes (as in some cases commanded by the Moysaicall law) are publickly shewne: and preserved by their parents as a testimonie of their incorrupted virginities.' The triumphant banner was flaunted at the end of a ruthless campaign of prevention: 'The Bridegroom entring the Church, sticks his dagger in the doore, held [believed] available against inchantments. For here it is a common practice to bewitch them: made thereby impotent with their wives, untill the charme be burnt, or otherwise consumed: insomuch that sometimes (as they say) the mother of the betrothed, by way of prevention do bewitch them themselves, and againe unloose them as soone as the mariage is consummated.'

The next busy port of call was the fertile island of Chios (where the Levant Company had an agent), in the Aegean, off

the west coast of Turkey. It appears to have served as an
entrepôt for the area, exporting spices, currants, silks, oils,
wines and carpets. 'Out of Syo a great Tribute of twentie
thousand Chicquins [sequins, zecchini: gold coins of Italy
and Turkey, then worth seven to nine shillings] ariseth unto
the Grand Signior, out of a principall Commoditie that this
Iland yeeldeth, viz. Masticke [*pistachius lentiscus*, a resinous
gum, then used in medicine and for chewing], which groweth
heere only of all the places of the World.' The women of
Chios had a reputation for beauty, 'I will not say
undeservedly', wrote Sandys, and Nicolas de Nicolay even
included in his book *Les Navigations* a picture of a Chiote
woman in her finery (the artist unfortunately failing to bring
out features attractive to a modern eye). William Lithgow,
after remarking that the monks here 'have a braver sort of life
for good cheare, fat Wines, and delicate Lechery, than any
sort of Friers can elsewhere find in the world', has a
characteristically sour note:

> The Women of the Citie are the most beautiful Dames (or rather
> Angelicall creatures) of all the Greekes in the World, and greatly
> given to Venery . . . They are for the most part exceeding proude,
> and sumptuous in apparell, and commonly goe (even Artificers
> Wives) in Gownes of Sattin and Taffetay; yea of Cloth of Silver and
> Gold, and are adorned with Precious Stones and Gemmes, and
> Jewels about their neckes and hands. Their Husbands are their
> Panders, and when they see any stranger arrive, they will presently
> demand of him, if he would have a Mistris: and so they make
> whoores of their owne wives, and are contented for a little gaine,
> to weare Hornes. If a Stranger be desirous to stay all night with
> them, their price is a Chicken [chequin] of Gold, nine shillings
> English, out of which this companion receiveth his supper, and for
> his paines, a belly full of sinful content.

It is remarkable how generally Lithgow seems to know about
such things. Modest, serious Coryate says nothing of such
matters; while staying at Chios, he rode out with three
English residents, hoping to see the tomb of Homer (claimed

by at least five other Greek cities), but got only as far as the Greek monastery of Nea Mona. There, he was most impressed by the sight of an eight-foot-high wax candle, 'so bigge as my middle, for I measured it with my girdle', but was unimpressed by the monks' ignorance of classical Greek (they not having been to Oxford).

After Coryate had sailed north-east through the Aegean and past the Dardanelles, his classical interests dictated his next stopping place, when on 22 February he landed, with fourteen other Englishmen and a dragoman (a guide-interpreter), 'all well weaponed for fear of any hostile invasion by the Turkes', at what he believed was the site of the ancient city of Troy, but was actually Alexandria Troas, about 14 miles to the south-west. Once one of the important trading centres of the Graeco-Roman world, it was now chiefly remarkable for its extensive ruins, which Coryate enthusiastically identified with the various buildings of the true Troy, with many broken pillars, marble tombs with obscured inscriptions, tumbled stones, fruit trees, and vaults filled with cattle dung. Other Englishmen visited the place, including Lithgow and George Sandys, who commented on it briefly. Classicist Coryate was extremely enthusiastic, and examined it with care, writing some 4,500 words of detailed description: credit to him for the effort, even if mistaken. After they had been there for some time, a friend, Robert Rugge (probably the versifier, R.R.), observing the trouble that Coryate had gone to,

in a merrie humour drew his Sword out of his Scabberd, and ascending to one of these great stones that lye in the open part of this middle Gate, Knighted mee, that kneeled upon another stone on my right knee, by the name of the first English Knight of Troy, and at the Knighting of mee, pronounced these wittie Verses extempore:

Coryate no more, but now a Knight of Troy,
   Odcombe no more, but henceforth Englands Joy.
Brave Brute of our best English wits commended,
                    [Brutus, reputed founder of Britain]

> True Trojane from Aeneas race descended.
> Rise top of wit, the honour of our Nation,
> And to old Ilium make a new Oration.

Coryate never needed a second invitation to make an oration; after reassuring two poor Turkish bystanders, who thought Rugge had been going to behead him, and after two celebratory volleys of shot, he provided an answering verse:

> Loe heere with prostrate knee I doe embrace
>   The gallant title of a Trojane Knight.
> In Priam's Court which time shall ne're deface;
>   A grace unknowne to any Brittish Wight.
> This noble Knighthood shall Fames Trumpe resound,
>   To Odcombes honour maugre Envie fell,   [despite]
> Till that my mournfull friends shall ring my knell.

He wrote out the entire oration, which Purchas entitled 'Quintessence of Coriat'. One can imagine fourteen Englishmen, probably still cumbered with their muskets and swords, together with a few uncomprehending Turkish peasants, standing or sitting about in a stony, windy field, while the little man, perched on a large stone, harangued them at length. After celebrating their arrival 'after so many bitter stormes, and cruell conflicts of the winds, in the most renowned place of the whole world (only Gods sacred Citie of Jerusalem excepted)', he reflects how, after Troy's ancient greatness, 'this grievous desolation may justly draw both sorrow from the hearts and teares from the eyes of all such as are endued with a true instinct of humanitie', as an illustration of the mutability of fortune – human transience and mortal oblivion his recurrent concern. After a review of ancient empires, he concludes how Troy's fate provides a warning against lechery, 'for Adulterie was the principall cause of the ruines of this Citie', and takes occasion to pray to Jehovah, 'which is the rewarder of Chastitie, and severe punisher of incontinence, to avert the punishment from our new Troy (for indeed, London was in former times called Troynovant) which

I think is as much polluted and contaminated with extravagant lusts as ever was this old Troy'.

Finally, he and another Englishman persuaded a farmer ploughing his field to let them do some ploughing, 'that if wee live to be Old men we may say in our old age, we had once holden the Plough in the Trojan Territorie' (remembering a line in Ovid's *Heroides* to the effect, 'Corn now grows where once Troy stood'). William Lithgow, who visited the place in 1614, was more jaundiced, and sceptical as to its identity: 'Well I wote, I saw infinite old sepulchres, but for their particular names and nominations I suspend, neither could I beleeve my Interpreter, sith it is more than three thousand and odde yeeres agoe that Troy was destroyed', but he too came up with his Ovid: 'Nunc seges est ubi Troia fuit.' Tom, however, was overjoyed, declaring that he would have forgone £500 to have been there: 'Therefore let me advise all my Country-men that meane to travell in the world for observation to see this famous place in their Travels, as being farre the most worthiest of all the ruined places in the world that are not Inhabited.'

A day or so later they called in at the little island of Cyzicus in the Sea of Marmora, and inspected more Graeco-Roman ruins. Coryate picked up a white marble head, of which he later boasted to the antiquarian Sir Robert Cotton, in one of his Indian letters; what became of it is not known – he probably left it, to be collected on his way home, at the residence of the English Ambassador in Constantinople, their next destination.

> White founts falling in the courts of the sun,
> And the Soldan of Byzantium is smiling as they run . . .

The city at which Coryate arrived, late in March 1613, was the capital of the great Ottoman Empire, then perhaps just past its very peak. The famous battle of Lepanto in 1571 (in which Cervantes took part), when over 220 Turkish galleys and galliots were captured, over 40 sunk and 12,000 Christian slaves released, as eloquently celebrated in G.K. Chesterton's poem quoted here, was perhaps the turning point, though the Turkish fleet and control of the eastern Mediterranean were soon restored, and the Empire appeared undiminished for several years. Richard Knolles, in his monumental *Generall Historie of the Turkes* (1603, 1700), describes the Sultan keeping

> four great Armies, two at Land, the one against the *Persians*, his antient Enemy, the other (consisting in a manner all of *Tartarians*) against the King of Poland . . . And two naval Armies, the one in the Black Sea against the Cossacks or Russians, who made daily Incursions into the Othomans Country [in log canoes] . . . The Turks fourth army is in the white Sea, as they call it, employed either to conduct the Caravan which brings the Tribute from *Egypt* to *Constantinople*, or in search of the Gallies of *Malta* and *Florence*, which scoure those Seas continually to annoy the Turk.

The Empire's territory stretched northwards through Greece, the Balkans and Hungary as far as Vienna, eastwards through Turkey to the Persian Empire, southwards through Palestine towards Egypt, westwards along the north coast of Africa, with its fleets and the Barbary corsairs, raiding the Venetians, southern France and Spain, and reaching out into the Atlantic. (A prayer was introduced into the English liturgy in 1565: 'O Almighty and Everlasting God, our Heavenly Father, we thy disobedient and rebellious children, now by thy just judgment sore afflicted, and in great danger to be oppressed by thine and our sworn and most deadly enemies the Turks . . .'; in 1630 the Turks captured six ships near Bristol, and even in 1645 raided Fowey in Cornwall, enslaving 240 inhabitants.) The wealth of the vast empire flowed into Constantinople (captured in 1453), itself one of the great world cities, an urban monster of well over 400,000 inhabitants (George Sandys estimated a population of 700,000, half Turkish and half Jews and Greek Christians), depending for sustenance on the flocks of sheep in the Balkans, rice, beans and corn from Egypt and oxen, camels and horses from Asia Minor, and maintained by slaves from the Caucasus, the Balkans and northern Africa. At its heart was the Sultan, or Grand Signior, in his magnificent palaces. Apart from these, Santa Sophia and the palaces of the Bashaw nobles, Fynes

Moryson was not greatly impressed by the rest of the city: low, flat-roofed, flimsy buildings, frequently catching fire. The city was notorious for its frequent fires – there were three serious fires in five weeks while Coryate was there. He observed, 'it doth often happen that Janizaries [the Sultan's soldiers] doe of purpose set Houses on fire, even to the great endangering of the Citie, for prey and spoile sake, especially the houses of Jewes'. On 20 April a Bashaw (actually the chief Admiral of the Fleet) killed a janissary looting a house during a fire. There was an unusual fire-prevention policy: 'It is the Custome that whensoever any Fire riseth in the Citie, to Hang up him in whose House it beginneth, as now a Cooke in whose house it began was Hanged presently after the Fire ceased.'

The poor state of much of the building was explained as being due to the fact that the Sultan automatically inherited all the property of those dying 'in the hideous Gulfe of the Vast Empire', so that it was never worth while investing in or improving property. Moryson describes the ordinary buildings of the city as having

> no magnificence, being partly of a matter like bricke, but white, and (as it seems) unhardened by fire, partly of timber and clay . . . The streetes of this Citie are narrow, and shadowed with pentises of wood, and upon both sides the way is raised some foot high, but of little breadth, and paved for men and women to passe, the middest of the street being left low and unpaved, and no broader then for the passage of Asses or beasts loaded. In many places of the streetes lye carcases, yea sometimes the bodies of dead men, even till they be putrified, and I thinke this uncleanlinesse of the Turkes (who otherwise place Religion in washing their bodies, and keeping their apparrell, especially their Tulbent [turban] pure and cleane) is the chief cause that this Citie, though most pleasantly seated, yet above all the Cities of the world is continually more or less infected with the plague.

William Lithgow, in poetic mood, described the city as

> A painted whoore, the maske of deadly sin,
> Sweet faire without, and stinking foule within.

English trade with the Ottoman Empire had developed in the later sixteenth century; in 1580 a trading treaty was signed, and the Levant Company was given the trade monopoly. In 1582 the Company appointed an agent, effectively the English Ambassador, in Constantinople, who supervised the importation there of English cloth, furs, skins and tin, and the export to England of spices, currants, silks, carpets and so on. He also had the pleasure of being host, in his hill-top house with pleasant walled garden and large field, set outside the city, to English visitors, including at various times Moryson, Lithgow, Sandys and Coryate. Economical Tom appears to have enjoyed free board with the then Ambassador, Paul Pindar, for ten months, besides being taught Turkish and Italian (the 'lingua franca' of the Mediterranean) by the English chaplain, William Ford. Irritatingly, Purchas did not print all Coryate's account of his time in the city, presuming it would duplicate other accounts that he had already printed, to some of which we have to turn to provide a context for Coryate's writing.

Peter Mundy, who was there in 1617, is the most eloquent and enraptured about the palace:

The Seraglio [not just the women's quarters, but the extensive private apartments of the palace] is the pallace of the Gran Signior inclosing as much ground as St James parcke: Large Courts: Spacious gardens, embattled walles, stored with Artillerie . . . in the middest there riseth a Core of three or four Roomes with Chimneys whose mantle trees [chimney-breasts] are of silver, curiously glazed, protected with an Iron grate all gilt over most gloriously. The whole frame soe set with Opalls, Rubies, Emeralds, burnisht with gold, painted with flowers and graced with Inlaid worcke of porphyry, marble, Jett, Jasper and delicate stones, that I am perswaded that there is not such a bird cage in the world. Under the walles are stables for sea horses, called hippopotamie, which is a monstrous beast taken in Nilus: Elephants, tigres and Dolphins: Sometimes they have Crocodiles and Rinoceros. Within are Roebucks, white partridges, and turtles, the bird of Arabia, and many beasts and fowle of Aphrica and India. The walkes are shaded with Cipresse, Cedar, turpentine [terebinth tree], and trees which we only know by their names.

Mundy is also probably the most informative about life within the palace, describing the beautiful audience chamber, with its delicately carved fountains, sofa with carpets of gold and crimson velvet embroidered with pearls, and walls covered with silver plate decorated with gold. The women's quarters contained, he estimated, some 2,000 women, the 'young virgins taken and stollen from forren Nations' – often from Circassia, north of the Caucasus, an area famed for beautiful women; theoretically Islam forbade the enslavement of Muslims, Christians and Jews, but there were ways round this, by taking prisoners, receiving human gifts, or buying those already enslaved by others. (Knolles wrote that the Sultan, Achmet I, 'was much given to Sensuality and Pleasure: for the which he entertained three thousand Concubines and Virgins in a Seraglio, being the fairest Daughters of the Christians. His Mother was a Christian of Bosn[i]a, or of Cyprus, and therefore it is thought he was somewhat favourable to the Christian'.) The young women were supervised and trained by older women, and kept in large dormitories. When the Sultan was in the mood, a selection was lined up, and he signified his choice by wordlessly giving a handkerchief to the chosen one; that night she was brought to his bed (the bedposts silver, topped with crystal lions, the canopy, bolsters and mattresses covered in cloth of gold); in the morning he left behind his clothes and any money in them, and sent her a present, in proportion to 'the satisfaction and content which he received from her that night'.

The Sultan's daughters, sisters, aunts and female cousins ('whom he reckons up by dozens') lived in the palace until married off to the Bashaws (noblemen), whom they completely dominated – at dagger point, if need be; the unmarried remainder 'live and dyet with the rest, wasting their youthfull dayes amongst themselves in evill thoughts (for they are too well lookt unto to offend in Act)'. Indeed, any phallic objects, such as 'cucumbers, gourds, or such like meates . . . are sent in unto them sliced, to deprive them of the meanes of playing the wantons; for, they all being young, lustie, and lascivious Wenches, and wanting the societie of Men (which would better instruct them) are doubtlesse of themselves inclined to that which is naught, and will be possesst of unchast thoughts'.

Mundy also tells us of the better parts of the city, where the 'Bashaws houses, mosques, Conduits, tombes and monuments are even as it were a storehouse of magnificent worcks . . . heapes of Ostentation and fabriques of great delight . . . to these you may adde the Besistene, a place like our Exchange, for varietie of merchandise, market of Virgins, Selling of Slaves, ducts under ground fenced with Iron gates to secure their treasure'. Most visitors commented on the slave market; Fynes Moryson saw 'captives to be sold and the buyers had as much freedom to take the virgins aside to see and feele the parts of their body as if they had bene to buy a beast'. While he was walking near the market, an old woman offered to buy him from his janissary guide, for 'an hundred Aspers, that is some eight shillings fower pence English', but for a sturdy young servant man was prepared to pay 400 aspers. Lithgow described the slaves as mostly 'Hungarians, Transilvanians, Carindians [Carinthians], Istrians and Dalmatians', and relates how he and a French sea captain resolved to buy and release one or two Christian captives. Lithgow wanted to save an old man or woman, but the Frenchman wanted to buy 'some virgin or young widdow, to save their bodies undefloured with Infidels. The price of a virgin was too deare for him, being a hundred Duckets, and widdows were farre under and at an easier rate. When we did visite and search them that we were mindfull to buy, they were strip'd starke naked before our eyes, where the sweetest face, the youngest age, and whitest skin was in greatest value and request.' They bought a young widow for 36 ducats; the captain took her off to Galata (on the other side of the straits), and used her sexually that night, to her distress. When Lithgow found out, he threatened the captain, who released her to him and sailed off; Lithgow gave her her liberty, and got her a job in 'a Tavern' (whatever that may mean).

Eunuchs were also for sale; it having been found that mere gelding was not sufficient to guarantee incapacity, in some cases boys were completely castrated, Sandys writes, 'making all smooth as the backe of the hand (whereof divers do die in the cutting) who supply the uses of nature with a silver quill, which they weare in their Turbants'. The slave market was every Wednesday, 'and every one comes freely, to buy for their several uses', reported Robert Withers (*Pilgrimes*, Book X) 'some for Nurses, some for Servants, and some for their Lustfull appetites'. Coryate remarks how 'the Turkes are exceedingly given to Sodomie, and therefore divers keep prettie boyes, to abuse them by preposterous [backwards] venerie'. Sandys also describes the Turkish baths, with separate rooms for men and women; after describing the bathing, the scrubbing clean of the men with rough cloths, and the anointing of the women with an ointment from Chios, he concludes: 'Much unnaturall and filthie lust is said to be committed daily in the remote closets of these darksome Bannias [bagnios, bath-houses]: yea women with women; a thing incredible, if former times had not given thereunto both detection and punishment.'

Coryate, however, was more concerned with religious practices among Catholics, Muslims and Jews, all exotic and intriguing, and to be disapproved of by a Protestant clergyman's son. One of the first things he saw, on Thursday 1 April, was a public flagellation ceremony: 'certaine fellowes prostrating themselves in the middle of the Quire of the Church, directly before the high Altar, whipped themselves very cruelly, and continued in the mercilesse punishment of themselves at the least an houre and a halfe.' They were not friars, as he had thought at first, but slaves, acting as proxies for others' penances, in order to buy their liberty by this means. Purchas has a sharp marginal note: 'These hypocrites which doe Penance by others must goe to Heaven by proxie too.' The flagellants 'did endure such bitter chastisement which they inflicted upon themselves, that I could scarce behold them with drie eyes', wrote Coryate. Their faces were veiled, but all the middle part of their backe was naked which they lashed with certaine Napkins, at the ends whereof . . . were inclosed certaine little sharp peeces of Iron, made like the straight part of the rowell of a Spurre, which at the very first blow that it layd upon the skinne did easily draw blood . . . one of them that dealt somwhat roughly with himselfe by redoubling his blowes a little faster than the rest, did fetch off all the skin from the middle part of his backe, which was a very dolefull and tragicall Spectacle, and when he had very bitterly whipped himselfe, there came a certaine fellow with a Cloth in his hand steeped in Vinegar, with which he wiped away the blood that it should not rankle [fester] . . . This severe Discipline being now ended, one of the Friers ascended the Pulpit and made a Sermon in the Italian Tongue concerning the Passion of Christ.

Such spectacles of pain are generally popular, and several 'gentlemen of Qualitie', including the French ambassador, were keen spectators; actually, galley slaves in Venice could buy out their liberty by similar means, and Montaigne once saw an equivalent, 500-strong mass flagellation in Rome.

From Rome, to Islam: on 9 April Coryate observed the ritual of the whirling dervishes (Sandys confirms that these ceremonies took place on Tuesdays and Fridays). He had to earn his entertainment, with patience:

A certaine Singing-man sitting apart in an upper roome began to sing certaine Hymnes, but with the most unpleasant and harsh notes that ever I have heard, exceedingly differing from our Christian Church singing, for the yelling and disorderly squeaking of them did even grate mine eares. Whensoever he pronounced the Name of Mahomet, all of them did cast downe the Heads to the knees. After hee had done, the Interpreter of the Law ascended into a Chaire, and read a certaine Turkish Booke for some halfe houre to the Assembly . . . Almost a quarter of an houre before he had done, three Pipers sitting in the roome with the Singer, began to play upon certaine long Pipes not unlike Tabors, which yeelded a very ridiculous and foolish Musicke, and continued so very neere a quarter of an houre after the Clergie man had ended his Lecture . . . Having played very neere a quarter of an houre, upon a sodaine they sounded much louder then ordinarie, whereupon some five and twentie of the two and fiftie Dervises suddainly rose up bare legged and bare-footed, and casting aside their upper Garment some of them having their brests all uncovered, they began by little and little to turne about the Interpreter of the Law turning gently in the middest of them all, afterward they redoubled their force and turned with such incredible swiftnesse, that I could not chuse but admire it. . . . This turning they kept for the space of one whole houre at the least: during which time, sometimes they turned exceeding swiftly, sometimes very gently. After they had halfe done, the Singer in the upper roome began to singe againe, at the pronunciation of some of whose words, the Darvises sodainly mumbled out certaine strange tearmes, with a most hideous kind of murmuring that did in a manner terrifie and astonish us that were meere Strangers to these Ceremonies . . . This exercise now driving to an end, one of the Dervises beginneth some prayer in Arabicke, and continually turning about with the rest of the Company, pronounceth it with a very audible voyce, and his Prayer being ended, there is an upshot of this ridiculous and Ethnicke devotion for this time.

Coryate attended various Jewish religious ceremonies, about which he was equally ignorantly hostile: 'I found the irreverence of the Jewes in Venice and those of Constantinople to be like in the service of God. They neither uncover nor kneele the whole time of their Prayer.' One ceremony that he was pleased to attend was the circumcision of the infant son of 'an English Jew, called Amis, born in the Crootched Friers in London':

The whole company being desirous that we Christians should observe their ceremonie, called us to approach neere to the child. And when we came, a certaine other Jew drawing forth a little Instrument made not unlike those small cissers that our Ladies and Gentlemen doe much use, did with the same cut off the Prepuce or fore-skinne of the child, and after a very strange manner unused (I beleeve) of the ancient Hebrewes, did put his mouth to the childs yard, and sucked up the bloud.

After the child had been powdered and given some wine to comfort him, 'the Prepuce that was cut off was carried to the Mother, who keepeth it very preciously as a thing of worth'.

There was also a notably more spectacular ceremony marking the circumcision of three of the Muslim Vizier's teenage sons,

> the custome being such, that when the Sonnes of any eminent Turke is circumcised, a little before they performe the act upon him, he rideth up and downe the City with great solemnity with divers Jewels of great prize in his Turbant, his long locke hanging downe behind his back artificially woven and wrought in curious pleites and tresses, and adorned with Diamonds and other sparkling stones of great value. Likewise they have two long Pendants made of Gold Plate . . . In their Turbant beside their Jewels they weare blacke Ostridge-feathers. Some of them weare upper Vests of cloth of Gold, and Cimiters by their sides . . . Before the youths certaine Gemilands walke afoot, carrying certaine strange devices . . . Likewise neere to them goe certaine Flutes that yeeld a very ridiculous and squeaking Musicke.

After the ceremony, the Vizier laid on a spectacular firework display, with rockets shooting 'as high as the highest steeple in Constantinople', with other fireworks reflected in the water, while 'among the rest of these fire-works I observed some made upon the very shoare itselfe with singular cunning resembling the shape of Cypress-trees, a very pleasing and delectable object to behold'.

The most magnificent ceremony he witnessed was the triumphal entry into the city of the Grand Sultan, on 28 April. Sultan Achmet I had succeeded to the throne in 1604 aged 15, after the usual family slaughter. His father, Mahomet III, on his accession, had had all his nineteen brothers strangled, and, Knolles relates, 'at once to rid himself of the fear of all Competitors . . . caused ten of his Fathers Wives and Concubines, such as by whom any Issue was to be feared, to be all drowned in the Sea'. Later, suspecting his eldest son, Mahomet, of planning a coup, he had him strangled in front of him; finding him to have been innocent, he hanged the

Bashaw who had carried out the execution. Knolles describes Achmet as 'not so cruel as many of his Predecessors', and only one brother had to be strangled. At this time Achmet had been engaged in campaigns in Hungary and Transylvania, but had to return to deal with problems in Anatolia, and Turkish rebels. As the city was suffering one of its recurrent attacks of plague, he waited in Adrianople until it had died down. 'He then came unto the City,' reports Knolles,

whereas he made a very stately entry; before him there marched his ordinary Guard of five and twenty or thirty thousand Janizaries, all the Bassaes of the Court followed him in very great Pomp . . . Passing before the Mosques, the Talismans or Priests of his Law made Sacrifices in his Presence for his Prosperity, they slew Sheep and Oxen upon Altars erected for that purpose, then they cut them in pieces, and gave them unto the people.

Coryate watched the great procession: 'The pompe of it was so gallant that I never saw the like in my life . . . the people that attended upon his person at that time were said to amount to the number of 15,000. First rode the Subbashaw of Constantinople and Galata, with one hundred men on horseback,' followed by footsoldiers with muskets, some 120 renegade French soldiers, some carrying model galleys ('a very strange and ridiculous conceit; for indeed everie one laughed heartily at it'); then came 'Squibsters' (possibly grenade-throwers) and young footsoldiers, 'whereof one had a feather sticking in his flesh, even in his face somewhat neere to his eye', then the Sultan's gold coach (empty – the Sultan had entered the city earlier, with a few companions), 'then a Delee, that is a foole with a Bears skinne upon his back'. (Fynes Moryson gives a fuller account of the Dellis, light horsemen armed with scimitars: 'wearing a Gippo or Jackett, and breeches of the skins of lyons and beares, with the hayre outward, and Capps of the skins of ownees [ounces?] and leopards covered with an Eagles Wing, which wings they also fasten to their bucklers, and the hinder parts of their horses are

covered with skinns of lyons and wilde beasts, affecting
thereby to seeme terrible to their Enemyes.') Then came 200
cha'usches (middle-ranking officers employed as messengers:
the word entered the English language as 'chiause' – see Ben
Jonson's *The Alchemist* of 1610 – to mean a fraud or impostor,
after one was sent on a diplomatic mission to London in 1607
and was mistakenly treated with the dignity of a full
ambassador); then came seven more coaches, and then more
than 4,000 mounted janissaries. These were men largely
forcibly recruited from Turkish-occupied territories, especially
in the Balkans, converted and trained from 10 years old as
Muslim warriors, dedicated to the Sultan personally but
otherwise largely independent (and as such somewhat of a
force for disorder – on his accession, Achmet had had to buy
them off with large sums of money). Some of them became
figures of enormous authority throughout the Ottoman Empire,
others could be hired as 'security forces', available as guards
and guides but a menace to unprotected non-Muslims and
even to other Muslims, being largely outside the law. Sandys
describes how they

> serve with harquebushes [heavy muskets, supported on props],
> armed beside with cymiter, and hatchets. They weare on their
> heads a bonnet of white felt, with a flap hanginge downe behind to
> their shoulders, adorned about the browes with a wreathe of
> metall, gilt, and set with stones of small value; having a kind of
> sheathe or socket of the same erected before, wherein such are
> suffered to sticke plumes of feathers as have behaved themselves
> extraordinary bravely.

On and on went the procession: horses with leather water
bags; long-haired, ragged holy men; a black elephant; 112
ladies on horseback with 300 attendants; the Mufti; eight head
Viziers with 100 chiauses; musicians; dervishes; 100 pikemen;
more ladies; 100 greyhounds and more chiauses; a man with a
green taffeta streamer with Arabic writing, another with a
battle standard of a horse's tail; archers; and so on.

Coryate did not know of a plot by the janissaries, as reported by Knolles, to murder the Grand Vizier during the procession,

> as he should enter in at the North Gate coming from *Adrianople*, [having] placed themselves there for the effecting of what they had intended; but coming near unto the Gate, the Sultan (being ignorant of what was intended against the Visier) called for him to speak to him, keeping him by him until he was entered into the City, by which means he escaped the intended practice. Soon after, Nassuff [the Vizier] invited the Sultan to a sumptuous Feast, and within a few days after the Emperor feasted the Visier; who, presuming upon his great credit, caused all the Crosses in the Church of St *Sophia* . . . to be thrown down, and all the Images to be defaced, the which had stood intire ever since the Christians Government.

Knolles also reports a curious episode that took place shortly after:

> The Grand Seignior being returned to *Constantinople* after the great Plague, notwithstanding the Turks hold a firm Opinion of Predestination, and that they shall not die before their appointed time, and that the time of their Death is written in their Foreheads; yet, apprehending the Infection, by the advice of some about him, he commanded all the Dogs in the City of *Constantinople* to be transported unto *Scutary* in *Asia* . . . and for the due Execution thereof, every Housholder was to bring his Dog first to the Cadi (which is the Judge of the Place) and to receive from him a Tuscary or Ticket for his Passage, or else he was to pay four Chequines; by which means there were transported to the number of fifty thousand Dogs.

Overwhelmed by so many dogs, the people of Scutari were near rebellion, until the dogs were removed to an uninhabited island nearby, where they all died. 'Before their sending away, the Grand Seignior had propounded to his Muphti, to have them all slain; who made answer, That every Dog had a Soul, and therefore it was not fit to kill them.' In Coryate's version, it was the Christians and Jews had to surrender their dogs; however, there were not enough dogs for all the Christians and Jews to deliver, so various (or, as Coryate would say, certain) shrewd operators in Galata collected more dogs and brought them over to Constantinople to sell on at inflated prices: 'Mungrels and masterless Curres that before strayed up and downe the Citie, being now worth twenty or thirty Aspers.' (Rabelais may have known of Constantinople's large number of dogs, and its propensity to burn, when in Book Two he had Pantagruel escape from the Turks by setting the city on fire, though pursued by 'more then thirteen hundred dogs great and small'.)

Coryate discusses the animal life of the area – 'the strangest Bird that ever I saw in my life, a Pellican', the bill of which, they found, could hold a small dog; locusts in June and July, covering the fields, rooftops and streets – 'a man cannot passe in the streets of Constantinople or Galata but hee shall everie where tread upon them'; huge, colourful butterflies 'as big as reare-mice [bats]'; fireflies, that scientist Tom experimented on ('having taken one of them and opened his bellie, I found a certaine bright and glistening sparke of fire in his taile, which I never saw before'); and his old enemies, lice: 'those kind of Flies that troubled me in Italy, did in the night time as much infect mee in Constantinople . . . I meane the Cimices, after that being once taken and bruised upon the naile of a man, doth cover the whole naile with bloud and stinke.' ('I thought', writes Thomas Nashe in *The Unfortunate Traveller*, 'cimices . . . were no more but things like lice, which alive have the most venemous sting that may be, and being dead do stink out of measure; Saint Au[gu]stine compareth heretics unto them.')

'The true Musulman wil scarce kill a louse, if he find him in his apparell, but throwes him away, affirming, that it is contrarie to the rules of charitie to kill him,' observes Coryate; unfortunately, this clemency did not apply to human beings. Non-Muslims, especially Christians, could be treated very severely. 'It cannot be expressed what great injuryes the Turkes will doe unto Christians uppon the lightest causes,' reported Moryson, who made a point of going with eyes lowered submissively; those wearing European clothes might be

attacked, and he and his friends left their swords behind in
Venice, 'travelling through all Turky with our hands in our
hose' (whatever that may mean). William Biddulph, there a
few years earlier, reported that 'greene they account Mahomets
colour; and if they see any Christian wearing a garment of that
colour, they will cut it from his back, and beat him, and ask
him how he dare presume to wear Mahomets colour . . . One,
for having but green shooe-strings, had his shoes taken away.
Another wearing green breeches under his gown, being espied,
had his breeches cut off and he reviled and beaten.' Coryate
likewise writes that 'they hold it a bad omen when the Grand
Signior on any occasion goeth out of Constantinople to meet in
his way a Christian, for which onely fault one of Sir Thomas
Glovers men [the previous Ambassador] was taken and had so
many blowes on his buttockes (his breeches betwixt) that he
died thereof within few daies after'.

Commentators generally remarked on the severity of
punishments in the Ottoman Empire, whether for religious
offences ('If in the space of this Ramazan any Turke should bee
found drunke hee is punished with death, as it happened to
one when I [Coryate] was in Constantinople, who by the
expresse commandment of the Visier [Nassuff] had hote
burning Lead powred into his mouth and eares'), or moral
lapses (fornication between a Muslim woman and a Christian
man was punishable by death, though he might be saved by a
prompt conversion – followed by painful circumcision), or
crimes of varying degrees of seriousness. Peter Mundy
describes the punishment for robbery, staking,

which is by driveing with a great Sledge a bigge, longe, sharpe,
poynted pole in att their Fundament quite through their Body, untill
it come forth betwene head and shoulders . . . Then they sett the Pole
on end, where the body is to remaine three dayes, and continueth
alive ordinarily Eight or nine houres, sometymes more. Myself was
present att one of theis Executions at Constantinople, where I heard
the blowes of the Mall, and the most horrible and fearfull Crye of the
Tortured wretch; but he sodainely left off, even as the Stake was

through his Body, all though he lived and spake many howres after. I could not well come neere to see him for the presse of people.

John Sanderson, who was there in 1599, describes concisely (*Pilgrimes*, book IX) another punitive public entertainment, gaunching,

> which is, to be stripped unto their Linnen Breeches, with their hands and feet bound all foure together at their backs, and so drawne up with a rope by a pullie upon the Gallowes, and let fall upon a great Iron hooke fastned to a lower crosse Barre of the Gallowes, most commonly lighting upon their flanke and so through their thigh, there they hang sometimes talking a day or two together, but if they be Gaunched through the belly and back, then are they dead in two or three houres.

Such – presumably frequent – horrors do not appear in what remains of Coryate's notes (though they may well have been there originally), which instead describe the charming lamps and fireworks around the (750, he estimates) mosques at Ramadan ('a passing glorious and refulgent Spectacle'), and the Christians celebrating the new vintage in their vineyards around the Bosphorus

> with good cheere, Musicke, &c. During the time of their Raccolta, whatsoever strangers come into their Vineyard might freely take as many Grapes as they were able to eate, which at another time they could not doe, for if before that they should be apprehended stealing Grapes in a Vineyard by any Janizaries, and carried to the Subbashaw of Galata, perhaps he might have twentie or fortie blowes upon the feet. Besides an Imposition of a thousand Aspers.

Memories of his grape-gathering outside Worms. However, 'for exercise sake' he helped in some grape picking and trampling underfoot; he might have got a drink or two out of it.

Early in Coryate's visit, Paul Pindar had introduced him to a Turkish fortune-teller, who, amazingly, told him that he was 'a man desirous to Travell into remote Regions . . . that I should travell farre . . . come to a great Cittie (perhaps he meant London) where many would flocke about me to heare me Discourse of the things I had seene and done in my Travels'. Now, at last, Pindar was able to say farewell to his guest, who departed on Friday 21 January, 'in as tempestuous and extreame a season as ever I travelled in my life, either by land or water, for the snow which fell incessantly for the space of almost two dayes and two nights': once again, 'a cold coming [they] had of it, I Just the worst time of the year I For a journey' (as Lancelot Andrewes and T.S. Eliot were to write of the Magi), setting off at last for the Holy Land.

The ship he sailed in was English, the *Great Defence*, which had recently caused a stir by sailing from Chios to Constantinople in only forty-two hours, unlike Coryate's previous ship, the *Samaritan*, which had taken almost six weeks (but it may have been an old, weak ship: back in 1590 John Sanderson sailed from Dartmouth for 'East India' in the *Samaritan*, but had to put back because of dangerous leaks caused by Atlantic storms). Despite the numbing cold and contrary winds,

> when we came within three or foure miles of Gallipoli, by tacking about and turning to windward, as they call it (those are nauticall words) [he announces, proudly] . . . with some kind of difficultie we entred into the Port. After we were come in, a certaine Jewe that was in our Ship perceiving that wee sailed so bravely against the winds, told me that the Englishmen by reason of their dexteritie in sailing might bee not improperly called the fishes of the Sea.

(There are several contemporary references to British – and other Channel-experienced – sailors coping better than others with rough weather; their expertise considerably improved the performance of the Barbary corsairs.) There they were delayed for three days, by Turkish customs officials, and sea fog.

On 14 February they landed at Lesbos (Mytilene) – 'The people flocked about us, many of them women, the ugliest sluts that ever I saw, saving the Armenian trulls of

Constantinople'; on the 18th they called in at Chios, then sailed past Patmos and Cos; on the 23rd they mistakenly thought they could see the top of Mount Ararat, and the next day they arrived at the notoriously unhealthy port of Iskanderun (also known as Alexandretta). Peter Mundy described it as set 'in a great marsh full of boggs, foggs, and froggs', and Coryate remarked on 'the infectious aire caused by foggie clouds after Sun-set, and till nine in the morning hovering about the mountaines, and letting fall an unwholsome dew, the waters being also pestiferous; which cause many to leave their carkasses there to be devoured by Jackals, which scrape them out of their graves. I saw one somewhat like a Mastive [mastiff] Dog, but somewhat lesse, his taile as long as that of a Foxe.' The buildings were few and rotten – 'about fortie Houses, the poorest Cotages that ever I saw, being but a few boards weakly compact and covered with Reeds'; eventually the Levant Company had to stop sending its agents there to die in 'the merry dance of death and trade . . . in a still and earthy atmosphere as of an overheated catacomb' (in Joseph Conrad's words), despite it being the port for Aleppo. The *Lonely Planet* guide to Turkey describes it as still 'just a sailors', brokers' and shippers' town', with nothing to attract the tourist.

Aleppo, however, was a very pleasant, busy, cosmopolitan city (Christians were even allowed to ride horses there). The English Consul, another Somersetshire man, took religious-sightseer Coryate to look at the Valley of Salt at nearby Jebbul, generally associated with that mentioned in 2 Samuel 8: 13: 'The Poole where the Salt is made is twenty miles long, and two broad, exceedingly frequented with plentie and varietie of Fowle. The water continueth all the yeere saving July, August, September, at which time it is quite dried up . . . and then is there nothing but a hard massie Salt, which appeareth like hard Ice digged thence with mattocks . . . it yields 20,000 dollars yeerly to the Grand Signior.' On the way they passed through several Bedouin villages, unattracted by 'sluts painted under the nosthrills and ringed on the right nosthrill unto the spoyle of kissing', and saw a sort of mirage: 'wee seemed to see a Towne standing like an Iland in water, and when we came thither found no waters, but a kind of shrub like withered Time, which covering the Mountaine made with the white sprigs a shew of water afarre off.'

Exasperatingly, Purchas briefly breaks off his transcription from Coryate's notes very shortly after this: 'I dare not obtrude Master Coryats prolixitie on the patientest Reader. He was indeed a curious viewer of so much as his bodily eyes could comprehend, to which he added (not so faithfull intelligence of) his inquisitive eares.' Nevertheless, he summarizes the next section of Coryate's report ('in as rare a stile of big swolne strange-attired travelling words expressed'). Coryate had to wait until 15 March before he could join a caravan travelling to Jerusalem, walking with an Englishman, Henry Allard, with some Armenians and their Patriarch, with a blue and white turban and a hazel-wood crucifix on his crozier, leading the way. Caravans were essential for safe travel throughout Palestine and the Middle East, and even they were under frequent attack by Arab raiders. Some Arabs may have been, theoretically, keepers of the roads, extorting three times more in duty than they should have, but, in practice, they were robbers, operating just beyond the reach of the law. Moryson offered an interesting analogy: 'The Arabians are not unlike the wild Irish, for they are subject to the great Turke, yet being poore and farre distant from his imperiall seat, they cannot be brought to due obedience, much lesse to abstaine from robberies.'

William Lithgow's experience of travelling from Aleppo to Jerusalem a few years later gives a fair idea of Coryate's:

The number of my company were about nine hundred Armenians, Christian pilgrimes, men and women: sixe hundred Turkes, trafficking for their owne businesse: and one hundred Souldiers, three Schowsses [chiauses], and six Janisaries to keep them from invasions.

Betweene Aleppo and Damascus we had nine days journey, in five of which we had pleasant travelling, and good Canes [khans:

secure, walled compounds] to lodge in, that had been builded for
the support of Travellers, and are well maintained. But when we
passed Hamsek, which is a little more then mid-way, wee had
dangerous travelling, being oft assailed with Arabs, fatigated with
rockie Mountaines, and sometimes in point of choaking for lacke
of water. The confusion of this multitude, was not onely grievous
in regard of the extreame heate, providing of victuals at poore
villages, and scarcitie of water to fill our bottles, made of Boare
skinnes, but also amongst narrow and stonie passages, thronging,
we oft fell over one another, in great heapes, in danger to be
smothered; yea, and oftentimes, wee that were Christians had our
bodies well beaten by our conducting Turkes.

Damascus was a relief and a delight, 'the Capitall Citie of
Syria', writes Lithgow,' beautified with many rivers on each
side . . . excellent Orchards, and all other naturall objects of
elegancie; that for scituation, Artizens, all manner
Commodities, and varietie of Fruits, in all the Asiaticall
Provinces it is not paraleld'. He also reports on the city's
famous arms industry: 'The onely best Shables or short
crooked swords that be in the world are made here; and so
are all other their weapons, as halfe Pikes, Bowes and
Arrowes, and Baluckoes of Steele, that Horse-men carry in
their hands: their shafts being three foot long, their heads
great and round, and sharply guttered; wherewith they use
to braine or knocke downe their enemies in the field.'
Coryate, on the other hand, was enraptured with the
dervishes' monastery and gardens, the great mosque with its
thousand pillars, and, ever keen on economy, food so cheap
that 'at a Cookes', he and Allard dined well for three
farthings each: 'an earthly Paradise: for which cause it is
said the Grand Signior may not reside there, least he should
forfeit his hopes of a future Paradise.'
From Damascus onwards, for the next six days the travellers
were in Christian site-seers' paradise: they crossed the Jordan
by Jacob's Bridge (where reputedly Jacob had wrestled with
the angel), climbed Mount Tabor to view the scene of Christ's
Transfiguration, and visited Nazareth to see the ruin of the

Virgin Mary's house. (Lithgow remarked sardonically how the Armenians 'carried away above five thousand pounds weight [of stones from the "ruinous lumpe"] to keepe in a memoriall thereof'. It did not help that he had previously been at Loreto in Italy, which also claimed to possess Mary's house, specially flown over from Palestine by four angels: 'A divellish invention', he thundered, 'to deceive the blind-folded people, and to fill the Coffers of the Romane Priests. Now thou bottomless Gulfe of Papistry, here I forsake thee, no Winter-blasting Furies of Satans subtile stormes can make ship-wracke of my Faith on the stony shelfes of thy deceitfull deepes.' Powerful stuff; especially with what H.G. Wells's Mr Polly called 'Allitrition's Artful Aid'.) 'The whole Territorie of Canaan', observed Lithgow, 'is inhabited with . . . Moores, some Turkes, civill Arabs, and a few Christians and scattered Jewes. The Arabians are for the most part Theeves and Robbers, the Moores cruell and uncivill, hating Christians to the death: the Turkes are the best of all three, yet all sworne enemies to Christ.'

On arrival at Jerusalem (Coryate entered on 12 April 1615) travellers had to pay a fee (probably two zecchines each) to the Turkish guards on the gate, and then were welcomed, had their feet washed, and were put up by Franciscan friars (who depended on Christian pilgrims for their income). Not everyone was impressed by Jerusalem. Henry Timberley, who was there in 1601 (*Pilgrimes*, book IX), observed,

A man may goe twentie miles before he finde a place to feed a horse or a cow . . . Jerusalem it selfe is the most barren that I saw in all my travells, the desarts excepted. I cannot compare any place in England to it, except the barrenest place in Cornewal, where is nothing but rocks and stones, and daily by the report of the Inhabitants, the stones grow more and more . . . I am of opinion that it is quite forsaken of God; for the more sort of Turkes there inhabiting use all filthinesse, that the Christians are forced to marry their children very young, yea even at ten yeeres of age; boyes they keepe openly, and shew them at their doores which hath the fairest.

Fynes Moryson in turn wrote that the inhabitants were

> either Tailors, Shoemakers, Cookes or Smiths . . . and in generall
> poore rascall people, mingled of the Scumme of divers Nations,
> partly Arabians, partly Moores, partly the basest inhabitants of
> neighbour Countries, by which kind of people all the adjoining
> Territorie is likewise inhabited. The Jewes in Turky are
> distinguished from others by red hats, and being practicall doe live
> for the most part upon the sea-coasts, and few or none of them
> come to this Citie, inhabited by Christians that hate them, and
> which should have no traffique [business], if the Christian
> Monasteries were taken away. Finally, the Inhabitants of Jerusalem
> at this day are as wicked as they were when they crucified our
> Lord, gladly taking all occasions to use Christians despitefully.

He went on to complain how in 'Hierusalem wee were forced
to beare a thousand injuries, hardly keeping the very boyes
from leaping uppon our shoulders from the Shopps and higher
parts of the way while their Parents looked on, and
commended them for so doing'. Coryate was struck by the
city's relative emptiness: 'Jerusalem is but meanly peopled,
there being scarce 10,000. So few walking in the streets as
except in Padua he hath not seen in any Citie.'

Coryate did everything the devout Christian pilgrim might
do. Edward Terry, who knew him later in India, relates that he
was tattooed on the left arm with 'the arms of Jerusalem, a
Cross Crossed, or Crosslets', that is, a cross with smaller
crosses set in each corner, and on the right wrist with a single
cross and the words 'Via, Veritas, Vita' (the Way, the Truth, the
Life), with which he was very pleased, quoting Galatians 6: 17,
'I bear in my body the marks of the Lord Jesus.' He explained
how the tattoo was 'made by sharp needles bound together,
that pierced only the skin, and then a black powder put into
the place so pierced, which became presently indelible
characters to continue with him so long as his flesh should be
covered with skin; and they were done upon his arms so
artificially as if they had been drawn by some accurate Pencil
upon parchment'. With a party from the monastery, he visited

the Temple of the Holy Sepulchre (the Turks normally charged Western Christians an entrance fee of nine zecchines, which was rather expensive), spending the night in the upper gallery, with blankets and food provided by the monastery. They were awoken by the 'very clamorous noyse' of a Greek Orthodox procession, with banners of silk and cloth of gold, streamers and a gilded cross; 'a world of Lamps was carried before and behind them, men, women, and children confusedly, crying Kyrie eleeson'. The next Sunday, from 11 a.m. there were further processions by the Armenians, Maronites, Jacobites, Copts and Abyssinians, with some 2,000 worshippers:

They walke round about till five of the clocke in the afternoone without intermission, most of them carrying a bundle of white wax Candle in their right hands, bound about with the holy thred or garters which have touched holy places, about forty in a bundle lifted over their heads, invocating the holy Ghost, the Greeks crying Kyrie Eleison, the rest in Arabian, with such stentorian outcries, for that sixe houres procession, thinking therewith to pierce the Heavens, as hath not elsewhere been heard.

The Armenians seemed to put on the best show:

Their Patriarche wore a cope of cloth of Gold, a Miter of like cloth on his head beautified with many rich stones, with a Crucifix in his hand beset with Diamonds, Rubies, Amethists, Saphires and other Stones of great worth; his Priests also sumptuously attired, wearing embroidered Caps of Velvet and Sattin with Crosses on the tops. . . . some of the Priests went before the Patriarch backward perfuming him.

Before the ceremony of the descent of the Holy Fire, Coryate was shocked by the 'buying and selling in the Temple of girdles, garters, bread &c., they then remaining there eight and forty houres; yea, they defiled it with their excrements, and made it a metamorphosis of Ajax, and that not for want of necessarie places, which there were publicke and common, but through meere beastlinesse in superlative degree'. (In 1596

Sir John Harington celebrated his transformation of a lavatory
– a jakes – into a water-closet, with a poem, 'The
Metamorphosis of Ajax'.)

> About three quarters of an houre after foure, the door [of the
> Sepulchre] was unlocked, and the Patriarchs of the Greekes and
> Armenians went in, with an Abassine. This last entreth into the
> grotta, and there in hugger-mugger contriveth his businesse, and
> having been there a quarter of an houre, cometh forth with his
> bundle of lights lighted, and leaping furiously forth is caught by
> the zealous people ravished with joy at this appearance, the Priest
> in danger of stifling whiles each strives to light his candle first.

Whilst Tom always enjoyed a good spectacle, as a sound
Protestant he would not have been impressed by the rest of the
performance. William Lithgow related how, on Palm Sunday
afternoon, the Christian Guardian went with twelve friars to
Bethphage, where he mounted an ass and rode into Jerusalem,
the people 'dispoyling themselves almost to the skinne',
strawing the way with branches and crying "Hosanna, the
Sonne of David, blessed is hee that commeth in the Name of
the Lord"'. Lithgow did not approve.

Coryate also visited other tourist holy sites in the city and
surrounding area, notably the River Jordan, some 15 miles
from Jerusalem. Lithgow (unlike Coryate) complained how
difficult it was to get there, through 'such deep sandie ground,
that the Mulets were not able to carrie us through, whereupon
we all dismounted, wrestling and wading above the middle
part of our bodies, and sometimes falling in over our heads, we
were in great danger of perishing. Even in the middest of this
turmoyling paine (the night being darke) the unwelcommed
Arabs invironed and invaded us with a storme of Arrowes . . .
yet they prevailed nothing'. At the river, Coryate related, 'all
made great applause; men, women and children stripped
themselves starke naked, having opinion that that water
washeth away all their sinnes. It is very muddy.'

It appears that, from there, Coryate and Allard headed
north towards Mount Lebanon, with returning Maronite

Christians probably giving them protective company, and then walked on to Aleppo. There, Coryate wrote up his voluminous notes, which Allard took with him back to England; eventually they found their way to the hands of Samuel Purchas, who printed some of them (the rest being lost or thrown away). Coryate stayed on, waiting for another caravan, preparing for his greatest walk yet, eastward through modern southern Turkey, Iraq, Iran and Afghanistan, to India and the court of the Great Mughal.

ELEVEN

A Passage to India

The journey that Coryate now proposed, from Aleppo all the way to the court of the Great Mughal in northern India, through rocky, barren deserts and rugged mountains, beset by bandits and slavers, was a long and dangerous one, attempted by very few Englishmen before him. In 1600 John Mildenhall and John Cartwright went out, the former eventually arriving in 1603, to ask for trading privileges at the Court, and returning in 1606. In 1611 Mildenhall set out again, with trade goods entrusted to him by others, with which he apparently ran off, before being caught and made to return the goods. One of his pursuers, Richard Steel, whom we shall encounter later, went on with him to India, where Mildenhall died in Ajmer in April 1614 (his tomb in the Roman Catholic cemetery in Agra is the oldest English monument in India).

Coryate had to wait three months in Aleppo for a large caravan bound for Persia, eventually departing, he later reported in a letter from India (some letters are in *Pilgrimes*, part I, book IV), in September 1614, shortly afterwards 'passing the noble river Euphrates (the cheefest of all that irrigated Paradise, where-hence, as from their original, the three other rivers were derived [Genesis 2: 11–14: Pison, Gihon and Hiddekel]) about foure dayes journey beyond Aleppo, on that further side of which I entered Mesapotamia alias Chaldea'. Two days later he thought they had reached the ancient city of Ur (though actually it was Urfa, 'a very delicate and pleasant Cittie', he reported, but a different place, 'the West part standing on the side of a rockie Mountaine' according to

Cartwright in his *The Preachers Travels*, 'and the East part . . .
replenished with Vineyards, Orchards and Gardens . . . and for
the galantnesse of the Site, it was once reckoned the
Metropoliticall seat of Mesopotamia'). Abraham was supposed to
have been born in Ur; not surprisingly, Coryate's predictably
diligent searches found no trace of him. After four more days
they reached the mountain fortress city of Diarbekr (modern
Diyerbakir, in Turkey), set in a vast, rock-strewn plain, where it
was normal practice for caravans to camp below, while mules
carried the merchandise up the steep, narrow tracks to the
market's crowded alleys; apparently Coryate went in, and,
disastrously, was robbed of his money 'both golde and silver (but
not all, by reason of certain clandestine corners where it was
placed) . . . by a Spahee, as they call him, that is, one of the
horsemen of the great Turk'. Interestingly, the modern author of
the *Lonely Planet* guide to Turkey advises solitary visitors here to
exercise caution, having 'had a few reports of robbery attempts'.

On they went, through rocky mountains and dramatic
gorges. At one point on the route, reported Cartwright,

> for the strangenesse of the site, the Turkes have builded three
> Bridges in the midst of these Rockes, to passe from one to another,
> thereby to behold Natures wisedome in framing so wonderfull.
> Wee went to view the same, but through the huge over-falls, which
> came farre off within those Mountaines, and the steepnesse of the
> same, together with the hideous noise, and whistling murmuring,
> were found not so great contentment above, as wee did beneath,

presumably looking up at the waterfalls. En route, Coryate's
caravan encountered another caravan, taking presents to the
Great Mughal,

> beeing Elephants, whereof there were 31 and of those two so
> gloriously adorned, as I never saw the like, nor should see the like
> again while I live. For they wore four chaines about their bodies all
> of beaten gold: two chaines about their legges of the same:
> furniture for their buttocks of pure gold: two Lyons upon their
> heads of the like gold: the ornaments of each amounting to the

value of almost eight thousand pounds sterling: and the whole Present was worth ten of their Leakes [lakh: 100,000 rupees], as they call them; a Leake being ten thousand pounds sterling; the whole, a hundred thousand pounds sterling.

Also around this time Coryate was tricked out of money by some Armenians, though he was curiously unwilling to go into details.

Four days later they forded the River Tigris: 'in the same where I crossed it, I found it so shallow that it reached no higher than the calfe of my legge: for I waded over it afoot' (his whole journey was done on foot). Then it was on, and up, into Armenia, hot and hilly, with a distant glimpse of Mount Ararat. It was not pleasant going: 'A great part of the Turks land is extreme barren and sterill as I have observed in my peregrination thereof, particularly in Syria, Mesopatamia and Armenia; many large portions thereof being so wonderfull fruitlesse that it beareth no good thing at all, or if any thing there "infelix lolium et steriles dominantur avenae" [Virgil: "the unhappy darnel and barren oats hold sway"].' Then they passed through lower Media, and in six days were in 'Ecbatana, the summer seat of Cyrus his Court, eftsome mentioned in the Scripture, now called Tauris [Tabriz, in Azerbaijan]', which he found, after many years and wars between Turkey and Persia, to be 'in wofull ruins'. Cartwright, there in 1600, described it as having a population of almost 200,000, with a 'most beautifull and flourishing Garden, large and spacious, replenished with sundry kinds of Trees, and sweete smelling Plants, and a thousand Fountaines and Brookes, derived from a pretie River'. This sounds more like a former emperor's summer residence. However, the city had been captured by the Turks in 1585, and then reconquered by the Persian king, Abbas I, in 1602, so it may not have been looking its best when Coryate got there.

Two days' journey took them on to Casbin, and four more, through snow-capped mountains, to Qazvir, an important trading centre for Persian carpets, Indian spices and jewels, Venetian glass and even English cloth, where they stayed

overnight. Twenty-three more days' steady progress brought
them at last to 'Spahan [Isfahan] in Parthia, the place of
residence of the Persian king. But at my being there, he was in
the Countrey of Gurgistan [Georgia], ransacking the poor
Christians there with great hostility, with fire and sword'. Here
Coryate had to stay for two months awaiting another east-
bound caravan, learning Persian and sorting out his notes; a
large bundle of these was left here, to be transported back to
Aleppo and England, but disappeared without trace.

Isfahan was a large city of some 200,000 people (including
merchants from England, the Netherlands, Portugal, Poland and
Russia, as well as Armenians, Georgians, Turks and Jews), 'most
pleasant in its situation, elegant as to building, populous for
inhabitants, rich in trade, and noble by being the usual residence
of the court', wrote Thomas Herbert in his *Travels in Persia* in
1628: the 'metropolis of the Persian monarchy . . . seated in the
Parthian territory (now called Ayrac [Iraq]) and as umbilic to that
spacious body which at this day is awed by the Persian sceptre'
(Herbert was afflicted with a fancy style on occasion).

> The Maydan [he writes] is without doubt as spacious, as pleasant
> and aromatic a market as any in the universe . . . resembling our
> Exchange, or the Place-Royal in Paris, but six times larger . . . of
> sun-dried brick . . . arched above (in cupolas), terrace-wise framed
> at the top, and with blue plaster pargeted . . . The North aisle of the
> Maydan hath eight or nine arched rooms, usually hung with lamps
> and latten candlesticks, which being lighted . . . give a curious
> splendour. Thither the Potshaw [prince] and others frequently
> resort for pastime, as tumbling, sleight-of-hand, dancing girls, and
> painted catamites (that *nefandum peccatum* being there tolerated).

The King's palace was also 'pargeted and painted with blue
and gold, embroidered with posies [poesies, verses] of Arabic,
which after the grotesque manner makes it shew very
pleasant'. The rooms were arched, painted red, white, blue
and gold; the extensive gardens (the Char Bagh) were 'made
fragrant with flowers, filled with airy citizens privileged from
hurt or affrights, and for which they return their thankful

notes in a more melodious concert and variety then if they were in the exactest vollyere [aviary] in the universe'. Clearly, the city was delightful, with flower-filled gardens with summerhouses, artificial lakes, fountains, streams and shady avenues: 'Gardens here for grandeur and fragour [Herbert's coinage, for fragrance] are such as no city in Asia outvies; which at a little distance from the city you would judge a forest, it is so large; but withal so sweet and verdant that you may call it another Paradise.'

John Cartwright has an extensive account of the people, whom he found remarkable for

> their continuall riding. They ride on horse-backe for the most part, on horse-backe they fight with the Enemie, they execute all Affaires as well publike as private on horse-backe, they goe from place to place on horse-backe, they buy and sell, and on horse-backe they conferre and talke with one another; and the difference between the Gentleman and the slave is, that the slave never rideth nor the Gentleman never goeth on foote. Besides, the nature of the people is arrogant, seditious, deceitfull, and very unquiet, but the fierceness of their nature is much restrayned by the Kings severe government. To sensualitie they are much inclined, having three sorts of women, as they terme them, viz. honest women, halfe honest women and courtezans; and yet they chastise no offense with like extremetie as Adulterie, and that as well in the halfe honest woman as in the honest . . .

(Nothing is said about the men.)

At last Coryate was able to get away, in February 1615, with another large caravan. He later explained the caravan system, in a letter to his mother:

> A Caravan is a word much used in all Asia: by which is understood a great multitude of people travelling together upon the way with Camels, Horses, Mules, Asses, &c. on which they carry Merchandizes from one country to another, and Tents and Pavillions; under which instead of houses they shelter themselves in open fields, being furnished with all necessary provision, and

convenient implements to dresse the same: in which Caravans I
have ever most securely passed between Jerusalem and this Towne
[Ajmer, in India], a journey of fifteene months and odd days
[including time spent waiting for caravans].

Coryate reassures his mother about his security and comfort
in these travelling Ideal Homes; it seems unlikely, however,
that our lone footslogger was able to carry any tents or
pavilions, or was much furnished with provisions, but in all
probability had to sleep in a blanket on stony ground under
the stars, on a level with the various snakes or multi-legged
stinging and biting creatures patrolling the desert surface, and
had to buy or cadge what food he could from better-supplied
travellers. The caravan in which he travelled from Isfahan to
India comprised, he reported, some 2,000 camels, 1,500
horses, over 1,000 mules, 800 asses and 6,000 people – the
equivalent of a small, fly-bothered, rather smelly town spread
out over a couple of miles, straggling slowly, at walking pace,
through the long, hot days, and resting up around camel-dung
fires in the chilly nights.

From Isfahan they would have passed through Yezd, some
180 miles to the east; after that, there were two favoured routes,
one going southward to Kerman before trekking northward to
Farah, the other, slightly more direct, through Tabas to the
north-west, to Farah; this was the route used by Richard Steel
and John Crowther (*Pilgrimes*, book IV) on their return journey
from Ajmer to Isfahan. At Tabas, they reported, all caravans
rested for at least four or five days to recover from the strains of
the journey; Farah (high up in western Afghanistan) had a
sunbaked brick-walled fort, four-square and a mile round, with
'a pretty Bazar vaulted over-head to keepe from raine . . . good
soil and plenty of water'. All caravans passing through
(especially those going west) were forced to stay for between
seven and ten days, for the benefit of the town traders, while
the Royal Treasurer mulcted them on their goods at the rate of 3
per cent of value; 'at their going into India they use all
extremetie, searching them to the skinne for gold [but Tom had

his "clandestine corners"], which to transport, or any coyne of silver out of Persia, but the Kings, is death'.

Somewhere along the way, on the border between Persian and Indian territory, Coryate's caravan encountered another, westward bound, remarkable at first sight for including two elephants and eight antelope (the first he had seen, though, as he said, he was to see plenty more at the Great Mughal's court). These animals were intended as presents for the Shah of Persia from the English adventurer-diplomat, Robert Sherley, making a slow and circuitous return from England, sailing from Gravesend in the inappropriately named *Expedition* in January 1613, via the Cape of Good Hope and India, before proceeding overland to Isfahan (which he reached in June 1615). Sherley, one of the famous Sherley brothers, was a Catholic convert who had gone abroad during the reign of Elizabeth, become, like his brothers, involved in Eastern politics, and for some years had acted as ambassador for the Shah; remarkably, he had been at James I's court in 1611 (seeking, among other matters, to negotiate a contract for the export of raw silk from Persia), when Coryate's *Crudities* and *Crambe* came out and were being talked about. He and his glamorous Circassian wife 'seemed to exult for joy to see me', claimed Coryate in one of his Indian letters, and there, in that distant, desert land, thousands of miles from England, did Sherley 'shew mee, to my singular contentment, both my Bookes neatly kept'. Sherley promised to show them to the Shah, 'to the end, I may have the more gracious accesse unto him after my returne thither' on his way, as he intended, to Aleppo, 'for he is such a jocond Prince, that he will not be meanlie delighted with my facetious hieroglyphicks if they are truely and genuinely expounded unto him'. Sherley may have found Shah Abbas (1587–1629) a 'jocond Prince', but few others did: known as cruel and despotic, given to gouging out his enemies' eyes with his own hands, Abbas had his eldest son killed, before, in a fit of remorse, ordering the assassin to bring him his own son's head; two other sons were blinded, on his orders. His 'forceful rule' (to use a historian's bland phrase), however, not only pushed back the Ottoman Empire in the west and the Uzbeks in the east, but brought order to the country: turbulent mountain tribes were subdued, while the sight of thieves being buried alive or dragged with trailing entrails through the streets discouraged crime. Whatever Sherley's professed hopes for Coryate's future treatment, his wife seems to have assessed more accurately Coryate's immediate situation and, more practically, gave him the equivalent of forty shillings in Persian money (and, with him, a little meant a lot, and went a long way – literally).

Kandahar, now in south-east Afghanistan, then part of the Mughal Empire, was set in a dangerous, mountain area, 'inhabited', wrote Steel and Crowther, 'by a fierce people called Agwans or Potans [Afghans, Pathans], very strong of bodie, somewhat whiter than the Indians, great Robbers, accustomed to cut off whole Caravans', and indeed to pick off stragglers and sell them as slaves. The Great Mughal had to maintain a garrison of 12,000–15,000 horsemen to restrain their activities and protect the caravan trade, which had increased recently as a consequence of wars along the coastal route between India and the Levant. Here also caravans were forced to contribute to the local economy by staying twenty-six to thirty days, 'whereby it is much inhabited by lewd people, as all such places of resort commonly are'.

After two weeks, Coryate's caravan got out of Kandahar, laboured somewhat breathlessly through the high mountain passes, where the Afghan tribesmen were notorious nuisances, and at last descended into the broad and fertile plain of the Indus, a river 'as broad againe as our Thames in London, and hath his originall out of the Mountaine Caucasus, so much ennobled by the antient both Poets and Historiographers, Greeke and Latine' (as scholarly, instructive Coryate reminds us). Two days later they arrived in Multan, 'a great and ancient Citie', reported Steel and Crowther, which 'yeeldeth white linnen and Diaper. All Caravans are constrayned to stay at this River eight, ten, or twelve dayes before they can get leave of the Governour to passe.' It may have been here that Steel and Coryate encountered each other; they were to meet once more. In any case, here Coryate's Christian zealotry got out of control, in an extraordinary outburst. As he related later, in a letter to Sir Edward Phelips, he met an Italian-speaking Muslim who (presumably in the course of one of Coryate's futile religious disputes) called him a Giaour, or infidel, which Tom would not permit. He, he claimed, was the true believer, in believing in Christ, and the Muslim therefore only a pseudo-believer, a pseudo-Mussulman. He went on to denounce the Koran and the life and career of Mahomet, trotting out all the errors and beliefs common in Europe at the time:

What thy Mahomet was, from whom thou dost derive thy religion, assure thy selfe I know better than any one of the Mahometans amongst many millions; yea, all the particular circumstances of his life and death, his nation, his parentage, his driving camels through Egipt, Siria, and Palestina, the marriage of his mistris by whose death he raised himselfe from a very base and contemtible estate to great honor and riches, his manner of cozening the sottish people of Arabia, partly by a tame pigeon that did fly to his eare for meat, and partly by a tame bull that hee fed by hand every day, with the rest of his actions both in peace and warre, I know as well as if I had lived in his time, or had been one of his neighbours in Mecca. The truth whereof if thou didst know aswell, I am perswaded thou wouldest spit in the face of thy Alcoran and trample it under thy feete, and bury it under a jaxe [jakes], a booke of that strange and weake matter that I my selfe have already written two better bookes (God be thanked) . . .

He concluded this eloquent persuasion by condemning the futility of Muslim prayer – 'your praiers doe even stinke before God, and are of no more force than the cry of thy camell when thou doest lade or unlade him' – whereas Christian prayers as 'a sweete smelling sacrifice are acceptable to God' and effective in producing rain or stopping plague. What made matters worse was that, as he wrote, 'I pronounced the speech before an hundred people, whereof none understood it but himself [the Muslim]; but he afterward told the meaning of some part of it as far as he could remember it to some of the others also'. He does not indicate what the bystanders' reaction was, but admits, 'If I had spoken thus much in Turky or Persia against Mahomet, they would have rosted me upon a spitt; but in the Mogols dominions a Christian may speake much more freely than hee can in any other Mahometan country in the world.' As he failed to note, the sects in Christian Europe would have permitted no such freedom – or abuse – of religious expression.

In any event, he got away with it, and moved on to the caravan's main destination, Lahore, with which, like most travellers, he was greatly impressed: 'one of the largest Cities of the whole universe . . . it containeth at the least xvi [16] miles in compasse, and exceedeth Constantinople it selfe in greatnesse' – a place, reported Edward Terry, 'as I have often been told by Tom Coryat and others, of very great trade, wealth and delight, lying more temperately out of the Parching Sun than any other of his [the Grand Mughal's] Cities do' (in May and June, the temperature round here can reach 120° F). Steel and Crowther are informative about the great trading activity that traveller Coryate was caught up in here:

> From this place came the Treasure of the Portugals Trade when they had peace, as being the centre of all Indian Traffique. And here they embarqued the same down the River for Tatta, whence they were transported for Ormus [on the Arabian Sea] and Persia. . . . At this present the Merchants of India assemble at Lahore, and invest a great part of their monies in Commodities, and joyne themselves in Caravans to passe the Mountaines of Candahar into Persia, by which way is generally reported to passe twelve or fourteen thousand Camels lading. . . . These Merchants are put to great charges betwixt Lahore and Spahan (besides great cold in Winter and heate in Summer, and the badnesse of the way, spending six or seven moneths betwixt those two places).

William Finch, who was here in 1609–10, gives a good sense of the wealth of the city and palace (*Pilgrimes*, book IV): 'one

of the greatest Cities of the East, containing some 24 course
[*corse*: 2–2½ miles] in circuit . . . The Castle or Towne is
inclosed with a strong bricke wall, having thereto twelve faire
gates, nine by land, and three openings to the River: the streets
faire and well paved, the inhabitants most Baneans [Hindus]
and handicrafts men; all white men [Muslims] of note lying in
the suburbs.' Gardens and orchards around the city were filled
with 'Apples, but small, Toot [Indian mulberries] white and
red, Almonds, Peaches, Figges, Grapes, Quinces, Orenges,
Limmons, Pomgranats, Roses, Stock-gellow-flowers,
Marigolds, Wall-flowers, Ireos [iris], Pinkes white and red,
with divers sorts of Indian Flowers'.

He goes on to describe a magnificent palace, of many
courtyards:

In the Gallery where the Prince useth to sit, are drawne over-head
many Pictures of Angels, with Pictures of Banian Dews [gods], or
rather Divels, intermixt in most ugly shape, with long hornes,
staring eyes, shagge haire, great fangs, ugly paws, long tailes, with
such horrible difformity and deformity, that I wonder the poore
women are not frighted therewith . . .

Before this Gallery is a faire paved Court, with stone
gratings, and windowes alongst the waters side; at the end a
faire marble Jounter [*chattri*: a small pavilion with a dome on
columns], convexed over-head [the earliest citation for 'dome'
in the *OED* is 1656], looking over the River, beneath it a
Garden of pleasure; behind, the Kings lodgings very sumptuous
the walles and seelings all over-laid with pure gold; and round
about the sides, about a mans height, some three foote distant
are placed faire Venice Looking-glasses, three and three above
each other: and below these alongst the walls, are drawn many
pictures of this mans Ancestors, as of Acabar [Akbar] his father
[1542–1605], Hamoune [Humayun] his Grand-father [1508–56],
Babur his great Grand-father [1483–1530], who first set foote
into India.

Outside the city was a remarkable monument to one of Akbar's
wives or concubines,

with whom it is said Sha Selim [Akbar's son, later the Emperor Jahangir] had to do (her name was Immacque Kelle, or Pomgranate Kernell) upon notice of which the King caused her to be inclosed quicke [alive] within a wall in his Mohol [*mahal*: palace], where she dyed; and the King in token of his love, commands a sumptuous Tombe to be built of stone in the midst of a four-square Garden richly walled, with a gate, and divers rooms over it: the convexity of the Tombe he hath willed to be wrought in workes of gold, with a large faire Jounter with rooms over-head.

No doubt it was of interest to other royal wives.

Akbar appears to have had whimsical ways with his wives; Coryate also tells of how 'Ecbar Shaugh had learned all kinds of Sorcery, who beeing once in a strange humour to shew a spectacle to his Nobles, brought forth his chiefest Queene, with a sword cut off her head, and after the same perceiving the heavinesse and sorrow of them for the death of her (as they thought) caused the head, by vertue of his Exorcismes and Conjunctions [conjurations?], to be set on againe, no signe appearing of any stroke with his Sword'. How they must have laughed.

Now Coryate had to push on alone, down the long road to Agra, where he expected to find the Great Mughal's court, a journey of twenty days, passing 'through such a delicate and even tract of ground as I never saw before'. Indeed, 'all the Countrey betwixt Agra and Lahore', Steel and Crowther write, 'is exceeding well tilled and manured, being the best of India, and plentifull of all things . . . Here all the way is set on both sides with trees, the most of them bearing a kind of Mulbery.' William Finch has a story to explain this remarkable avenue. When, shortly after Jahangir's accession to the throne in 1605, his eldest son Khusrau led a rebellion at Lahore, Khusrau was captured in Kabul and 'as some say' had his eyes burned out, though others said that he was only permanently blindfolded (with his father's seal) and imprisoned in the castle at Agra: 'All alongst on both sides the way from Cabul to Agra, a reasonable distance, the King caused trees to be planted to shade the way, in remembrance of this exploit.' Finch chooses words unexpectedly: 'love' and 'exploit'. At least there was shade from the burning sunshine to shelter the 'broad river of life' – camel trains, bullock carts, villagers with flocks of goats, women in bright saris with great burdens balanced on their heads, horsemen from the court, naked holy men – that flowed along what would much later become part of the Grand Trunk Road, celebrated in Kipling's *Kim*.

Steel and Crowther tell us more of the conditions of Coryate's trek down the great road:

> It is dangerous in the night for Theeves, but in the day secure. Every five or six Course there are Seraes built by the King or some great men, very faire for the beautifying of the way, memory of their names, and entertainment of Travellers. In there you shall have a Chamber and place to tye your Horses, also store of Horsemeat [fodder for horses]. . . . In the morning, about day breake, all men make readie to depart together, and then are the gates opened. Before, no man is suffered to depart for feare of Theeves. This was a tedious travaile: for within two houres after the Sunne-rising, we were scarcely able to endure the heate.

Halfway along the road, Coryate was told, there was a mountain 'verie neere ten miles out of the way on the left hand: the people that inhabit that Mountaine observe a custome very strange, that all the brothers of any familie have but one and the self same wife: so that one woman sometimes doth serve 6 or 7 men'. The classical scholar remembered having read in Strabo of something similar in 'Arabia Felix'.

Frustratingly, he found that the Emperor's Court had removed from Agra to the hill town of Ajmer, to the south-west, another ten days' trudge in heat and dust along dirt tracks and through mud and wattle villages for Coryate (a distance of some 200 miles, which gives an indication of the pace he could keep up, hour after hour, day after day). There, in July 1615, he found, to his delight, 'a Cape Merchant of our English men, with nine more of my Countrimen, resident there upon termes of Negotiations, for the right worshipfull

Company of Merchants in London that trade for East India';
and there he stopped.

One cannot but wonder what kind of figure Coryate
presented to his wondering countrymen after so many months'
arduous travel. Spenser's description of a pilgrim (*The Faerie
Queene*, I.vi) probably gives a fair idea:

> A silly man, in simple weeds forworne,   [innocent]
> And soild with dust of the long dried way;
> His sandals were with toilsome travell torne,
> And face all tand with scorching sunny ray,
> As he had traveild many a sommers day
> Through boyling sands of Arabie and Ynde.
> And in his hand a Jacobs staffe, to stay   [pilgrim's]
> His wearie limbes upon: and eke behind
> His scrip did hang, in which his needments   [bag]
>   he did bind.

In a letter to his friend Laurence Whitaker, Coryate related that
his journey from Jerusalem to Ajmer had taken fifteen months
and odd days (including time waiting for caravans),

> al which way I traversed afoot, but with divers paires of shooes
> [picking up on the teasing he received for using only one pair in
> his European journey], having been such a Propateticke . . . that is,
> a walker forward on foot, as I doubt whether you ever heard the
> like of in your life: for the totall way betwixt Jerusalem and the
> Moguls court containeth two thousand and seaven hundred
> English miles

— an uncharacteristic underestimate: it was certainly several
hundred more. He had been on the road for about nine months,
averaging some 70 miles a week, on foot, on rough tracks,
through desert and mountain, often in severe conditions. He
continues, 'My whole perambulation of this Asia the greater is
like to bee a passage of almost sixe thousande miles. For if God
grant me life and health, I meane to make it a voyage of full
seaven yeares before I come home' (the idea being, to equal

Ulysses in taking ten years to get home). He developed plans to travel on to Tartary and Samarkand, 'to see the Sepulcher of the greatest Conqueror that ever was in the worlde, Tamberlaine the Great' (once again, the interest in the memorial defeat of death's oblivion, and his own achievement as the greatest walker that ever was in the world), before at last returning via Persia, Babylon, Nineveh, Cairo, Alexandria, Venice and Germany. Another boast, that he repeated in his last letter to his mother, was of his extraordinary economy:

> A matter verie memorable; I spent in my ten moneths travels betwixt Aleppo and the Moguls Court, but three pounds sterling, yet fared reasonable well everie daie; victuals being so cheape in some Countries where I travelled, that I oftentimes lived competentlie for a pennie sterling a day: yet of that three pound I was cousened of no lesse than ten shillings sterling, by certaine lewde Christians of the Armenian Nation: so that indeed I spent but fiftie shillings in my ten moneths travailes.

He then outlined his travel plans, telling her she should not expect any more letters until he had finished 'these Mahometan Travelles', when after two years or more, he would write from Ragusa (modern Dubrovnik) or Venice, and concluded, 'Your dutifull, loving, and obedient sonne, now a desolate pilgrim in the world.'

Coryate had fallen on his weary feet at the little British encampment, with the East India Company agent, William Edwards, 'an honest man that useth me with verie loving respect', allowing him free board and lodging, 'not spending one little peece of money, either for diet, washing or any other thing'. Here he rested and recovered, wrote up his notes, and wrote some letters back to England, eventually printed in London in 1616, in two versions with slightly different titles: *Thomas Coryate, Traveller for the English Wits: Greeting from the Court of the Great Mogul . . .*, and *Thomas Coryate, Travailer for the English wits, and the good of this Kingdom: To all his inferiour Countreymen, Greeting . . .* (both volumes have a picture of Tom perched on a rather frisky elephant, incorrectly showing him in

European dress, when he habitually wore some approximation of local dress; Terry records how, by contrast, the English company 'kept to our English habits, made as light and coole as possibly we could have them', in red-trimmed green taffeta).

His first letter, of Michaelmas Day 1615, was to his erstwhile patron, Sir Edward Phelips, wondering whether after so long he would recognise the handwriting, but confident of his recognising the style, like that of his 'Linsie-woolsie [tangled, confused] Orations' and 'extravagant discourses' when they knew each other in Somerset. He boasts (pardonably) of his achievements, that have surprised even himself: 'Now, though there hath itched a very burning desire in mee, within these few yeares, to survay and contemplate some of the chiefest parts of this goodly Fabricke of the World, besides mine owne native Country: yet never did I thinke it would have broken out to such an ambitious vent.' Nevertheless, he continues, 'such is my insatiable greedinesse of seeing strange countries: which exercise is in deede the very Queene of all the pleasures in the world', that he proposes to travel seven more years, to equal Ulysses. The next letter, to Laurence Whitaker, provides a detailed report on his journey from Aleppo to Ajmer, and an account of Jahangir, before asking Whitaker to forward letters to his mother and to his 'unkle William', encouraging uncle '(with such convenient termes and patheticall perswasions as your discretion shall dictate and suggest unto you) to remember me as his poore industrious peregrinating kinsman, neerest unto him in blood of all the people in the world . . . with some competent gratuitie, if God should call him out of the world before my returne into my native Countrie'. In the meantime he encloses some verses by John Browne, a London merchant resident at Amadavers, 'To the Odcombian wonder'. Browne exclaims

> What though thy *Cruder* travels were attended
> With bastinadoes, lice, and vile disgraces?
> Have not thy glorious acts thereby ascended
> Great Brittaines stage, even to Princes places,
>> Led on in triumph by the noblest spirits
>> That ever deignd to write of anies merits?

before anticipating further travels through China, Arabia and
elsewhere in India, concluding:

> But by the way, forget not Gugurat,   [Gujerat]
> The Lady of this mighty kings Dominion:
> Visit Baroche, Cambaia, and Surat,
> And Amdavar; all which in my opinion
>   Yeeld much content: & then more to glad yee,
>   Weele have a health to all our friends in Tadee.
>
>   [toddy: palm wine]

People liked Tom Coryate, and were kind to him.

There is the letter to his mother, quoted earlier; of unusual
interest is the letter addressed mostly to his old writing–
drinking friends in London, particularly 'To the high
Seneschall of the right Worshipfull Fraternitie of Sirenical
Gentlemen, that meet the first Fridaie of every Moneth, at the
signe of the Meremaide in Bread Street . . .'. He thanks them
for the mock 'safe-conduct' letter they had given him, which
he says he may make use of in 'venerous Venice' where he will
'decantate, yea and blazon' their praises. He asks to be
remembered to some twenty friends and acquaintances –
almost everyone he can remember, it seems – including John
Donne, Christopher Brooke, Inigo Jones, 'Samuel Purkas [a
spelling that confirms pronunciation], the great collector of the
Lucubrations of sundry Classical authors, for the description
of Asia, Africa and America', several notable lawyer-writers,
the King's goldsmith, William Stansby, the printer of the
Crudities and *Crambe*, and 'also to his childless wife', and the
booksellers around St Paul's churchyard (the chief book-
selling area in London). Coryate seems to be feeling his
isolation, far from home, family and friends, miles and miles
and years away.

However, the letter to Whitaker also happily announces the
arrival, on 18 September 1615, in Surat near the west coast,
not so very far away, of 'a very generous and worthy Knight, a
deare friend of mine, Sir Thomas Rowe . . . This newes doth
refocillate (I will use my old phrase so well known to you) my

spirits: for I hope he will use me graciously, for old acquaintance sake.' Roe, slightly younger than Coryate, had had a court appointment under Elizabeth, had been knighted by King James in 1605, and had been on good terms with Prince Henry, at whose court he probably became acquainted with Coryate; his cousin had done Coryate a good turn in Frankfurt in 1608; they had friends in common, notably Ben Jonson and John Donne. He was coming to Ajmer: things might pick up now for Tom Coryate.

The little group of Englishmen that Roe was joining constituted a far-flung, Indian outpost of the East India Company, as it was later to be known though originally more concerned with the East Indies. The official English trading monopolists for the area, the Company's agents and ships were frequently in violent conflict with the well-established Portuguese and Dutch; the to-and-fro of trade struggles eventually brought the first English ship to land in India to moor off Surat in the Gulf of Cambay, in August 1608. The captain, William Hawkins, quickly began negotiations for trading rights with the Mughal Empire, and to set up a 'factory' or trading centre at Surat, despite the non-cooperation of the Emperor's local agent and the active opposition of the Portuguese. In 1609 Hawkins went to the Court at Agra, where Jahangir took to him, providing him with money, a Court position and an Armenian Christian wife, as well as promising (without actually confirming) permission for a factory at Surat, to which Hawkins returned in 1611, having fallen out of favour. Another agent, Henry Middleton, then took over, whilst setting up an important anchorage nearby at the unpromisingly named Swalley Hole (Suvali). In 1612 the Company sent two more ships to Surat, under Thomas Best, who continued the seemingly endless negotiations, whilst soundly defeating a larger Portuguese fleet, which impressed the Mughal spectators on land. Relations improved, and in 1613 Best was able to send back a ship laden with a new cargo, of Indian cloth; oriental fabrics were soon to figure largely in English vocabulary – 'cotton' and 'muslin' derive from Arabic, 'taffeta' from Persian, and 'calico', 'chintz' and 'cashmere' are Indian in origin. With trade and profits improving, the Company persuaded King James to send an ambassador to the Great Mughal (at their expense) to secure trade relations, and in September 1615 Sir Thomas Roe came, to a land which he described disgustedly as 'a miserable and barren Countrey, the Townes and Villages all built of mudde, so that there is not a house for a man to rest in'.

On 22 December he arrived in Ajmer, not feeling too well, which may have increased his distaste for the 'base old Citie, wherein is no house but of mudde, not so great as a Cottage on Hownslo-heath: only himselfe [the Emperor] hath one of stone. His Lords live in Tents.' Here, as he recorded, 'Master Edwardes the Agent mett me, accompanied with the famous unwearied walker Tho. Coryatt (who on foote had passed most of Europe and Asya, and was Now arrived in India, beeing but the beginning of his purposed travells) and some other Christians residents in Adsmere'. Coryate welcomed him with (we are told) 'a long, eloquent oration'. Roe seems to have viewed Coryate with a wry amusement, as in a later letter to Lord Pembroke, remarking how

the fates have sent him hither to ease mee, and now lives in my house [with an eye to both his comfort and status as the King's representative, Roe had quickly added to his 'mudde walls, upon canes, a doozen thatched rooms']. He came heither afoote: hath past by Constantinople, Jerusalem, Bethlem, Damascus, and (breefly) through all the Turkes territory: scene every post and pillar: observed every tombe; visited the monuments of Troy, Persia, and this Kings dominions, all afoote, with most unwearied leggs: and is now for Samarcand in Tartarya, to kisse Tamerlans tombe: from thence to Susa, and to Prester Jhac [John] in Ethiopia, wher he will see the hill Amara, all afoote: and so foote it to Odcombe. His notes are already to great for portage: some left at Aleppo, some at Hispan – enough to make any stationer an alderman that shall but serve the printer with paper. And his exercise here, or recreation, is making or reapeating orations, principally of my Lady Hartford.

The orations come as no surprise, unlike Lady Hertford. As mentioned earlier, she was a well-known Court beauty, whose second husband had been Lord Lieutenant of Somerset and Wiltshire in 1602 and 1608, when Tom might have encountered her; now, miles and years away, she could have been no more than a (possibly wistful) memory, an occasion for rhetorical exercise, a chance to amuse Sir Thomas.

Sir Thomas had begun his arduous and frustrating diplomatic efforts promptly. Outside the Daulat Khana palace there is a signboard that records: 'In this Fort, Sir Thomas Roe, the accredited ambassador of King James 1 of England, was given the first official audience by the Emperor Jehangir on January 10th 1616 AD.' Coryate also was busy; as he remarked in a letter, he had 'many irons in the fire', particularly in learning languages, in which he had considerable facility: to his original Latin and Greek he had added Turkish and Italian in Aleppo, and was now improving his Persian and Arabic. He confessed that a fourteen-month stay in Ajmer was too long (though he was getting free lodging, and eating rather better at Roe's expense than he had been used to: Edward Terry, Roe's chaplain, mentions buffalo beef and milk, butter, cheese, mutton, poultry, geese and wild fowl, bananas, mangoes, oranges, dates, melons, etc.):

> Yet for two principall Causes it was very requisite . . . first to learne the languages of those countries through which I am to passe betwixt the bounds of the territories of this prince and Christendome, matters as availeable [important] to me as mony in my purse, as being the chiefest or rather onely meane to get the mony if I should happen to be destitute, a matter very incidentall to a poore footman pilgrime as my selfe, in these heathen and Mahometan countries through which I travell, secondly, that by the helpe of one of those languages (I meane the Persian) I might both procure unto my selfe access unto the King, and be able to expresse my minde unto him.

As his friend Ben Jonson put it, 'Language most shewes a man: speake that I may see thee.' For Coryate, language was vital – throughout his life as the expression and overflow of a lively, quirky and eccentric mind, but also as the means of engaging the sympathy and support of the wealthy and powerful, essential for his travel research and the writing intended to make him famous. To the Mughal Emperor, his Court and country, Coryate now had to turn.

TWELVE

To the Field of Bones

The empire over which Jahangir ruled was of relatively recent origin, established by the Mongol leader Babur (a descendant of Tamburlaine and Genghis Khan) in 1525–30; his son Humayun became Emperor in 1530, ruling territories from Afghanistan and the Punjab up to the Himalayas and the Delhi plain as far as Allahabad. When Akbar, who succeeded to the Peacock Throne in 1556, died in 1605, the Mughal Empire covered Northern India, stretching from Kabul and Kandahar, across via Lahore and Kashmir to the Bengal coast in the east, and south to the borders of Golconda (until the eighteenth century the world's only source of diamonds) and Ahmadnagar, to roughly the latitude 20° North. This huge territory produced enormous wealth, funnelled to the princes and royal families (as in Turkey, all property reverted to the monarch on the death of the owner; as Sir Thomas Roe observed, 'He is every mans heire when he dyeth, which maketh him rich, and the Countrey so evil builded'). Edward Terry remarked that 'the Great Mogol, considering his most large Territories, his full and great Treasures, with the many rich Commodities his Provinces afford, is the greatest and richest known King of the East, if not of the whole world'. Coryate estimated that the Emperor's annual revenue 'exceedeth the Turk and the Persian his Neighbour by just halfe: for his Revenues are 40 millions of Crownes of six shillings value, by the yeare [£12 million]', but William Hawkins put the annual value nearer £56 million, which seems not unlikely – this at a time when the English king might have had access to half a million.

The succession did not go smoothly: while Akbar was away
fighting in the Deccan, his son Salim staged a coup, forcing his
hurried return; Akbar had intended to name Salim's son,
Khusrau, as heir, but died before he could enact that, possibly
of dysentery, possibly of natural causes. Soon after Salim's
accession, when he took the name Jahangir ('World-Seizer'),
Khusrau made his own bid for power (like father, like son),
with the consequences for himself indicated in the previous
chapter. Purchas quotes a story by Coryate, of other
consequences of the rebellion:

> After Shaof Freed had wonne the Battle of Lahor by a stratagem, the
> Captaines being taken by the King, and hanged upon Flesh-hookes
> [presumably the equivalent of the Turkish practice of gaunching] and
> Stakes, made an entrance for the King to Lahor, his son Cursaroo
> being then taken Prisoner, and riding bare-footed upon an Elephant,
> his Father demanded him how he liked that Spectacle of his valiant
> and faithfull Captaines hanging in that manner, to the number of two
> thousand: hee answered him, that hee was sorrie to see so much
> Crueltie and Injustice in his Father, in executing them that had done
> nothing but their dutie; for that they lived upon his Bread and Salt:
> but he should have done right if hee had saved them, and punished
> him which was their Master,

which, it appears, he did.

Apparently unwilling actually to kill his troublesome son,
Jahangir preferred to be safe rather than sorry. Coryate
records that

> during his imprisonment, the king intending to make a hunting
> Progresse of foure moneths [being at least as keen on hunting as was
> King James] consulted how to keepe him safe in his absence; at last
> resolved to build a Towre, and immure him within it, without gate,
> doore or window, except some small holes to let in Ayre higher than
> he could come unto; putting in sorts of provision whatsoever, both
> fire, cloathes, &c. with some servants to abide with him for that time.
> While this was building, his [Khusrau's] Wife came and fell at the
> Kings feete, and never would let goe till she had obtayned leave to
> bee shut up with him: the King much perswading to enjoy her

libertie; she utterly refused any other comfort, then to be the companion of her Husbands miseries; amongst which this was the greatest, that if any of those that were immured, being in number fiftie, should have dyed in the Kings absence, there was no meanes to burie them, for that no man was admitted to come neare the Towre.

Her reward was both to have her request granted, and to be Khusrau's only wife.

This was the man that Coryate hoped to impress: keen on hunting, blood sports, cruel punishments and too much wine, caught up in court ritual, tolerant in religion and controlled by his wife. Coryate tells us,

> an olive colour his face presenteth: hee is of a seemely composition of bodie; of a stature little unequal (as I guesse not without grounds of probabilitie) to mine [Coryate seems to have been of less than average height], but much more corpulent than myselfe [hardly surprising, considering their respective recent diets] . . . It is said that he is uncircumcised, wherein he differeth from all the Mahometan Princes that ever were in the world . . . a verie worthy person, by name Selim . . . 53 yeares of age [46, actually], his nativitie daie having beene celebrated with wondefull pompe since my arrivall heere for that daie he weighed himselfe in a paire of golden Scales, which by great chance I saw the same day (a custome that he observeth most inviolablie every Year) laying so much golde in the other Scale as countervaileth the weight of his body, and the same he afterward distributed to the poore.

Sir Thomas Roe saw the ceremony in September 1616, when Jahangir (apparently weighing 1,173 pounds) was weighed against jewels, gold, silver, cloth of gold, cloth of silver, silk, butter, rice and fruit (the poor might have got some of the food, at any rate): 'He was so rich in Jewels, that I must confesse I never saw together so unvallewable wealth.' Edward Terry, who was present, reported:

> When the Mogol is thus weighed, he casts about among the standers by thin pieces of silver and some of Gold, made like flowers of that Countery, and some of them are made like Cloves,

and some like Nutmegs, but very thin and hollow. Then he drinks to his Nobles in his Royal wine . . . he drank to my Lord Ambassadour, in a Cup of gold most curiously enameled, and set all over the outside with stones (which are small Rubies, Turkesses, and Emeralds) with a Cover, or Plate to set it in, both of pure Gold . . . which he then gave unto my Lord Ambassadour.

Jahangir liked to get lots of presents: pictures, 'especialy if there were faire and beautifull women portrayed in them' (though, to be fair, he enjoyed and encouraged art: he admired a miniature of Roe's by Isaac Oliver, and had it copied perfectly), swords, rapiers, embroidery, jewels and anything expensive – Roe was to find that he could not keep up with rival Eastern ambassadors and potentates. Coryate recorded a present from the King of Bijapur in August 1615:

One of the richest presents that I have heard to be sent to my prince in al my life time. It consisteth of divers parcels, one beeing elephants, whereof there were 31, and of those two so gloriously adorned as I never saw the like, nor shal see the like again while I live. For they wore foure chaines about their bodies all of beaten gold; two chaines about their legges of the same; furniture for their buttocks of pure gold; two lyons upon their heads of the like gold; the ornaments of each amounting to the value of almost eight thousand pounds sterling; and the whole present was worth a hundred thousand pounds sterling.

Roe was very critical in his comments on the town of Ajmer, even though it had a pleasant setting with wooded hills and several large lakes, but even he must have been pleased by the sandstone Daulat Khana palace in the Daulat Bagh gardens, with its cypress trees, and the castle, which William Finch described as

seated upon the top of an inaccessible Mountaine of 3 course ascent, being a Fort invincible ['1½ mile in circuit, taken in with a strong wall . . . and a pretty Massit' (Masjid, mosque), according to Peter Mundy, 'also little gardens and Fresh greene trees and flowers'] . . . without the wals [of the town] are many Antiquities [the Mughals let older buildings, especially those now owned but not wanted by the Emperor, decay], amongst which some 2 course toward Agra is a very faire Tanke [very large stone-walled reservoir]. This place is only famous for the Sepulchre of Hoghee Mundee [Khwaja Muin-ud-din-Chishti], a [Sufi] Saint much respected by the Mogols, to whom . . . the Acabar [Akbar] made a Romery [pilgrimage] on foot from Agra to obtayne a Sonne [Mundy has a nice story of Akbar's humble progress being barefoot but on carpets, the carpet he had just walked over being quickly brought round again before him]. Before you come to this Tombe, you passe three faire Courts . . . the doore is large and inlayed with Mother of Pearle, and the pavement about the Tombe is of interlayed Marble; the Sepulchre very curiously wrought in worke of Mother of Pearle, and Gold, with an Epitaph in the Persian Tongue.

Jahangir's way of life in Ajmer is suggested by Roe's description of the Great Mughal riding to his hunting camp:

His sword and buckler set all over with great Diamonds and Rubies, the belts of gold sutable: another hung on his quiver with thirty arrowes, and his bow in a case (the same that was presented by the Persian Ambassador), on his head he wore a rich Turbant, with a plumbe [plume] of horne tops, not many, but long: on one side hung a Rubie unset, as big as a Walnut; on the other side a Diamond as great; in the middle an Emerald like a heart, much bigger. His Sash was wreathed about with a chaine of great Pearle, Rubies and Diamonds drild: about his necke he caryed a Chaine of most excellent Pearle thrice double, so great as I never saw: at his elbowes armelets set with Diamonds, and on his wrists three rows of Diamonds of severall sorts: his hands bare, but on almost every finger a Ring; his gloves were English, stucke under his girdle; his coat of cloath of Gold, without sleeves, upon a fine Semian as thinne as Lawne: on his feet a paire of embroydered buskins with Pearle, the toes sharpe and turning up. Thus armed and accommodated he went to the Coach, which attended him with his new English servant [sent out to drive this gift of a coach, which, however, was not thought sufficiently richly ornamented and fitted], who was cloathed as rich as any Player [English actors often wore courtiers' cast-offs], and more gaudy, and had trained foure horses, which were trapped and harnished in Gold Velvets.

This was the first he ever sate in, and was made by [copied from] that sent from England, so like, that I knew it not but by the cover, which was a Gold Persian Velvet. He got into the end, on each side went two Eunuches, that carried small Maces of Gold, set all over with Rubies, with a long bunch of white-horse-taile to drive away flyes: before him went Drummes, ill Trumpets, and loud musick.

Wiliam Finch relates how Jahangir went hunting in closed royal game reserves: the game taken was sold and the money given to the poor; on the other hand, any men, 'poor inhabitants of these woods and desarts', caught in these forbidden areas might be enslaved and sold off in Kabul.

Coryate, Roe and Terry all record various instances of Jahangir's severe punishments. In July 1616 a woman from the extensive harem (one, wrote Terry, that 'he had formerly touched and kept Company withall, but now she was superannuated, for neither himself nor Nobles (as they say) come near their wives, or women, after they exceed the age of thirty years, though they keep them and allow them some maintenance') 'was taken in the Kings house', writes Roe, 'in some action with an Eunuch; another Capon that loved her, killed him; the poore woman was set up to the arme-pits in the earth, hard rammed, her feet tied to a stake, to abide three dayes and two nights without any sustenance, her head and armes exposed to the Sunnes violence: if she dyed not in that time, shee should be pardoned: the Eunuch was condemned to the Elephants [to be torn apart and trampled]'. She survived, reports Terry, 'almost to noon on the second day, crying out most lamentably when she was able to speak in her language . . . Ah my head, my head!' In another instance, a group of some hundred bandits was sentenced to death; the leader and thirteen others were chained and then torn to pieces by ravening dogs, whilst the others had their hands bound to their feet, and their necks cut with a sword, 'but not quite off, and so left naked, bloody and stincking to every mans vew and incommodytie'.

Coryate also remarked on Jahangir's piety and religious tolerance: 'He speaketh very reverently of our Saviour, calling him in the Indian tongue, Ifazaret Eesa, that is, the great Prophet, Jesus: and all Christians, especiallie us English, he useth so benevolently, as no Mahometan Prince the like.' Coryate was later to abuse this toleration, in Agra, as Edward Terry related:

Tom Coryate upon a time having heard their Moolaes [mullahs: priests] often (as before) so to cry . . . [in the mosques, 'in Arabian: *La Illah, illa Allah, Mahomet Resul-Alla*: that is, no God but one God, and Mahomet the Ambassadour of God'] . . . got him upon an high place directly opposite to one of those Prophets, and contradicted him thus. *La illa illa alla, Hasaret Eesa Ben-alla*, that is, no God but one God, and the Lord Christ the son of God, and further added that Mahomet was an Impostor: and all this he spake in their owne language as loud as he possibly could, in the eares of many Mahometans that heard it. But whether (circumstances considered) the zeale or discretion of our Pilgrim were more here to be commended, I leave to the judgment of my reader.

That he did so, I am sure, and I further believe how that bold attempt of his, if it had been acted in many other places of Asia, would have cost him his life with as much torture as cruelty could have invented. But he was here taken for a mad-man, and so let alone.

Coryate's attention-seeking performances, here as self-elected champion of Christianity, were becoming more extravagant – and risky; but not even devout Muslims would take him seriously.

There were limits to Jahangir's toleration, where he felt confronted by insincerity. He once asked an Armenian Christian if he knew of any converted by the Jesuits out of real conviction rather than by profit-seeking (the Jesuits, who had been active in the area for some years, offered converts a pension of three pence a day), and was told of this man's servant, who was then interrogated but would not yield despite offers of bribes and threats of whipping and torture, for which Jahangir praised him, 'giving him a rupia a day pension for his integritie'. Two months later, Jahangir summoned the servant to collect a wild pig that he had killed while hunting, to take to his master as a present; on the way home with the pig, the servant was so jeered at by 'Mohammedans' that he threw it away in a ditch, without telling his master. When later Jahangir enquired of the Armenian and learned that the pig had not been received, the whole story came out. 'Now,' said Jahangir, 'I see thou art neither good Christian nor good Mahumetan, but a dissembling knave with both. While I found thee sincere, I gave thee a pension; which now I take from thee, and for thy dissimulation doe Command thee to have a hundred stripes.' He might also have been annoyed over the treatment of his present.

To some extent, Jahangir's religious tolerance may have been learned from his father. Coryate tells a story of how

> Ecbar Shaugh, a very fortunate Prince and pious to his Mother . . . never denied her anything but this that shee demanded of him, that our Bible might be hanged about an Asses necke, and beaten about the Towne of Agra, for that the Portugals having taken a ship of theirs at Sea, in which was found the Alcoran among the Moores, tyed it about the necke of a Dogge, and beat the same Dogge about the Towne of Ormuz: but hee denied her request, saying, That if it were ill in the Portugals to doe so to the Alcoran, being it became not a King to requite ill with ill, for that the contempt of any Religion was the contempt of God, and he would not be revenged uppon an innocent Booke; the morall being, that God would not suffer the sacred Booke of his Truth to be contemned amongst the Infidels.

Coryate's 'moral' fails to take Akbar's moral point. Elsewhere, he records pious actions by Jahangir that he observed: 'when at Asmere he went afoote to the Tombe of the Prophet Hod. Mundin there buried [as did his father], and kindling a fire with his owne hands, and his Normahal [his chief wife], under that immense and Heidelbergian-aequipollent Brasse-pot [as big as the great tun of Heidelberg], and made Kitcherie [*khichri*: kedgeree, made with rice, lentils, etc.] for five thousand poore, taking out the first Platter with his owne hands, and serving one; Normahal the second, and so his Ladies all the rest. Cracke mee this Nut, all the Papall Charitie vaunters.' A similar ceremony is still performed by rich men at the Urs Mela festival in October in Ajmer. Coryate also relates that when Jahangir was awake at night, he would call for 'certaine poore and old men, making them sit by him, with many questions and familiar speeches passing the time; and at their departure clothes them and gives them bountifull almes often, whatsoever they demand, telling the money into their hands'. Likewise, Roe describes Jahangir's benevolent treatment of an old fakir: 'This miserable wretch cloathed in rags, crowned with feathers, covered with ashes, his Majestie talked with about an houre with suche familiaritie and shew of kindnesse, that it must needs argue an humilitie not found easily among Kings.' The King also gave the old man a hundred rupees, fed him from his own banqueting table and embraced him.

Such performances were not Jahangir's main pastime. Finch tells how 'fighting of Elephants, Lyons, Bulles, killing of Deare with Leopards . . . is a custom on every day of the weeke, Sunday excepted . . . but Tuesday . . . is a day of blood, both of fighting beasts, and justiced men, the King judging and seeing execution'. Coryate describes the Emperor's

> abundance of wild Beastes, and that of divers sorts, as Lyons, Elephants, Beares, Antlops, Unicorns [rhinoceros]; whereof two I have seene at his Court, the strangest beasts of the world: they were brought hither out of the Countrie of Bengala . . . of Elephants the King keepeth 30,000 in his whole Kingdome at an unmeasurable charge . . . The King keepeth a thousand women for his own body, whereof the chiefest (which is his Queene) is called Normal.

Apart from his concubines and young boys, he also had eighteen official wives; apropos of this, Coryate tells of a curious bazaar:

> One day in the yeere, for the solace of the Kings Women, all the Trades-mens Wives enter the Mohal with somewhat to sell, in the manner of a Faire, where the King is Broker for his Women, and

with his gaines that night makes his supper, no man present (observe that whatsoever is brought in of virill shape, as instance in Raddishes, so great is the jealousie, and so frequent the wickednesse of this people, that they are cut and jagged for feare of converting the same to some unnaturall abuse [how big were the radishes?]): by this meanes hee attaines to the sight of all the prettie Wenches of the Towne: at such a kind of Faire he got his beloved Normahal.

It was not quite that simple. This was a beautiful and shrewd Persian woman, Mihr un-Nisa, whom Jahangir had been keen on for some time; somehow, she got married to an official who was then posted away to Bengal, where conveniently he soon died. She promptly returned, and married Jahangir a few months later, in 1611, when she deposed his then first wife and acquired the title Nur Mahal, or 'Light of the Palace', before becoming Nur Jahan, 'Light of the World'. Despite having to keep in the background, she became the centre of a dominating Persian clique at court; weakened by illness, indolence and alcoholism, Jahangir increasingly relied on his wife for decisions in government. Roe once caught a glimpse of her, at a jarokha [small, balcony] window, before an audience with Jahangir:

At one side in the window were his two principal wives, whose curiosity made them break little holes in a grate of reed that hung before it to gaze on me. I saw first their fingers, and after laying their faces close, now one eye and now another; sometimes I could discern the full proportion. They were indifferently white, black hair smoothed up; but if I had no other light, their diamonds and pearls had sufficed to show them. When I looked up they retired, and were so merry that I supposed they laughed at me.

This was the court and man that Coryate had to reach and impress. It was Jahangir's practice to show himself to his people three times a day, at dawn, at the jarokha or interview window, when the nobles performed Tessillam (obeisance), each bowing low and touching the ground with the back of the right hand before bringing the palm up to the crown of the head; then at noon, when he might behold Tamashan (entertainment), and then between three and four, when he might hear public matters and grant suits. (Any serious government business was done in the evening, in the 'ghusl khana' – literally, 'bathroom', equivalent to the Privy Chamber.) Coryate knew that Roe would disapprove of him going, so informed only one close friend, probably Terry, before attending, dressed in Indian clothing. Somehow he caught the Emperor's attention, and was permitted to make his oration – in Persian. He later transcribed this, together with a translation. It begins, 'Lord Protector of the World, all haile to you. I am a poore traveller and World-Seer, which am come hither from a farre countrie, namely England, which auncient Historians thought to have been scituated in the farthest bounds of the west, and which is the Queene of all the Ilands in the World.' He explains that he has come, first, to see 'the blessed face of your Majesty, whose wonderfull fame hath resounded all over Europe', secondly, to see the elephants, thirdly, to see the Ganges, 'the captaine of all the rivers of the world', and, fourthly, to obtain the Emperor's pass to travel to Samarkand, 'to visit the blessed sepulcher of the Lord of the Corners [by which he meant Tamburlaine] whose fame, by reason of his warres and victories is published over the whole world'. He concludes, 'So farre have I traced the world into this country that my pilgrimage hath accomplished three thousand miles; wherein I have sustained much labour and toile, the like whereof no mortall man in the world did ever perform, to see the blessed face of Your Majesty since the first day that you were inaugurated in your glorious monarchall throne.' Unfortunately, the Emperor told him that he could not help him to get to Samarkand, as there was no friendship between Tartary and himself, and warned him that the Tartars, hating all Christians, would certainly kill him if he entered their country; however, 'he concluded his discourse with me by a summe of money, that he threw downe from a window . . . an hundred pieces of silver, each worth two shillings sterling, which countervailed ten pounds of our English Money'.

According to Edward Terry, Jahangir had taken his strange orator for 'a Derveese, or Votary, or Pilgrim (for so he called him), and such as bear that name in that Countrey seem not much to care for money, and that was the reason (I conceive) that he gave him not a more plentiful Reward'. As Coryate had anticipated, Roe (who was very careful of his dignity as English Ambassador) was not at all pleased with him, telling him it was discreditable for an Englishman to have behaved 'in that beggerly and poore fashion to the King, out of an insinuating humour, to crave Money of him: But I answered our Ambassadour in that stout and resolute manner, after I had ended my businesse, that he was contented to cease nibling at me, never had I more need of Money in all my life then at that time: for in truth I had but twentie shillings sterling left in my Purse'. He then went two days' journey to visit 'a certaine Noble and Generous Christian of the Armenian Race' (of whom we have probably heard before) and gave him another oration in Persian, and received money to the value of forty shillings (£2). His linguistic skills – which appear to have been considerable – were not exercised solely for profit, but sometimes out of sheer exuberance: 'He having got a great mastery likewise in the Indostan or more vulgar language,' Terry remembers, 'there was a woman, a Landress, belonging to my Lord Embassadors house, who had such a freedome and liberty of speech, that she would sometimes scould, brawl and rant from the Sun-rising to Sun-set; one day he undertook her in her own language, and by eight of the clock in the morning had so silenced her, that she had not one word more to speak.' For vocabulary, invention and sheer vivacity, that beats any stuffy, prepared oration.

Life in Ajmer, even if more comfortable than Coryate's life on the road, had its drawbacks for the little English community. The houses were, as Roe had complained, flimsy, of mud and lath, not particularly secure against wind and rain; fires were frequent, fed by the dry grass and hay stored nearby as fodder for the animals. The English factory, containing valuable merchandise, was seriously threatened by fire in May, so that Roe had it rebuilt more securely in brick and loam; in August, torrential rain produced severe flooding, surrounding the building and again threatening the goods inside, until Jahangir arranged for a sluice to be opened, lowering the water level. 'All was soe moyled with dust and water that I could scarce lye drye or safe, so that I must be at chardge in reparations,' complained Roe. 'Thus were we every way afflicted, with fires, smokes, floodes, stormes, heate, dust, flyes, and no temperate or quiett seasons.' He was not a happy man.

It is not surprising that Coryate was keen to get away for a while, and see more of the country. On 12 September he left Ajmer, with some English merchants, to go to Agra, when (in recognition of his straitened circumstances – and what he might do to alleviate them) Roe gave him, as he reported in his October letter to his mother, 'a piece of Gold of this Kings Coyne worth foure and twentie shillings', so that, as he calculated, since he came into the country he had received 'twentie markes sterling, save two shillings eight pence', as well as Lady Sherley's gift, which he now valued at 33 shillings and four pence. 'At this present I have in the Citie of Agra, where-hence I wrote this letter, about twelve pounds sterling', which, at his usual rate of expenditure of two pence a day ('such is the cheapnesse of all eatable things in Asia, drinkable things costing nothing, for seldom doe I drinke in my Pilgrimage any other liquor than pure water' – though the water was not likely to have been as pure as he thought), would, he estimated, maintain him for three more years' travel.

His intention was to stay in Agra for six weeks, before going on to Hardwar (modern Haridwar), to watch thousands of 'the gentle people of this Countrey called Banians [Hindus]' bathe in the Ganges and 'sacrifice a world of Gold to the same River, partly in stamped Money and partly in massie great lumpes and wedges, throwing it into the River as a sacrifice, and doing other strange Ceremonies most worthy the observation . . . Superstition and Impietie most abominable in the highest degree of these brutish Ethnicks, that are aliens from Christ

and the Common-wealth of Israel'. After the reference to
'gentle people', the last sentence comes as a shock; it may be
only the automatic condemnation expected of a clergyman's
son writing to a clergyman's widow. The letter includes a list
of people to whom he wishes to be remembered – not the
smart, London literary set, but Somersetshire people: the
Reverend Hancoke, his wife, their sons and their wives, the
widow Darby, old Master Dyer and his son, 'I had almost
forgotten your husband' (!), his old patrons Sir Edward and Sir
Robert Phelips, and even his old legal foe, Master Starre of
Yeovil, the 'vilipendious linnen draper' – a once familiar,
small-scale, provincial milieu, remembered now from far
away, among strangers.

Agra itself was one of the great cities of northern India
trading in indigo, silks from Bengal and Bihar, musk from
Bhutan, shawls, saffron and walnuts from Kashmir, diamonds
and spices from Golconda; none of Coryate's notes on it
(which would have been extensive) has survived (that he did
not mention in his letter to his mother the great plague in the
city when he was there is hardly surprising). William Finch
and then Peter Mundy evoke it:

> spacious, large, populous beyond measure, that you can hardly
> passe in the streets, which are for the most part dirty and narrow,
> save only the great Bazar and some few others which are large and
> faire. The city lyeth in manner of a half-moone, bellying to the
> land-ward some 5 corse in length, and as much by the Rivers side,
> upon the banks whereof are many goodly houses of the Nobility,
> pleasantly over-looking Gemini [River Jamuna], which runneth
> with a swift movement . . . the Castle [founded by Akbar, built
> 1565–73], one of the finest and admirablest buildings of the East,
> some three or foure miles in compasse . . . loftie and stately,
> garnished with handsome Compleat battlements on the wall; about
> it appearinge divers of the Kings places of residence some of
> whose upper Coveringe are overlaid with gold.

Mundy praises the many gardens, with orange, mulberry,
mango, cocoanut, fig and banana trees, roses and marigolds, and

the great fruit, vegetable and meat market, while also
mentioning another very active market area, 'the common
stewes . . . each of them every evening is like a faire, where they
resort, make their bargaines, take and choose the whores sittinge
and lyeinge on their Cotts att their balcones and doores'. Coryate
did tell Terry about the Palace 'Turrets about ten foot square
covered with massie Gold', while the English merchants
described to him the great 'Throne . . . ascended by divers steps,
which are covered with plate of silver, at the top of which
ascent stand four Lions upon pedestals (of curiously coloured
Marble) which Lions are made of massie silver, some part of
them guilded with Gold, and beset with precious stones. Those
Lions support a Canopy of pure Gold under which the Mogol
sits, when as he appears in his greatest state and glory.' Mundy
described the Peacock Throne: 'all of pure gold, curiously
engraven, enamelled and sett off with diamonds, Rubies,
emralds, Saffiers, etts., prettious stones', estimated as worth £1¼
million. It is not known where Coryate would have stayed when
visiting Agra: possibly in the homes of sympathetic merchants,
or in the *padri tola*, the Roman Catholic residential complex, or
even in the Nur Mahal Ki Sarai, the travellers' lodge just outside
the city, where Mundy stayed in 1632.

Coryate was busy with (non-Christian) religious sightseeing
elsewhere: the Hardwar bathing festival, as Terry confirms,
where the Ganges passed through a rock that Hindus thought
looked like a cow's head, 'which of all sensible Creetures they
love best' (and Sir Thomas Roe's map of the Mughal Empire,
actually drawn by William Baffin, mapmaker, surveyor and
mate of the *Anna*, in which Roe returned to England, shows
Hardwar with a cow's head; likewise, the indication of
'Jallamakee, the pilgrimage of the Banians', derives from
Coryate). There were also Akbar's tomb at Sikander, 'built
high like a Pyramus with many curiosities about it . . . [the]
most sumptious Pile of all the structures that vast Monarchy
affords'; Nagarkot in the north-east Punjab, the silver-plated
shrine of Mata Devi, where, he reported, the faithful 'out of
the officiousness of their devotion, cut off some part of their

Tongues to offer unto [the idol] as a Sacrifice, which (they say) grow out again as before' (but Terry doubted that); and the volcanic eruptions at Javala Mukhti (modern Jawalamukhi), 'where, out of cold Springs that issue out from amongst hard Rocks, are daily to be seen continued Eruptions of Fire, before which the Idolatrous People fall down and worship . . . these places were seen and strictly observed by Mr Coryat'.

It would soon be time to be moving on; on 20 July 1617 Roe wrote from the old fortress city of Mandu, Jahangir's latest base, to the English merchants at Agra, warning them of possible developments – negotiations with Jahangir were, as ever, proving frustrating, and Roe thought (hoped) he might be recalled, or sent on to Persia – and asking whether Coryate was 'for England, or stay; or if I take any new course, whither hee will goe with me'. This was kind of Roe: Coryate had been out a long time, and was showing the effects: on Michaelmas Day 1615 he had boasted of enjoying 'at this time as pancraticall [strongly exercised] and athleticall a health as ever I did in my life', but 'pure' water and 'Delhi belly' had taken their toll; now he could be helped on an overland return journey, or even get back sooner, by sea. Four hundred miles' solitary tramping later, at some time in late August or early September, leg-stretcher (and surely leg-weary) Coryate trudged through the gate of Mandu. The last part of the journey might not have been the least tiresome: 'From all parts that lye about [Mandu] but one,' wrote Terry,

the ascent is very high, and steep; and the way to us seemed exceeding long, for we were two whole dayes Climbing up the Hill with our Cariages [how was it for a lone walker?] . . . That Hill on which Mandoa stands is stuck round (as it were) with fair trees . . . that there is much delight in beholding them either from the bottom or top of that Hill. In those vast and far extended woods, there are Lions, Tygres, and other beasts of Prey, and many wild Elephants. We lay one night in that wood with our Carriages, and those Lions came about us discovering themselves by their Roaring.

Where, and how, did Coryate spend his solitary night on the slopes of the forest? Was he still relishing his sightseeing?

To this day, Mandu's rocky plateau and steeply sloping sides are covered with thick, green vegetation, while in the ancient city great, beautiful palaces and mosques crumble beside old water tanks and lovely gardens; beyond, beneath a bleached sky and its drifting kite hawks, an endless vista of sun-baked plains and huddled mud villages stretches away to the horizon. In these respects, it would have been much the same then. Here, at any rate, camped in a disused mosque and tomb enclosed in a walled courtyard (not, as Roe's little dog was to discover, secure against marauding lions) on the other side of the city, looking toward the River Narbada, he found what might be called the English Embassy and its disenchanted Ambassador. Here too he met the Revd Edward Terry.

Terry (1590–1660) was in his late twenties, a devout Oxford graduate who had been taken on as ship's chaplain in an East India Company merchantman; after an exciting voyage round the Cape to India, which included a particularly savage battle with a Portuguese carrack, he reached Swalley Road in Cambaya Bay in September 1616, when Roe persuaded him to take over as embassy chaplain (his predecessor having died of dysentery, as had, worryingly, the English cook. 'Death', wrote Terry, 'made many breaches into my Lord Ambassadours family, for of four and twenty wayters, besides his Secretary and my self, there was not above the fourth man returned home. And he himself by violent Fluxes was twice brought even to the brink of the Grave'). When Coryate arrived at Mandu he was put to share quarters, for ten or twelve weeks, with Terry, to whose book, *A Voyage to East-India*, we owe much of our knowledge of Coryate's later activities in India.

Coryate must have been glad of someone to talk to during those long, hot afternoons and cool evenings, while Terry, who clearly respected his achievements while recognising his weaknesses, recorded some of his words and activities, so that people might remember him 'who while he lived was like a perpetual motion, and therefore now dead should not be quite forgotten'. In doing this, he helped to fulfil what he knew was Coryate's great desire: ''Twas fame, without doubt, that stirred up this man unto these voluntary but hard undertakings, and the hope of that glory which he should reap after he had finished his long travels made him not at all to take notice of the hardship he found in them. That hope of name and repute for the time to come did ever feed him and feast him for the time present.' He went on to provide a (not over-generous) character assessment:

> He was a man of a very coveting eye, that could never be satisfied with seeing (as Salomon speaks, Eccles. ii.8), though he had seen very much; and I am perswaded that he took as much content in seeing, as many others in the enjoying of Great and Rare things. He was a man that had got the mastery of many hard languages . . . in which, if he had obtained wisdom to husband and manage them, as he had skill to speak them, he had deserved more fame in his generation. But his knowledge and high attainments in several Languages made him not a little ignorant of himself, he being so covetous, so ambitious of praise, that he would hear and endure more of it than he could in any measure deserve; being like a Ship that hath too much sail, and too little Ballast; yet [and this seems a very shrewd observation] if he had not fall'n into the smart hands of the Wits of those Times, he might have passed better.

Those early years performing as the pedantic clown, the Holofernes entertaining the supercilious wits of Prince Henry's court and the Mermaid Tavern, showed him how to get the attention he craved, without showing him how to present himself, and get taken, seriously; having, like Hamlet, 'put on an antic disposition', perhaps he could never quite discard it.

In any case, the hardy little footslogger was becoming noticeably frailer. Terry records how, one day at Mandu, Coryate

> there standing against a stone pillar, where the Embassadour was and myself present with them, upon a sudden he fell into such a swoon that we had very much ado to recover him out of it. But at last come to himself, he told us that some sad thoughts had

immediately before presented themselves to his fancy, which (as he conceived) put him into that distemper; like Fannius in Martial [who killed himself to escape a mortal enemy]: *Ne moriare mori*, to prevent death by dying. For he told us that there were great expectations in England of the large accounts he should give of his travels after his return home; and that he was now shortly to leave us, and he being at present not very well, if he should dye in the way toward Surat, whither he was now intended to go. . . . he might be buried in obscurity and none of his friends ever know what became of him, he travelling now, as he usually did, alone.

Always, and now more than ever, there was the fear that his achievements would go unrecognised, and that he might easily slip out of life, little known and soon forgotten, like most of us.

Jahangir's move to Mandu had been intended to provide some support for Prince Khurram and his forces in his campaign in the Deccan, to the south. On 2 October Khurram made a triumphal entry into Mandu, being awarded the title Shah Jehan ('World Ruler'); on 5 October came the unwelcome news from England that Roe was to stay on and continue negotiating; and by the 26th Jahangir had decided to move on, taking his court with him on a leisurely (but for others, exhausting) excursion before settling again. This meant that Roe and the others, including Coryate, would have to pack up and follow him, Roe himself complaining that he was 'very weak, and not likely to recover upon daily travell in the fields with cold raw muddy water'. When they caught up with the travelling court on 31 October, the camp was not yet in good order; Jahangir had gone off hunting, leaving it all 'divided and scattered into many parts; ill water, deare provisions, sicknesse and all sorts of calamitie accompanying so infinite a multitude', as Roe complained.

Progress was slow and difficult, with paths having to be cleared through jungly woodland, and water and supplies obtained off the land, at the expense of the poor local inhabitants. The earlier arrival of Jahangir's whole court at Mandu had caused a desperate water shortage (though he is unlikely to have noticed, let alone cared). Terry preserved a note by Coryate: 'Remember the charitie of two great men that in the time of this great drought were at the charge of sending ten camels with twentie persons every day to a river called Narboda for water, and did distribute the water to the poor.' Coryate knew about need, the difficulties of survival, and dependence on the whims of the mighty.

Peter Mundy's account of how a noble Indian and his entourage might travel gives some idea of the complications involved in Jahangir's progress:

First . . . they send away their Peshconna (which is a Sutte [suite] of Tents, cannatts [cloth walls] etts accommodation) to the place where they meane next to rest, hee in the meane tyme remaininge in another sute of Tents, etts. The which, when hee begins to sett forth, is carryed 2 dayes Journey forward, vizt. where he intends to stay the morowe. When himselfe is on the way, There first goe certaine Elliphants before him about ¼ mile distance with flaggs, then the measurer of the way, then troopes of horses, and among them other Eliphants with drumms on their backs, continually beating a kind of March; and now and then the Trumpetts sound. Then a great number of flaggs carried by footemen. Then cometh himselfe, either in a palanqueene [an Oriental covered litter] . . . els on horseback or upon an Eliphant, Several servants about him, some to beat away flyes, others carrye fanns to keepe away the Sunne, others with Coole water, with divers others. Then come his favourites, then the Cohouri or maine bodie of horse and foote; then after all, his Lumberment [baggage train] and people of service, as Cookes, Housekeepers, Frosts [farrash: carpet-layers] or Tent settlers, water bearers, Cahares [= cohouri], etts., there being of these alsoe gon with the former Peshconna . . . haveing also of drumms with them on Cammells.

The procedure for Jahangir and his court, including many such noblemen, was even more elaborate, with frequent diversions and halts. The 'leskar' or camp for some hundred thousand people was 20 to 30 miles in circumference, yet was so well organised that, according to Roe, it could be set up in four hours (perhaps he meant just the Emperor's section), Jahangir's red pavilions and 10ft high screens (cannats) rising up in the centre, to contain his entourage of wives, courtiers and servants, while the rest of the camp would be laid out on the same plan every time, like a small town, with designated areas for courtiers, bazaars, guards and so on.

The decision to move on was announced by drumbeats at midnight. 'When that the King removes from one place to another, for the space of twelve hours a broad passage is continually filled with passengers and Elephants, and Horses, and Dromedaries, and Camels, and Asses, and Oxen (on which the meaner sort of men and women with their little Children ride),' wrote an apparently overwhelmed Terry. Sometimes the whole circus might go as far as 10 miles in one day, sometimes less, depending on local water supplies and hunting possibilities (where these were good, they might stay for three or four days); then a camp site had to be got ready, clearing out and grubbing up trees and bushes over a large area, and the pavilions prepared, before the Emperor, his wives, eunuchs and house servants could move in.

Apart from his worsening health, Coryate was not having a good time. Early in November they were joined by Richard Steel, returning from England with a present of pearls for Jahangir, who cruelly told Tom 'that when he was in England, King James (then living) enquired after him, and when he had certified the King of his meeting him on the way, the King replied, "Is that Fool yet living?" which, when our Pilgrim heard, it seemed to trouble him very much, because the King spake no more nor no better of him; saying, that Kings would speak of poor men what they pleased'. So indeed would others, even when being helpful. Roe gave Coryate a note for £10 to be redeemed at Aleppo, with a covering note to the Consul there, that read, 'Mr Chapman, when you shall hand these letters, I desire you to receive the Bearer of them, Mr Thomas Coryat, with curtesy, for you shall find him a very honest poor wretch.' Coryate was very hurt, complaining, 'My Lord had even spoyled his Curtesy in the carriage thereof; so that if he had been a very Fool indeed, he could have said very little less of him than he did, Honest poor Wretch!' Roe kindly rewrote the letter more to Coryate's sense of his own dignity. Terry commented how 'any thing that did in any measure eclipse him in those high conceivings of his own worth did too much trouble him'. Over sensitive he might have been thought, but a little respect would not have come amiss. Dogged Ulyssean traveller he might be, but, as far as English society was concerned, he had made little progress: still the King's fool and my Lord's wretch.

In the meantime, it became apparent that Jahangir was heading for Gujarat, which did not suit poorly Coryate's plans, so, in mid-November, at Dhar (about 30 miles north of Mandu) Coryate separated from the others (Roe giving him a bill of exchange for 35 rupees, to be paid by the English factors at Surat), and set off on what was to be his last, long, lonely trek: 'My Lord willed him to stay longer with us' wrote Terry, defensively, 'but he thankfully refused that offer, and turned his face presently toward Surat, which was then about three hundred miles distant from us'. There is no information as to his route, but he could well have headed south over minor tracks to the River Narbada, that flows near Mandu, and then gone down river to the river port of Broach (modern Baruch) and then by the trade road to Surat.

Surat, some 12 miles up the River Tapti from Swalley Hole (Suvali), was a trading town of increasing importance, used by the Portuguese before becoming the main base for the English, and an embarkation point for pilgrims to Mecca; it seems to have been an attractive town in those days. The English merchant William Finch provides a very appealing account:

The Citie is of good quantitie, with many faire Merchants houses therein . . . Some three miles from the mouth of the River . . . is the Barre, where ships trade and unlade, whereon at a Spring tide is three fathoms water. Over this, the Channell is faire to the Citie side, able to beare vessels of fiftie tunnes laden . . . As you come up the River, on the right hand stands the Castle [erected in 1540 by the Sultan of Gujarat] well walled, ditched, reasonable great and faire, with a number of faire peeces, whereof some of exceeding greatnesse. It hath one gate to the Green-ward, with a

drawbridge and a small Port on the River side . . . Before this lyeth
the Medon [Maidan], which is a pleasant greene, in the middest
whereof is a May-pole to hang a light on, and for other pastimes on
great Festivalls. On this side, the Citie lyeth open to the Greene,
but on all other parts is ditched and fenced with thicke hedges, of
which one leadeth to Variaw, a small Village, where is the ford to
passe over for Cambaya way. Neare this village on the left hand
lieth a small Aldea [hamlet or villa] on the River banke very
pleasant, where stands a great Pagod, much resorted to by the
Indians . . . Hard without Nonsary gate is a faire [water-]Tank . . .
inclosed on all sides with stone steppes, three quarters of an
English mile in compasse, with a small house in the middest. On
the further side are divers faire tombes, with a goodly paved court
pleasant to behold: behind which groweth a small grove of Manga
trees, whither the Citizens goe forth to banquet. Some halfe cose [a
mile or so] behind this place is a great Tree much worshipped by
the Banians, where they affirme a Dew to keepe [a god inhabits]
. . . Neare to the Castle is the Alphandica [custom-house], where is
a paire of staires for lading and unlading of goods. Within are
roomes for keeping goods till they be cleared . . . Without this gate
is the great Gondores or Bazar. Right before this Gate stands a Tree
with an Arbour, whereon the Fokeers (which are Indian holy men)
sit in state. Betwixt this and the Castle, on the entrance of the
Greene, is the market for horse and cattell. A little lower on the
right hand over the river is a little pleasant Towne, Ranele . . . the
houses are faire therein, with high steps to each mans doore, the
streets narrow; they are very friendly to the English. Heere are
many pleasant Gardens, which attract many to passe there their
time; and on the trees are infinite number of those great Bats
which wee saw at Saint Augustines [in Africa], hanging by the
clawes on the boughes, making a shrill noise.

Peter Mundy also reports seven city gates, notably 'Baroche
Gate, out of which goe many an Englishman that never returne,
it being the way to our place of Burial'. The English factory, he
writes, was 'of the best sort in Towne, very faire and stronglie
built, the Rooffs in general flatt and terrassed alofte to walke on,
very substantiallie done with lyme, etts., so that noe rayne can
peire [harm] it, and below a faire hall, Chambers and roomes for

the President and Councell, etts. . . . a garden with long walkes and alleys, a water-tank with a fountain'. Here were ten or twelve Company officers and merchants, a preacher, a surgeon, a steward, cooks, etc., comprising some twenty-six 'persons English', who were pleased to see Coryate: people liked him and were kind to him. Terry tells us what happened:

He lived to come safely thither, but there being over-kindly used by some of the English, who gave him sack which they had brought from England; he calling for it as soon as he first heard of it, and crying: 'Sack, sack, is there such a thing as sack? I pray give me some sack'; and drinking of it (though, I conceive, moderately, for he was a very temperate man), it increased his flux [probably dysentery] which he had then upon him. And this caused him within a few days, after his very tedious and troublesome travels (for he went most on foot) at this place to come to his journey's end, for here he overtook Death in the month of December 1617, and was buried (as aforesaid ['on the banks of the river at Swally']) under a little Monument, like one of those are usually made in our Church-yards.

Suvali seems an odd choice for his burial; Terry was not there at the time, and is not always wholly accurate in his recall; but a mile north of Suvali stands a domed Muslim monument, which came to be known as 'Tom Coryate's Tomb', and used to be so marked on British Admiralty charts. On the other hand, the well-used English graveyard outside Surat (now 'melancholic' and 'weed-choked', with some 400 graves, according to the Rough Guide to India) seems a more probable burial place. In November 1627 Thomas Herbert, then in the retinue of a new ambassador travelling to Persia, saw the body of a Persian nobleman, who had died on board ship, 'entombed' at Surat, 'not a stone's throw from Tom Coryate's grave, known by two small stones that speak his name, there resting till the Resurrection'. Another Englishman, John Fryer, later saw the Persian's tomb outside Surat's Broach Gate, near the English graveyard, 'not far from whence, on a small hill on the left hand of the road, lies Thomas Coriat, our English fakier (as they name him)'. Today – of one who wrote out so many memorials – there is, however, no trace.

Roe bundled up some of Coryate's notes and got them back to England. Terry wrote a weak verse 'epitaph' for 'the Wanderer of his age, I Who . . . spent full many pretious daies I As if he had his beeing I To wast his life in seeing' but at last 'Fell blinded in this narrow Tombe'. He concluded more eloquently in prose (the theatrical metaphor he employed was conventional, but may have seemed particularly apt, recognising the performer and role-player in Tom's character):

Sic exit Coryatus; hence he went off the Stage, and so must all after him, how long soever their parts seem to be: For if one should go to the extremest part of the World East, another West, another North, and another South, they must all meet at last together in the Field of Bones, wherein our Traveller hath now taken up his lodging, and where I leave him.

True enough; but rather than leaving him lost in anonymous dust, let Tom, with a characteristic flourish and modest fanfaronade (he would have liked the expression), sign off for himself, as he did to his London friends:

Farewell noble Sirenaicks.
Your generosities most obliged Countreyman,
ever to be commanded by you, the Hierosolymi-
tan-Syrian-Mesopotamian-Armenian-Me-
dian-Parthian-Persian-Indian Legge-
Stretcher of Odcombe in Somerset,

THOMAS CORYATE

Bibliography

(Place of publication is London, except where indicated.)

THOMAS CORYATE
Coryats Crudities (1611); repr. 2 vols (Glasgow, James MacLehose, 1905).
Coryats Crambe (1611).
Letter No. 1 (15 Nov. 1610, to Sir Michael Hicks), in Samuel Egerton
   Brydges (ed.), *Censura Literaria*, vol. 8 (1808).
Letters No. 2, 3, 4, 5 (1615), in *Thomas Coriate, Traveller for the
   English Wits* (1618).
'Notes Made in India', in Samuel Purchas (ed.), *Purchas his
   Pilgrimes*, part I, book IV (1625); repr. 20 vols (Glasgow, James
   MacLehose, 1905–7).
'Master Thomas Coryates Travels to . . . Constantinople . . .
   Jerusalem', in Samuel Purchas (ed.), *Purchas his Pilgrimes*, part II,
   book X (1625); repr. 20 vols (Glasgow, James MacLehose, 1905–7).
Letter No. 6 (1616), in John Taylor, *All the Workes of John Taylor the
   Water-Poet* (1630).

CONTEMPORARY WRITING
Anon., *The Odcombian Banquet* (1611).
Aubrey, John, *Aubrey's Brief Lives*, ed. Andrew Clark, 2 vols (Oxford,
   Clarendon Press, 1898).
Cartwright, John, *The Preachers Travels* (1611).
Dallington, Robert, *Method for Travel* (1605).
Estienne, Henri, *The Frankfort Book Fair*, ed., trans. and intro. James
   Westfall Thompson (1574; Chicago, Caxton Club, 1911).
Foster, Sir William (ed.), *Early Travels in India* (Oxford, Oxford
   University Press, 1921).
—— *The Embassy of Sir Thomas Roe to the Court of the Great Mogul,
   1615–1619*, 2 vols (Hakluyt Society, 1899).

Fuller, Thomas, *The Worthies of England* (1662); ed. and selected John Freeman (Allen and Unwin, 1952).

Herbert, Sir Thomas, *A Relation of Some Yeares Travaile in Persia* (1628), ed. Sir William Foster (Routledge, 1971).

Knolles, Richard, *The Generall Historie of the Turkes* (1603, 1700).

Lithgow, William, *The totall discourse of the rare adventures* (1614, 1623).

Moryson, Fynes, *An Itinerary* (1617); repr. 4 vols (Glasgow, James MacLehose, 1907).

—— *Shakespeare's Europe. Unpublished Chapters of Fynes Moryson's Itinerary*, ed. Charles Hughes (Sherratt and Hughes, 1903).

Mundy, Peter, *The Travels of Peter Mundy, 1608–1667* (1668); ed. Sir Richard Carnac Temple, 5 vols (Cambridge, Hakluyt Soc., 1907–36).

Nashe, Thomas, *The Unfortunate Traveller* (1592); ed. J.B. Steane (Harmondsworth, Penguin, 1972).

Nicolay, Nicolas de, *Les Navigations* (Paris, 1576).

Purchas, Samuel, *Hakluytus Posthumus, or, Purchas his Pilgrimes*, 5 vols (1625); repr. 20 vols (Glasgow, James MacLehose, 1905–7).

Sandys, George, *A Relation of a Journey* (1615).

Taylor, John, *All the Workes of John Taylor the Water-Poet* (1630).

Terry, Edward, *A Voyage to East-India* (1655).

Wood, Anthony à, *Athenae Oxonienses* (1721).

MODERN WRITING

Bates, E.S., *Touring in 1600* (Constable, 1911); repr. (Century Hutchinson, 1987).

Berinstain, Valérie, *Mughal India: Splendours of the Peacock Throne*, tr. Paul G. Bahn (Thames and Hudson, 1998).

Braudel, Fernand, *The Structures of Everyday Life*, tr. Siân Reynolds (Collins, 1981).

Chaney, Edward, *The Evolution of the Grand Tour* (Frank Cass, 1998).

Chew, Samuel S., *The Crescent and the Rose* (New York, Oxford University Press, 1937).

Colley, Linda, *Captives: Britain, Europe and the World, 1600–1850* (Jonathan Cape, 2002).

Howard, Clare, *English Travellers of the Renaissance* (J. Lane, 1914).

Keay, John, *The Honourable Company: A History of the English East India Company* (HarperCollins, 1991).

Maczak, Antoni, *Travel in Early Modern Europe*, tr. Ursula Phillips (Cambridge, Polity Press, 1995).

Moore, Tim, *Continental Drifter* (Abacus, 2001).

Moraes, Dom, and Srivatsa, Sarayu, *The Long Strider. How Thomas Coryate Walked from England to India in the year 1613* (New Delhi, Penguin, 2003).

Norwich, John Julius, *A History of Venice* (Harmondsworth, Penguin, 1983).

Penrose, Boies, *Urbane Travellers, 1591–1635* (Philadelphia and London, University of Pennsylvania Press and Oxford University Press, 1942).

Sells, A. Lytton, *The Paradise of Travellers: The Italian Influence on Englishmen in the Seventeenth Century* (Allen and Unwin, 1964).

Stoye, John Walter, *English Travellers Abroad, 1604–1667* (Jonathan Cape, 1952).

Strachan, Michael, *The Life and Adventures of Thomas Coryate* (Oxford University Press, 1962).

Strong, Sir Roy, *Henry, Prince of Wales, and England's Lost Renaissance* (Thames and Hudson, 1986).

Index

Abbas I, 218, 222–3
Abbeville,17
Achmet I, 195, 200, 201
Agra, 227, 249, 250–1
Aiguebelle, 31
Ajmer, 228, 240, 248
Akbar, Shah, 226–7, 238, 241,
    244, 251
Alboinus and Rosamunda, 84
Alciati, Andrea, 172
Aleppo, 208, 215
Alexandria Troias, 189–91
Allard, Henry, 209, 210, 214,
    215
Amiens, 18–19
Ascham, Sir Roger, 9, 151
Aubrey, John, 75, 178

Bacon, Sir Francis, 8, 40
Baden, Lower, 113, 157
Baden Upper, 101–3
Baffin, William, 251
Bancroft, Richard, Archbishop,
    169, 170
Basel, 103
Beaumont, Francis, 178
Bergamo, 89
Best, Thomas, 233
Biddulph, William, 205
Bingen, 127

Black Forest, 112
Bodley, Thomas, and Library,
    116, 175
Bonn, 132
Boppard, 127, 131
Boulogne, 15
Bragadin, Marcantonio, 63
Brescia, 87
Breughel, Jan, 16
Briare, 26
Brooke, Christopher, 156, 163,
    175, 176, 232
Browne, John, 231
Bueler, Mark, 96, 97, 101
Bullinger, Henry, 96
Burghley, Lord, 3
Burlington, Lord, 83

Calais, 14–15
Campion, Thomas, 164
Campodolcino, 93
Capra, Villa, 82
Cartwright, John, 216, 217, 220
Casaubon, Isaac, 20, 126
Chambéry, 30
Charles, Duke of York, 172,
    173
Châtillion, Admiral, 19
Chaucer, Geoffrey, 150
Chesterton, G.K., 191

Chiavenna, 93

Chios, 187–9

Chur, 95

Cigliano, 35

Clermont, 20

Cleveland, John, 81

Colleoni, Bartolomeo, 63, 89

Cologne, 132, 133–41

Conrad, Joseph, 208

Constantinople, 191, 192–6

Cooper, Henrietta, 3

Corbet, Richard, 164

corsairs, 14, 185, 192

Coryate, George, 2, 7, 169

Coryate, Gertrude, 3, 153

Coryate, Thomas:

  background:

    appearance, 167–8, 229

    birth, 3

    education, 3

    parentage, 2–3

  character:

    modest, 6, 167

    temperate, 106, 167

    thrifty, 106, 183, 194, 230, 249

  death and burial, 260–1

  discussed by:

    Ben Jonson, 160

    Edward Terry, 2, 254, 258, 261

    King James, 257

    Laurence Whitaker, 68, 161, 162

    Richard Martin, 67

    Robert Rugge, 184, 189

    Sir Thomas Roe, 234, 257

    Thomas Fuller, 162, 183

  drinking:

    English drinking, 107

    German drinking, 144

Piedmont wine, 35

Rhenish wine, 96, 117, 118

sack, 260

Swiss drinking, 106

Tun of Heidelberg, 117

water in India, 249

eating:

  in Basel, 105

  in Cremona, 42

  in Damascus, 210

  forks, 36

  German, 105

  in India, 235

  in Zurich, 100

fashions:

  Basel, 105

  fans, 41

  Italian peasants, 34, 35

  Savoyards, 33

  Swiss men and women, 99, 105, 111

  umbrellas, 41–2

  Venetian men and women, 49, 56, 70, 71, 72, 75

health, 252, 254

interest in animal life:

  antelope, 222

  butterflies and fireflies, 204

  elephants, 217, 240

  frogs, 92, 97, 114

  herons, 115

  jackal, 208

  lice, 204

  locusts, 204

  ostriches, 24

  pelican, 204

  snails and butterflies, 30

  storks, 24, 150

  unicorns, 245

interest in classics:
  amphitheatre, 85
  Cato, 122
  Cicero, 187
  Homer, 174, 188
  Livy, 46
  Martial and Catullus, 49–50
  Ovid, 191
  Priscian, 29, 122
  Strabo, 228
  Troy, 189–91
  Virgil, 31, 42, 135, 143
interest in relics, 18, 23, 38,
  39, 48, 81, 87, 88, 138,
  140, 141
  Hindu sites, 251
  steals image, 88
  tattooed at Jerusalem, 212
  visits Christian sites, 214
interest in religion:
  debate with French friar, 17
  denounces Koran and
    Mahomet, 224, 243
  with Turkish Moor, 28
  with Venetian Jews, 67
languages:
  Hindustani, 248
  Latin and Greek, 3, 17, 65,
    120, 168, 223, 235
  Latin pronunciation, 89
  Persian, Arabic, 235
  sailors' jargon, 184, 207
  Turkish, Italian, 194
London friends:
  disputes with John Taylor,
    179–82
  disputes with Joseph Starre,
    155–6
  Mermaid Club, 178, 254
  Mitre party, 175

love of Odcombe and
  Somerset, 1, 3, 5, 80, 113,
  132, 231
  donates clothes to church,
    153
love of travel, 158, 183, 229,
  231
observations:
  bathing at Baden, 102
  Festival of John the Baptist,
    35
  Mass at Calais, 14
  Mass at Paris, 22
  Mass in Venice, 65
  punishments in
    Constantinople, 205
  punishments in France, 16,
    20, 26, 27
  punishments in Germany,
    124, 132
  punishments in India, 242
  punishments in
    Switzerland, 99, 103
  punishments in Venice, 78
relationships with:
  Edward Terry, 1, 247,
    253–4
  Frances, Countess of
    Hertford, 235
  Prince of Wales, 6, 7, 163,
    170, 172
  Sir Thomas Roe, 234, 248,
    249, 252, 257, 258
rituals:
  dervishes, 198–9
  flagellation, 197–8
  Jahangir at Urs Mela, 244
  Jewish circumcision, 199
  Muslim circumcision, 200
  Pentecost in Jerusalem, 213

procession of Grand Sultan,
    201–2
weighing of Jahangir, 239
speeches and writings:
  to Armenian, 248
  Coryats Crudities, 2, 20,
    153, 171, 222
  Coryats Crambe, 4, 155,
    163, 173, 222
  dedication to Prince Henry,
    170
  Epistle to the Reader, 3, 158
  from India, 178, 216, 230
  in Isfahan, 219
  to Jahangir, 247
  to Laurence Whitaker, 231
  letter to Sir Michael Hicks,
    169
  letter to Sirenaics, 178, 232,
    261
  to mother, 220, 230, 249
  notes left in Aleppo, 215
  orations at Odcombe and
    Yeovil, 5, 182
  parodied, 180–1
  petition to King, 181
  to Prince Henry, 169, 172
  in Purchas, 184, 209
  to Royal Family, 172
  to Sir Edward Phelips, 224,
    231
  to Sir Thomas Roe, 234
  style, 14, 157, 158, 159, 170,
    209, 231
  at 'Troy', 190
travel experiences:
  beds, 33, 100
  fortune told, 206
  initiation ceremony, 130
  mock knighthood, 189

  robbed, 217, 218
  scare in Black Forest, 112
  stable in Bologna, 90
  threat near Worms, 119–21
  Venetian courtesan, 73–5
Cotton, Sir Robert, 191
Courtenay, Sir Edward, 47
Cranfield, Lionel, 162, 164, 168,
    176
Cremona, 42
Crowther, John, 221, 223, 225,
    227, 228
Cyzicus, 191

Damascus, 210
Day, John, 72
Diyerbakir, 217
Donne, John, 1, 67, 157, 163, 167,
    175, 176, 232
Dordrecht, 147–8, 150
Drayton, Michael, 162, 164, 168
Durlach, 113, 114–15

East India Company, 233, 234
Ecbatana, 218
Edward I, King, 66
Edwards, William, 230, 234
Eliot, T.S., 207
Elizabeth, Queen, 2, 71
Emmerich, 143,
Essex, Earl of, 27, 125
Estienne, Henri, 124
Ettlingen, 113
Euphrates, River, 216

Farah, 221,
Farnaby, Thomas, 153,
Finch, William, 225–6, 227, 240,
    242, 245, 250, 258
Flushing, 8, 150

Fontainebleau, 24–5
Ford, William, 194
Frances, Lady Hertford, 110, 235
Francis I, King, 41
Frankfurt, 124–7
Fryer, John, 260
Fuller, Thomas, 6, 162, 174, 179,
    183
Fusina, 50

Galileo, G., 45
galleys, 62, 191
Garda, Lake, 86,
Garnet, Henry, 141
Gifford, John, 167
Gilbert and Sullivan, quoted,
    150, 195
Goodyer, Henry, 167, 176
Googe, Barnabe, 13
Gorinchem, 145, 146–7
Grenville, Sir Richard, 183
Grisons, 92–5
Gruter, Jan, 116
Guiccardini, L., 157
Gutenberg, John, 123

Har(i)dwar, 249, 251
Har(r)ington, Sir John, 8, 214
Harrison, William, 76
Harvey, William, 45,
Hatto, Archbishop, 128
Hawkins, William, 233, 237
Heidelberg, 115
Henri IV, King, 18, 78
Henry, Prince of Wales, 6, 7, 78,
    157–8, 162, 163, 254
Herbert, Thomas, 219, 260
Hicks, Sir Michael, 169
Hildegard of Bingen, 128
Holland, 146

Hole, William, 153, 162, 164
Holland, Hugh, 163, 165, 176
Hooch, Pieter de, 146
Hoskyns, John, 163, 175, 176
Hospinian, Rudolph, 96

Ingram, Arthur, 169
Isfahan, 219–20
Iskanderun, 208

Jahangir, Emperor, 227, 235, 238,
    239, 241, 242–3, 258
James I, King, 1, 6, 8, 68, 78, 135,
    185, 222, 234, 235, 257
Jebbul, 208
Jehan, Shah, 255
Jerusalem, 211–12
Joan, Pope, 123
Jones, Inigo, 69, 164, 167, 176,
    232
Jonson, Ben, 12, 37, 49, 76, 120,
    160, 161, 162, 171, 179,
    201, 235
Jordan, River, 214

Kandahar, 223,
Kemp, Will, 8, 12, 153
Khusrau, Prince, 227, 238
Kipling, Rudyard, 183, 228
Kirchner, Herman, 95,
Knolles, Richard, 192, 195, 201,
    203
Köningsfelden, 101, 103

Lahore, 225–7
Lasnebourg, 32
Legnano, 44
Lepanto, Battle of, 191
Lesbos, 207
Levant Company, 8, 162, 184,
    187, 194, 208

Lichefield, Mr, 91
Lithgow, William, 9,17, 20, 46,
    49, 78, 91, 185, 186, 188,
    191, 193, 196, 209, 210,
    211, 214
Lodi, 40
Lombardy, 37
Loreto, 211
Luther, Martin, 2, 121, 122
Lyons, 27–9

Maccabean mother, 140
Magi, 136–8
Mainz, 122
Mandu, 252–3, 255
Mantua, 42–3
Margarite, Countess, 149
Marlowe, Christopher, 174, 185
Martin, Richard, 38, 67, 163, 175,
    176
Melancthon, Philip, 123,
Melville, Herman, 75,
Mereworth Castle, 83
Mermaid Tavern and Club, 37,
    178, 254,
Middelburg, 150
Middleton, Henry, 233
Middleton, Thomas, 36
Milton, John, 46, 183
Mirandula, 42,
Mitre Tavern, The, 175
Mol(l)e, John, 18
Montacute House, 6, 132
Montaigne, Michel de, 36, 100,
    198
Montargis, 26
Montreuil, 16–17
Moryson, Fynes, 9, 12, 15, 35, 40,
    44, 45, 46, 49, 50, 52, 54,
    62, 70, 72, 73, 78, 83, 87,

    90, 93, 94, 97, 99, 100, 102,
    103, 104, 105, 107, 108,
    112, 115, 120, 124, 126,
    144, 146, 150, 186, 187,
    193, 196, 201, 204, 209, 212
Moulins, 26
Mont Cenis, 29, 34
Mount Aiguebelette, 30
Mughal Empire, 237
Mughal, the Great, 237
Multan, 223
Mundy, Peter, 21, 44, 86, 87, 194,
    195, 196, 205–6, 208, 240,
    250, 251, 256, 259
Münster, Sebastian, 122, 128, 157

Nashe, Thomas, 10, 204
Nevers, 26
Nicolay, Nicolas de, 188
Nijmegen, 144
Norwich, John Julius, 61
Nur Mahal, Queen, 246

Oberwinter, 131
Odcombe, 1, 3, 5, 32, 113, 153
Odcombian Banquet, The, 173
Odcombs Complaint, 181
Ottoman Empire, 191–2

Padua, 8, 44–50, 81
Palavicino, Sir Horatio, 91
Palladio, Andrea, 69, 82,
Palmer, Sir Thomas, 8
Paris, 20–4
    Louvre, 21
    Notre Dame, 22
    St Denis, 23
Passo di San Marco, 91
Phelips, Sir Edward, 6, 132, 163,
    166, 231, 250

Phelips, Sir Robert, 6, 176, 250
Phelips, Sir Thomas, 6
Picquiny, 17
Piedmont, 34
Pindar, Paul, 194, 206
Pizzighettone, 41
Pope, Alexander, 83
Purchas, Samuel, 2, 184, 185, 194, 197, 209, 215, 232, 238

Qazvir, 218

Rabelais, François, 25, 204
Raleigh, Sir Walter, 159, 162, 175
Rees, 143
Remagen, 133
Reynolds, John, 175
Rheinberg, 142
Rheinfelden, 103
Rhine, River, 108
Roe, Sir Thomas, 8, 127, 232–3, 234, 237, 239, 242, 245, 246, 248, 249, 251, 252, 253, 255, 256, 257, 258, 261
Rooke, George, 45, 81
Row, Thomas, 127
Rowe, Richard, 156, 184
Rugge, Robert, 184, 189

Sackfield, Thomas, 125
St Gereon, 140
St Germain, 20
St Goar, 130
St Ursula, 138
Salmon, John, 153
Sanderson, John, 206, 207
Sandys, George, 186, 187, 188, 197, 198, 202

Sanguinetto, 43
Savoy, 29–33
Scaliger, Julius Caesar, 15, 20, 27, 84, 89, 115, 157
Schenkenschanz, 144
Schott, François, 38, 46, 81, 84, 157
Seward, John, 169
Shah Jehan, 255
Shakespeare, William, and creations, 1, 4, 6, 8, 10, 11, 12, 24, 29, 44, 46, 63, 71, 84, 85, 106, 107, 137, 153, 158, 166, 174, 179, 186, 254
Sherley, Lady, 222, 223
Sherley, Robert, 222
Sidney, Sir Philip, 8, 159
Simler, Josias, 95
Spenser, Edmund, 229
Speyer, 118
Spinola, General, 142
Splügen, 94
Stansby, William, 232
Starre, Joseph, 12, 155–6, 250
Steel, Richard, 216, 221, 223, 224, 225, 227, 228, 257
Strangways, John, 153
Strasbourg, 109–11
Suckling, Sir John, 20, 73
Surat, 233, 258–9
Suvali (Swalley Hole), 233

Taylor, John, 1, 179–82
Tell, William, 98–9
Terry, Edward, 2, 212, 225, 235, 237, 239, 240, 242, 243, 247, 248, 251, 252, 253, 254, 255–6, 257, 258, 260, 261
Thorpe, Thomas, 174

Tiepolo, Bajamonte, 60
Titian, 46, 59
Truchsess, Archbishop, 133
Tyndale, William, 121

Ur, Urfa, 216

Vadianus, Glareanus, 164–5
Valle Brembana, 91
Venetian Republic, 44
Venice, 51–80
  Basilica, 58, 61
  courtesans, 54, 69, 72, 73
  fashions, 49, 56
  galleys, 62–3
  ghetto, 65
  gondolas, 54, 55
  Grand Canal, 52
  Merceria, 57
  mountebanks, 76
  Piazza San Marco, 55
  punishments, 78
  Rialto, 53, 78
Vercelli, 35
Vermeer, 146
Verona, 84–6

Vicenza, 81

Wallenstadt, 96
Walsingham, Sir Francis, 45
Ward, John, 185
Waser, Gaspar, 97, 153
Wells, H.G., 211
Wentworth, Lord, 81
Wernerus of Wesel, 130
Whitaker, Laurence, 37, 68, 161,
      162, 163, 168, 178, 229,
      231
Willoughby, Richard, 45
Withers, Robert, 197
Wood, Anthony à, 2, 3, 7, 178
Worms, 119–22
Wotton, Sir Henry, 8, 45, 67–9,
      82, 117, 126, 175

Yeovil, 4, 153
Yezd, 221

Zaltbommel, 145
Zante, 186–7
Zurich, 96–101
Zwingli, Ulrich, 96, 97